For m

MW00962718

COLUMBUS
A Discoverer and his Conscience

_____

Richard Crosfield

Richard

FRONTIER 2000 SERIES

Frontier Publishing
Windetts, Kirstead, Norfolk
NR15 1BR

Columbus – A Discoverer and his Conscience
This paperback edition 1998

First Published in Great Britain by
Frontier Publishing 1998

ISBN: 1 872914 10 1

Cover: detail - (La Lettera Dellisole Che Ha Trovato Nuovamente. Florence, 1493)

Typeset by T&O Graphics, Bungay, Suffolk

PRINTED IN GREAT BRITAIN
Redwood Books, Trowbridge, Wiltshire

COLUMBUS

A Discoverer and his Conscience

_____

CONTENTS

	Preface	
1	TO GENOA	9
2	PORTUGAL	30
3	SPAIN	49
4	DISCOVERY	69
5	THE TAINOS	83
6	CANNIBALS AND CHRISTIANS	99
7	TRIUMPH	108
8	GOLD IS BEST	120
9	ON SLAVERY	130
10	FIRST GOVERNOR	140
11	FROM EDEN TO SHACKLES	146
12	TO THE ULTIMATE VICTORY	161
13	THE HIGH VOYAGE	170
14	LAST MONTHS AND THAT IMPOSTOR VESPUCCI	184
15	THE GREAT SEAFARER	195
16	TO THE DOMINICAN REPUBLIC: FATE OF THE TAINOS	204
17	TO THE DOMINICAN REPUBLIC: IN COLUMBUS'S FOOTSTEPS	215
	Notes	262
	Selected Bibliography	267

To my parents

PREFACE

Columbus was a controversial figure in his lifetime and biographers, with the warp of time, have merely added to the controversy. As two authoritative stories of his life were written by men who knew him – his scholarly younger son, Fernando, and the priest-historian Bartolomé de Las Casas – one might wonder what more of substance remained to be written. Biographies by the subject's contemporaries are rarely objective and assume a knowledge of the period, and later generations ask new questions which require new answers. Today's readers are far more interested in the indigenous inhabitants Columbus found in the Caribbean and their fate than readers of only thirty years ago, and I have written more about the Taino, Carib and other Indians who inhabited the Caribbean islands than any other book about the European discovery of America. Why and how the big Indian populations in the Greater Antilles died out so quickly is another subject which is rarely given more than a cursory airing, and this, with Columbus's role in their downfall, his views on slavery and gold, and the controversy over Amerindian cannibalism are all discussed in unusual depth.

To add colour and depth, I visited the places where Columbus spent most of his life – Genoa, in Portugal, Spain and Hispaniola – reporting them as a present-day traveller, but with one eye on how they would have seemed to Columbus at the end of the Fifteenth Century. This mixture of travel book and biography has, previously, only been undertaken by Morison and he concentrated on the sea. The last quarter of the book covers my visit to the eastern two-thirds of Hispaniola, the island he loved best. The Dominican Republic, with its people descended from Spanish conquistadors and African slaves, while retaining a strong identity with the Taino Indians they displaced, represents, in its purest form, the Columbian legacy.

Collingwood observed that, as the subject of biography was man and not thought, it was 'anti-history' and a form of literature. I would suggest that, since Columbus spent nearly all his life at sea or in port and would be unknown without his nautical achievements, a mariner with an interest in history is in a better position to write his biography than an historian with no interest in the sea. I have enough experience sailing small boats in big seas to describe Columbus's voyages and assess – perhaps summarize would be a better word – Admiral Morison's claim that Columbus's mastery of the sea was only equalled by Captain Cook.

It is, of course, a biographer's duty to provide the reader with conclusions drawn from the most recent research. Fortunately, in the run-up to the Quincentennial, Spanish scholars transcribed everything Columbus and his contemporaries wrote, which is now available in several volumes and accessible to any Spanish-speaking person. I thank those scholars who are listed in the Bibliography and from whose transcriptions I have based my translations into English. In this context I should mention the recent discovery of a thick wad of Columbus's letters which have not yet been used in any biography. The so-called *Libro Copiador*, or *Copybook*, sheds more light on those murky years at the end of the Fifteenth Century when Western man emerged as from a long sleep with the energy and curiosity that were to create the most brilliant period of his history, and whose maximum exponent in the field of practical discovery was Columbus.

Linguistic evidence has convinced me that Columbus came from a family of Spanish Conversos. Though this leads me into a hornet's nest of controversy, Columbus's Jewish origins can hardly be ignored since they do explain some of the mysteries which surround him.

Columbus was a prolific and interesting writer, and any biographer who chooses to paraphrase him does so at the reader's expense. Wherever possible, I have quoted from Columbus or his contemporaries, giving the reader an unrivalled flavour for the period. For some reason, Gresham's law applies to Columbus in the sense that, just as bad money drives out good, false information drives out true. For instance, Bill Bryson's *Made in America* (1994), otherwise a well-researched book devoted to myth-breaking, packs eight whoppers about Columbus into three short paragraphs, surely an achievement that would make even this sturdy writer blush:

Word of the existence of a land beyond the Ocean Sea, as the Atlantic was then known, was filtering back to Europeans long before

Columbus made his epic voyage. The Vikings did not operate in isola-tion. They settled all over Europe and their exploits were widely known. They even left a map – the famous Vinland map – which is known to have been circulating in Europe by the fourteenth century. We don't positively know that Columbus was aware of this map, but we do know that the course he set appeared to be making a beeline for the mythical island of Antilla, which featured on it.

Columbus never found Antilla or anything else he was looking for. His epochal voyage of 1492 was almost the last thing – indeed almost the only thing – that went right in his life. Within eight years, he would find himself summarily relieved of his post as Admiral of the Ocean Sea, returned to Spain in chains and allowed to sink into such profound obscurity that even now we don't know for sure where he's buried. To achieve such a precipitous fall in less than a decade required an unusual measure of incompetence and arrogance. Columbus had both.

He spent most of those eight years bouncing around the islands of the Caribbean and coasts of South America without ever having any real idea of where or what he was doing... He cost the Spanish crown a fortune and gave in return little but broken promises. And through-out he behaved with the kind of impudence – demanding to be made hereditary Admiral of the Ocean sea, as well as Viceroy and Governor of the lands that he conquered, and to be granted one-tenth of what-ever wealth his enterprise generated – that all but invited his downfall.

To set this little record straight: the *Viking* exploits west of Greenland were unknown outside Scandinavia until Thormodus Torfaeus published a Latin translation of the Vinland Sagas in 1705. The *famous Vinland Map*, whose discovery was announced with great pomp by Yale University on the eve of Columbus Day 1965, has been faked and anyway makes no mention of *Antilla*. No such map was *known to have been circulating in Europe by the fourteenth century*, for the simple reason that there was none; the earliest known 'Viking' map dates from 1590 and it makes no reference to *Antilla* either. In fact, in all Columbus's correspon-dence he never mentions Antilla. His often-stated objective was India, by which he meant South and East Asia. Columbus was never *relieved of his post as Admiral of the Ocean Sea*. After *he returned in chains* from the Third Voyage, the Spanish Crown reinstated virtually all of his privileges and financed a Fourth

Voyage of discovery. Nor did he die *in such profound obscurity* that people did not know where his remains were buried. Rather the confusion as to where his remains are buried is the result of his fame and the importance the Spanish state gave to them, moving them from cathedral to cathedral, from Santo Domingo (perhaps) to Havana, when the eastern two-thirds of Hispaniola was lost to France, and then to Seville when Cuba was lost to the United States. Contemporary chroniclers and historians – Peter Martyr, Las Casas, Oviedo, Bernaldéz – all took for granted Columbus's fame, while his elder son twice governed the Indies. None of Columbus's voyages *cost the Spanish Crown a fortune*: the Crown's contribution to the First Voyage was one-thousandth of their annual budget and all of that was loaned by a wealthy Converso. What was expensive was the maintenance of the first colony on Hispaniola, whose gold mines would pay handsomely for the initial investment. Before setting out on his First Voyage, Columbus came to a contractual agreement with the Spanish Crown which specified the titles and privileges he would be entitled to once he'd discovered *new islands and mainlands* – impudent, perhaps, but negotiated and accepted by Ferdinand and Isabella.

If I have devoted so much space to Bryson, it is to illustrate the deep anti-Columbus prejudice that rules in many circles in the United States and made the quincentennial celebration of the discovery of America such a strangely mute and polemical affair. This book, representing three years' research, answers many of the allegations which were made against Columbus at that time. Though, as Oscar Wilde observed, the truth is neither pure nor simple, *Columbus – A Discoverer and his Conscience* offers the reader a version of the discovery of America which is consistent with the known facts.

Madrid, 1998.

1

To Genoa

I drove in torrential rain – it was late October and winter had set in – down the autoroute towards Marseilles where it bends left at Aix, out of sight of the coast, for the Italian frontier. My objective was Genoa, Columbus's birthplace.

Italians have devoted books to prove that Columbus was born in Genoa, which would seem an awful waste of time knowing that all Columbus's contemporaries wrote that he was from Genoa, or at least Liguria. But wishful thinking and a wonderful disdain for facts, when they interfere with one's convictions, is one of the Latin peoples' endearing qualities. Both Portuguese and Spaniards have been promoting their own candidates for more than a century.[1] When I began this project, otherwise well-informed Spaniards would say, 'But aren't Colón's origins unknown?'

'No, they're well documented.'

'But no one knows where he came from, do they?'

'Well they do. He was born in or near Genoa in 1451 to Domenico Colombo and Susanna Fontanarossa and had three brothers and a sister. They lived for a time in a row-house on Vico Diritto, later lost in a suit for his sister's dowry to her father-in-law, Giacomo Bavarello. Columbus's father was a weaver turned taverner, and two of his brothers, Bartolomeo and Giacomo Colombo, became well known in Spain as Bartolomé and Diego Colón... ' By now my Spanish friends' eyes had glazed over as if I were rabbiting on about sightings of extraterrestrials or the virtues of astrology. Yet Columbus's origins are, in another sense, clouded in mystery. I will come to that later.

Driving along the A8 autoroute to the Italian frontier, pine forests and trifling hills merged into heavy clouds which looked as if they had settled in for the season. Somewhere to my right was the coast, hidden behind a curtain of rain which had no intention of lifting. According to the map, I was approaching the sea, but the only sign was a series of exits marked Cannes, Antibes, Cagne-Sur-Mer and Nice's disorderly stacked apartment blocks emerging optimistically white in the gloomy light. A signpost for Monte Carlo reminded me that I was approaching Columbus's homeland, and one of the Monegasque-Genoese Grimaldi family, Juan Francisco de Grimaldo, was banker to Columbus's sons in Seville.

In the 15th Century, the Republic of Genoa swept in a 300-kilometre crescent around the Italian Riviera, a land of pine-covered mountains tumbling down to the Ligurian Sea where settlements formed around coves and behind sandy beaches, looking outward over the water. Skilled as sailors and boat builders, the Genoese served the land-bound Duchy of Milan and Principality of Piedmont. The bigger towns of Genoa and Savona were entrepôts and centres of craftsmanship, and the Republic established trading colonies and posts from the Black Sea, around the rim of the Mediterranean and west, through the Pillars of Hercules, to the main Atlantic ports and the newly discovered islands of the Ocean Sea. By the late 15th Century, Genoa had become the greatest trading nation in Europe. Banking – the granting and collection of credit – followed the flag and became centred on the most important Genoese institution of Columbus's time, the Banco di San Giorgio, used by both Columbus and Fernando Colón. Formed in 1405 to take over the national debt, the Bank predated the Bank of England by 289 years.

126 kilometres beyond the Franco-Italian border is Savona, the other Ligurian port city which, thanks to various notarial documents, we know Columbus's family lived in from 1470 to about 1477. Domenico Colombo ran a business in cloth (he was a master weaver) and wine trading with the assistance of his sons. Columbus, then nineteen, jointly guaranteed a debt for wine delivered in 1470, proving that he was already a man of means. On three occasions Domenico sold part of his wife's land dowry, suggesting that the business was not a success. Columbus, according to further notarial documents and his own scanty recollections, spent part of the first five years at sea and part in Savona with his family. By 1476 he was established in Portugal.

Curling down off the autostrada, the first impression of Savona is inauspicious. Irregular mud-coloured blocks and streets fill the slope between the dark hills and docks. An enormous granite fortress, built to resist the Barbary pirates, lowers over a concrete promontory littered with derricks, warehouses, incomplete buildings and railway sidings, blocking the view to the west. The docks are sadly empty, derricks standing still and unused, silent witnesses to a city which seems to be in terminal decline. Behind a modern seafront frontage – tatty shops and cafés more suited to an English coastal resort than the Italian Riviera – are the unkept alleys of what remains of the medieval town, empty alley ways curving off the Paleocapa with the musty air of an unvisited museum. Beside the barred windows of the old library, a spray-painted graffiti warns Maradona that Savona hates him. Further inland, out of sight of the sea is the nineteenth-century New Town of broad avenues and apartment buildings. Here trees, shrubs and piazzas suddenly appear, and the air is sweet as if its better-off residents had it sprayed with *Pine Fragrance*.

That afternoon a sea breeze blew away the heavy clouds and a pale, autumnal sun lit up the city. Returning to the old town, I passed a solid, almost cowering Cistine chapel and Franciscan cloister, both new or reconstructed in Columbus's day. At the end of a grimy street a pair of medieval watch towers, built of grey and rose-flecked stone, stand in lonely isolation with a view, now, of nothing more distant than the docks. Beyond is a narrow channel leading to the reconstructed Pancaldo Tower, named after one of Magellan's pilots. Rebuilt in brick and dedicated in 1878 to Our Lady of the Sea, the original was a familiar landmark for Columbus, sailing in from the south. Largely destroyed by the Genoese in 1528 and heavily bombed in the last war, Savona seems to have lost its sense of civic pride, but in Columbus's day it strove, unsuccessfully, to rival Genoa. A 15th-century painting shows houses packed haphazardly inside walls acting as a corset on Savona's natural tendency to expand, in contrast to the sea which spreads so temptingly before it. Its port, a sloping beach protected by a sea wall, is a trifling affair compared to Genoa's of the same period; altogether an uninspiring town for a man with the ambitions of Columbus.

Avoiding another fifty kilometres of autostrada, I took the longer route along the coast to Genoa, leaving Savona behind me. Within five minutes I was driving by the shore in Albissola Marina, a long empty beach separating the dark sea from elegant villas, set in tidy, walled gardens, which had outlived the boom and bust of the Italian Riviera. Pretty resorts, quiet in the off-season, sat smugly at the foot of hills by a water which seemed altogether more calm and friendly. Celle Ligure, Varazze, Cogoleto (cited by Columbus's son, Fernando, as a possible birthplace) and Arenzano gracefully slipped by.

I turned a corner and was sucked into a far more monstrous version of Savona, and these were but the outskirts of Genoa. An autostrada plunges through tunnels and over viaducts, affording brief views of industrial chimneys and flat-topped warehouses leading down to what looked, in the evening gloom, a black oily lake which was the sea. I found my way down to one of the central thoroughfares, Via XX Settembre, and stopped outside the Bristol Palace Hotel, its entrance hidden behind a heavy grey stone arcade. In the cosy opulence of my room, I flipped through my notes of three of Columbus's contemporaries who linked him to Genoa (Taviani (1985) counted 62 Italians and 28 non-Italians, writing in the 16th and 17th Centuries, who refer to Columbus's Genoese origins).

Columbus lived for a year in the Sevillian house of priest and chronicler Andrés Bernaldéz, who wrote of his friend: *He was a man from the land of Genoa, a book dealer called Cristóbal Colón, a man of very high intelligence without much knowledge of letters, very skillful in the art of cosmography and in the composition of the world.*

Antonio Gallo, Chancellor of the Banco di San Giorgio and official chronicler of Genoa, knew the Colombo family and corresponded with Columbus. *Cristoforo and Bartolomeo Colombo, brothers, Ligurians by nationality, of plebeian Genoese parents who lived from the wages they earned as wool dealers (because their father was a weaver and, at times, their sons were wool-combers), reached great fame in Europe for an achievement of the greatest daring and of the greatest novelty in human affairs. Although little is known of their childhood, they dedicated themselves to navigation, as is the custom of their race, on reaching the age of puberty.*

Columbus's younger son, Fernando Colón, was intriguingly vague about his father's origins: *Some, who would dim his fame, say the Admiral was from Nervi, others from Cogoleto and others from*

Buyasco, all small settlements near to the city of Genoa and on the same coast. Others, who would enlarge it, say he was from Savona and others Genoa; and those who would raise him to the heights have him from Piacenza, where there are some honoured family members and sepulchers with the arms and epitaphs of Colombo, the surname of his ancestors. However he, depending on the country where he settled and began again, smoothed the word so that it conformed to the old one and yet distinguished it from those which preceded him; and so he called himself Colón. Considering this, I believe that, as in so many of his affairs which hold some mystery, the variation of his name and surname are not without mystery.

Born Colombo, Columbus *smoothed* his name to Colom in Portugal and to Colomo and later Colón, the accent to distinguish it from a part of his anatomy, in Castile. Genoese merchants in Lisbon and Castile only changed their surnames if they sounded odd to an Iberian ear, but Colombo is as easy to pronounce in Spanish as Colomo or Colón and in Portuguese as Colom. As three changes of name are at least one too many, there had to be more to the change than mere *smoothing*; a *mystery*, as Fernando wrote.

Though it was only about eight o'clock, Via XX Settembre was almost deserted. A stiff breeze pushed me down the wide street and I thrust my hands into my jacket pockets to keep them warm. Genoa was in a decidedly gloomy mood. The widely-spaced street lamps with their weak, white lights, threw long shadows, ideal cover for muggers, if they ever had anyone to mug. But there was only me, and I was a poor prey with only a Barclaycard and a small bundle of lira bills for booty. I missed the restaurants and bars, bright shop windows, the neon ads, even the headlights and noise of passing cars which you'd find at this time of night in any comparable street in London or Madrid. There wasn't even a bus. I tried the side streets and once passed a dark, lonely figure on the other side of the street who looked as lost as I did. Around the Piazza della Vittoria (over Venice in 1298 when Genoese forces almost captured the city) there was a little more activity – a cafeteria, two hotels, a well-lit travel agency and, the height of civilization, a taxi rank. Turning into the wind, I strode up the other side of XX Settembre, exploring the side streets in search of a restaurant. Seemingly decorated by a nurse with a fondness for strip lighting, white paint and chrome-legged chairs, it wasn't exactly what I had in mind, but proved no hindrance to good food. I lingered over my meal, ate and drank more than I should have, and returned to the Bristol Palace in an elevated state of mind.

The morning air was colder than ever and the overcast sky promised little in the way of relief. The tramontane, sucked down from the Alps, was of Arctic intensity and I could have done with a scarf and a pair of gloves. I strode up to the Piazza de Ferrari, avoiding the spray which flew off the fountain, and turned sharp left down the Via Dante to the Casa di Colombo.

What might have been Columbus's home – a notarial document identifies a house on Vico Diritto without specifying which one – is a grey, vine-covered brick box embellished with a stucco façade. As the city demolished all the other houses in the street, it stands small and lonely at the confluence of a widened road and a broad piazza. The upper and brighter floor is three paces wide and three paces deep, with two windows facing the street. Although the Colombos might have lived on this site, the construction dates, at the earliest, from the Seventeenth and not the Fifteenth Century, while the tall windows could have been added within the last fifty years. The original house, which the Colombos bought when Christopher was four, could not have occupied more land, though it might have risen as high as five floors. With the additional floors, this poor, airless dwelling in the weaver's quarter was, in terms of space, sufficient for a family and the weaver's material and frames.

From 15th-century chroniclers' reports, city plans and engravings collected in the *Raccolta Colombiana*, I reconstructed the city Columbus knew. In the 15th Century, the Colombos' house lay in a narrow street (and streets ranged from three to eight feet wide) of terraced houses caught between the inner and outer walls of the city. These heavy stone walls loomed high and grey and cast a shadow of fear over the neighbourhood – a massive section of wall and a gate stands within a stone's throw of the house – a reminder of the enemy outside, the Milanese, Catalans and of the French who had occupied the city when Columbus was a child. From the inner walls came the enemies' surrogates, the Fregoso, Fieschi, Adorno and Sforza factions. Inner and outer walls could be sealed, dividing the city in two. Four grey star-shaped fortresses, refuges for the four factions, sat like giant, fossilized toads at four points of the city. Wealthy citizens built tall towers (to a maximum permitted height of 80 feet) into their houses to shelter their families and retainers from factional warfare and brigandage; several still mark the skyline of the old city. Incessant conflicts created a fortress mentality and this city of walls, by making it divisible into defensible quarters, encouraged factional strife. The chronicler Faje protested that he couldn't record the revolts anymore, *because he would run out of paper, they were so many and short lived,* and Pope Pius wrote to Archbishop Paolo, now Doge, saying he was *amazed that you have accepted the rule of the city, which... is in a constant state of unrest and does not tolerate a Doge or Governor for any length of time.*

Vitale recorded the bloody murder of the Doge Pietro Fregoso near Columbus's house when he was eight. As his father was a member of the Fregoso faction, the murder of their patron would have left a strong impression on Columbus. From the vantage point of the now open square, I pictured Pietro Fregoso fleeing on his charger past their house towards the nearby gate. Blood streamed down his face, slashed open by mace blows from a knight of the Sforza faction. Finding the gate barred, Fregoso shouted for the guard to open it, but the only response was a hail of stones from the roofs of Columbus's neighbours. Some struck Fregoso and his charger, opening new wounds. Fregoso wheeled away from the gate, weak and unsteady now in his saddle, his cries smothered by abuse from the crowd that was forming in the street. Horse and man fled past Columbus's door. A hundred yards further on he dismounted at the steps of the Doge's Palace and collapsed. Retainers carried his dying body inside. Once still, the mob closed in, cursing and slashing at the corpse. Fregoso's troops tried to flee the city, but they were cut down in the narrow streets and murdered to a man.

The factional fighting and anarchy of his childhood left an indelible mark on Columbus, accentuating his flexible, accommodating nature. Frequently the focus of revolts and mutiny, as Captain of the fleet or Governor of the Indies, he would go to virtually any length to avoid confrontation and bloodshed, preferring negotiation even in the most hopeless moments. He was quick to pardon, even if he never forgot or inwardly forgave, the disloyalty of the men at his command. Columbus's instinct to negotiate where the alternative was war enabled the Spaniards to gain, virtually without a fight, a permanent foothold in the Americas over a century before the English, French or Dutch. Brought up with the permanent intrigue which marked out Genoa even from other Italian republics, Columbus was inclined to see intrigue everywhere and consequently trust no one but his brothers, sons and those few friends who had proven beyond doubt their loyalty to his person. To the less complicated, more extrovert Spaniard, Columbus seemed to be cold, calculating and interested only in gain for himself and his family. He was decidedly not *simpático*, a quality which is valued above all others in Spain. At sea, where his great skills were evident to the simplest seaman, this would rarely be a handicap, but on land, where the opportunities for gain seemed unlimited until the crude reality of a frontier life wore down even the strongest and most optimistic, Columbus's apparent lack of resolution coupled with his lack of charisma would spell disaster.

Inside Genoa's old city, I walked along streets less than an arm's span wide. It was like walking at the bottom of a drained moat as six or seven story houses, packed tight and seamless and curving inward at roof level, obliterate all but a sliver of sky. Today, with the maturity of centuries, they have a certain charm, but in the 15th Century noise, filth and pestilence filled the streets until, quite suddenly, a gate opened into the fresh air and open sky of the port and sea. *I have been more than forty years at sea,* wrote Columbus when he was fifty-one. With the example of his father's business failures, the sea was the only escape from the dull, poorly paid business of weaving in a city whose turmoil threatened the life of even its more modest citizens. With their eastern trading colonies (except Chios) lost to the Turks after the fall of Constantinople, Genoese traders now looked west, to the Atlantic, to new opportunities thrown up by the Iberian sugar plantations on Madeira and the Canary Islands, the Portuguese trading factory at El Mina and the growing commerce between Iberia, France, England and Flanders. Columbus would choose to make his home in the west, on the edge of the Ocean Sea.

I passed under the concrete elevated highway Aldo Moro

which embraces the waterfront. Built without the slightest concession to aesthetic values, the highway smothers the sea view and towers over what used to be Columbus's bank, the Banco di San Giorgio. Its painted façade dresses up the stone block of the Bank as a Renaissance palace, typifying, I believe, the Genoese character: as paint is cheaper than stonework, *trompe l'oeil* represents a compromise between art and commerce. Beyond are the docks. A dozen blue police cars and vans, filled with policemen, were parked in a no-man's land of concrete and swirling dust and litter, lifted and spread around by the wind. As there was not the smallest sign of public disorder, their immobility in an area of economic inactivity seemed a waste of the ratepayers' contributions. Or were they protecting the shiny yellow earthmoving equipment so incongruously on display around the former Bank?

Passing around the police wagons I entered the Porto Vecchio from where Columbus first embarked, as a cabin boy perhaps. The old mole, still sturdily seaworthy, has lost its imposing lighthouse surmounted by a wrought-iron weather vane. It is hopelessly diminished by an immense new wharf littered with empty exhibition halls in three conflicting styles: white imitiation sails inspired by the Sydney Opera House, yellowish stone Victorian blockhouse, and New University redbrick, staring at the sea from rows of blank, rectangular windows. All erected or conditioned to commemorate the fifth centenary of his discovery of America, which had been a commercial flop. The business of loading and unloading ships is done elsewhere and this desolate waterfront has been optimistically turned over to a *Centro Congressi*. I came across the only open door in the entire complex, belonging to a small, family-run trattoria. Over lunch I pondered Fernando's curious statement about Columbus.

Why would a man write of his father, *I believe that, as in so many of his affairs that had some mystery, the variations of his name and surname are not without mystery*? Fernando had lived for three years in the confinement of a sixty-foot caravel with his father, so it wasn't for lack of opportunity. Fernando was bright and inquisitive, so why hadn't Columbus answered his son's questions? Everyone knew he was from Genoa and yet, with one dubious exception, he never acknowledged this in writing, not even when he had the obvious opportunity while describing his past sailing ventures to Isabella and Ferdinand. Also, official records in Spain always refer to him as 'foreigner', never 'Genoese'. Why? Columbus last visited Genoa in 1479, when he was twenty-eight years old and working as a merchant for a Genoese trading house. He always maintained strong ties with the city: Genoese merchants employed him in Portugal, loaned him money in Lisbon and helped finance his voyages in Castile; he left his papers in custody of the Genoese Ambassador to Spain, used the Banco di San Giorgio and in the margins of his books he picked out references to Genoa. In practical matters he behaved like a good son of Genoa, so what did he have to hide from his son and the official records of Castile?

Reading and rereading everything which has survived of Columbus's letters and postils, I became convinced that the clue must lie in his surprising preference for Castilian Spanish which, as the eminent Spanish historian Menéndez Pidal acknowledged fifty-four years ago, was Columbus's first written language. But when did he learn to write it? And where – he wouldn't move to Spain until he was thirty-four years old? Was Spanish also his first spoken language? Ever since Menéndez Pidal concluded that Columbus learned Spanish in Portugal, arguing that the Infante Pedro (died 1449) had made it fashionable and for a time it replaced Portuguese as the language of poets and playwrights, the matter has been more or less closed.

However, in 1992, Juan Gil wrote, 'It is not credible that a sailor, for all the airs of a courtier he might want to acquire, would learn to speak and write Castilian Spanish in Portugal.' The language of merchants, mariners, map-makers and court officials, all the people Columbus was interested in, was Portuguese. Columbus never showed any interest in literature in any language, and his written Spanish has no literary pretensions. As he was married to a Portuguese and lived for years on the Portuguese islands of Porto Santo and Madeira, not exactly renowned for their literary set, surely he would have been busy learning Portuguese rather than Spanish. There is another generally ignored clue: King John of Portugal's only letter to Columbus, written when Columbus had already spent three years in Spain, is written in Portuguese. Surely this proves that the King and Columbus were accustomed to talking in

Portuguese in Portugal and not in 'fashionable' (which I suspect was no longer fashionable) Spanish. Also, the Portuguese playwright usually cited as making Castilian fashionable in Lisbon's literary circle, Gil Vicente, did not write until *after* Columbus left Portugal. This inconvenient fact forced Menéndez Pidal to the unlikely proposition that Columbus was in the vanguard of those Portuguese who preferred to write in Spanish.

Also in 1992, an expert in handwriting, Charles Hamilton, suggested that Columbus learned to write while young. There was a guild school he might have attended in Genoa where he could have learned to write Genoese, a dialect related to Provençal, and perhaps some Latin. Yet in none of his correspondence with his fellow Genoese, including his brothers, did he write in anything but Castilian Spanish. Further, nowhere does he write in any language other than Latin or Spanish – this is not quite true since he wrote two short postils in dreadful Italian, confirming his difficulty with this language – not even in the six-page annex, bound in with his copy of Pius II *Description of Asia* (and dated 1481), written three or four years before arriving in Spain. Evidently if he learned to write young, he learned to write Spanish before arriving in Portugal.

A less popular but alternative explanation of Columbus's preference for Castilian is that Columbus learned to write it at sea. Why Castilian and not Genoese, Italian, Portuguese or Catalan, the preferred languages of the mariners of the Western Mediterranean and Atlantic south of Lisbon? Why Castilian Spanish? As we know he sailed on Genoese and French vessels while there is no record of his having sailed on a Spanish ship before arriving in Spain, he had neither the incentive nor opportunity to learn Spanish.

Columbus's Spanish offers other clues.[2] The earliest texts, dating from 1481, four years before he was to move to Spain, are also written in the worst Spanish, almost a Castilian-Portuguese hash. Menéndez Pidal uses this as proof that Columbus must have been learning Spanish in Portugal; but isn't it equally possible that, after five years in Portugal following several years at sea, his Spanish was rusty from disuse? Columbus's letters written after his arrival in Spain, while occasionally salted with Portuguese, Genoese and Italian words and spellings, are clearly

Spanish. His Spanish is the sort of *patois* learnt phonetically at home, mixed with the language of the city where he lived (Genoa), adding useful words picked up elsewhere (Portugal, at sea). In this context it is worth noting that Columbus must have had a working knowledge of French (he sailed aboard French corsairs) and Italian as well as Portuguese, Spanish, Latin and Genoese. If Columbus learned Spanish while young, used it before setting foot in Spain and preferred it, to the exclusion of all other languages – except Latin for notes in Latin texts – for the rest of his life, where else could he have learned it but at home? Columbus's family had to come, perhaps three generations back, from Spain, and Spanish emigrants were almost all Jews escaping persecution, particularly the 1391 massacres. And there are other clues: Colombo happens to be the Italian variation of Colom, a common Jewish surname in eastern Spain where the 1391 massacres were most intense; and his mother's and grandfather's names – Susanna and Jacopo Fontanarossa – have, as the Genoese historian Taviani notes, a Jewish ring to them.

As Madariaga argued, once it is accepted that Columbus came from a family of Spanish Jews who had converted to Christianity three or more generations earlier, Fernando's mysteries are solved. Colombo was an adopted name Colom-Colomo-Colón was happy to jettison once he was established outside Genoa and, realizing the risk of being discovered as a Converso, he avoided all mention of his family in Genoa. I had another thought: Why did he change his name from Colom to Colomo when he came to Castile and then to Colón, when Colom is a common surname in Aragon? Looking back through my notes, the answer stared me in the face – Converso Coloms had suffered an auto-da-fé twenty years earlier and another family of Coloms were accused by the Spanish Inquisition of relapsing into Judaism in 1489. Castilian documents refer to Columbus as Colomo until 1487 but, by 1492, he was universally known as Colón. Surely this is more than a coincidence. The Jewish connection explains another enigma – why a man who was so eager to establish a family of Grandees in Spain never became a naturalized citizen of Castile: the Inquisition was directed at Spanish Conversos.

Unfortunately, any suggestion that Columbus came from a Sephardic family brings down the wrath of most non-Jewish scholars.[3] Let's review their main objections.

After three or more generations, they object, Columbus's Spanish would have been different, odd and antiquated. Indeed it was different – *he spoke like a foreigner,* wrote Las Casas. But Spanish, thanks to its phonetic pronunciation, has staying power. In a chic open-air discotheque on the Bosphorous I met a Turkish Sephardic Jew who spoke Ladino. Until then I had only read Ladino, whose spelling is utterly unSpanish (full of Ks which is not a Spanish letter), and listened to Sephardic songs, whose oriental tones sound strange to a Spanish ear. But here was young Yakob, who had never visited a Spanish-speaking country in his life, speaking a language that was perfectly intelligible to a Spaniard. His Ladino wasn't much more distant to Castilian than, say, Mexican Spanish.[4]

What about his Christian faith (as both his mother and father's families were property owners, they had to be Christian too)? Bartolomé de Las Casas wrote: *He was undoubtedly a Catholic and of much devotion. Almost in everything he would begin to do he prefaced, 'In the name of the Holy Trinity I will do this.' In whatever letter or other thing he wrote, he would head it,* Jesus cum Maria sit nobis in via, *and from these writings of his in his own hand I have many in my power… He fasted all the Church fasts with great observance; he confessed and took communion frequently; he prayed at all the canonical hours like a man of religion…* That contemporaries noted Columbus's devout (I was going to write 'good', but that has other connotations) Christianity is consistent with a good Converso, for Conversos were often the most pious of Christians. Many Conversos became priests and bishops – a friend of Columbus's even Inquisitor-General – and two, San Juan de Dios and Santa Teresa de Avila whose Converso grandfather was persecuted by the Inquisition, were sanctified.

Most scholars shy away from a Columbus of Jewish origins because he was so evidently a sincere Christian from a family of baptized Christians; but it was not inconsistent to be both, and goes some way to explaining his sense of being an outsider. Without the comfort of a normal social life or the security of a steady trade or career, he glimpsed an idea and nurtured it until it would become an obsession: to discover a new route to the Indies which would make his fame and fortune.

The Mayor's Office, containing the Columbian Archives, is at the Palazzo Tursi, a Renaissance palace in the Via Garibaldi, a street of splendid palaces all built within a hundred years of Columbus's death, and largely financed, as chance would have it, by the banking and commercial wealth brought via Spain from America. The Via Garibaldi is the one street with the architectural harmony, the detailed stonework and flourishes which one expects of an Italian city. Although there are splendid churches and palaces in isolated spots, in hidden piazzas and on the Via Balbi, I was coming to the conclusion that Genoa was bereft of the artistic inspiration of other Italian cities. After all, Genoa became as rich as Venice or Florence, and yet I couldn't name a single Genoese painter, though Van Dyck, Ruebens and Caravaggio all found a ready market here. The Via Garibaldi reassured me. I walked into the Palazzo Tursi where I had an appointment with the Curator of the Columbian archives.

Sr. Tarducci shook my hand with the light pressure of a diplomat. Tall, silver-haired, smooth-faced and elegant in his silver-grey suit, he had the air of a self-satisfied patrician. We mutually flattered the other on his national origin, the *Inglese* still respected for his nautical fame in this port city, though Tarducci was hardly likely to mention *i hooligans*, our best-known contribution to Europe's vocabulary.

We stood on a balcony overlooking a pink and white patio invaded by mature forest-green pot-plants. He led me through a dark corridor lined with small, gloomy offices, awash with papers and crammed with men working in the half-light, to a large, white, marble chamber finished in gold. Tall windows sucked in the light from the Via Garibaldi. It was empty but for a black functional table and chairs, and a six-foot marble column supporting a bust bearing a strong resemblance to Juan Carlos I of Spain. 'Not Columbus,' said Sr. Tarducci. Beneath the bust a Latin inscription in brass lettering read:

Here are the parchment letters Columbus
sent to his homeland. They were opened and
deposited here on his behalf.
Decreed by the Mayor of Genoa, MDCCCXXI.

Built into the column is a brass safe embossed with a scene of Mercury handing over something resembling a hand-grenade to a naked, feathered, Indian. The Indian received it with grave honour, as they at first received whatever trifle the Men-from-the-Heavens gave them, and I wondered what it was supposed to be. I asked Tarducci who smiled and said 'It was a gift.' I couldn't dispute that.

Tarducci inserted a key into the safe, extracted a carved walnut box, from which dangled a beautifully carved anchor, and placed it before me on the table. With the satisfaction of a magician, he withdrew from the box a Moroccan-leather purse and three silver-framed documents protected by glass. 'I show these to only a few people. The Spanish Ambassador, Senator Taviani, the former Minister, and the King and Queen of Spain.' I said I was honoured, wondering if my holiday dress of corduroy trousers, an old shooting-style jacket, leather boots and a thick pullover was quite up to this Columbian ceremony.

Columbus's handwriting was not as round and tidy as his postils, and the lower case rs almost flew off the page in imitation of seagulls. The black ink, based on iron salt and tannin, had faded to a rusty brown. As in all his correspondence, he wrote in Spanish, marked a cross at the head of each letter and signed, from 1494 onward, with the never-to-be-deciphered cipher:

$$\cdot S \cdot$$
$$\cdot S \cdot A \cdot S \cdot$$
$$X\ M\ Y$$

Xpo FERENS[5]

Tarducci asked me to read aloud from one of the letters. I selected the letter which warms the heart of all Genoese, for it is the only document signed by Colón-Columbus's own hand where he alludes to his Genoese origins. He addressed it to the *Prottetori del Banco di San Giorgio, Genoa.*

I read aloud, Tarducci listening with such an attentive expression that I could almost believe he had never read the letter before.

Seville, 2nd April 1502.

Very noble gentlemen: although my body walks here, my heart is constantly there... Messer Nicoló de Oderigo [Genoese Ambassador to Spain] knows more of my deeds than I do myself and to him I have sent my privileges and letters so that he may look after them.

And so he had. The Moroccan calfskin purse held one of the two extant copies of his *Book of Privileges*, still in mint condition. And suddenly, holding Columbus's book and thinking that it would be in equally good condition five hundred years from now, I was overcome with a sense of man's vulnerability. With our extraordinary gift for invention and capacity for hatred, would we even be around in half a millennium? And if we were, would the Sales and Stannards, authors of *The Conquest of Paradise* and *American Holocaust*, win the day and Columbus be remembered, if at all, as a wild Latino who would have better perished in mid-Atlantic? I studied the neatly-written pages with care, all directed at proving his rights and privileges contracted with and granted by Ferdinand and Isabella. At the end he had bound in a planisphere of the world, something no one had mentioned, an important discovery as it turned out, though its significance then escaped me.

While I handled the solid parchment book, Tarducci, in the casual stance of a man whose importance is self-evident, watched me. An inclination of his silver head, and he said, 'I'm afraid I can't leave you alone with these documents.' Of course he couldn't, and I said so.

Sr. Tarducci wanted to show me something else, and we walked back through the narrow corridor to the great reception room of the palace, flanked by two large mosaic portraits at either side of the entrance. Columbus looked at Marco Polo. Here, Columbus's dark eyes and black hair were typically Genoese whereas contemporaries described him as blue-eyed and reddish blond. Though his *Travels* had inspired Columbus, Marco Polo's presence surprised me. Genoa had kept him prisoner for half a year, coinciding with Rustichello to whom he related his travels. But if Genoa hadn't imprisoned him, would we or Columbus have known anything of Marco Polo? As Nehru once remarked, he himself had written all his major works in prison and would recommend it to an aspiring writer.

At the end of the reception room, on the left, Sr. Tarducci unlocked a small door leading to a dark, oak-panelled room. Behind a sheet of glass, one of Paganini's violins (four strings, of which two were loose) stood on an electrically-powered turntable. Sr. Tarducci set it in motion, watching it rotate with delight, as if it were a remarkable train set. As the violin rotated, patches of varnish rubbed thin by Paganini's shoulders, hands and jaw, testified to his loose, gypsy technique. On the same wall a crystal phial, hung inside a glass and gilt lantern, preserved a thimbleful of Columbus's ashes, suspiciously the colour of sawdust. Sr. Tarducci explained its provenance: 'Sixty years ago we sent a shipment of oil to Santo Domingo for Columbus's eternal flame, and they sent us back this phial of his ashes.'

'Have you noticed its colour?'

Tarducci glanced at the tiny phial and said they were, 'an interesting hue'.

It seemed churlish to press the point and remind him that Columbus would never have been cremated. Eminent institutions in Genoa, New York and Boston together with countless biographers had been duped by the Dominicans. The 'ashes' are the colour of recently cut pine.

As there was still an hour of daylight left, I walked back up the Via Garibaldi, plotting my roundabout, but necessary route to reach the vantage point known as the Villeta di Negro, named after a famous merchant family who had once employed Columbus. Plenty of people were about, all wrapped up in dark-coloured overcoats as if on their way to a funeral. I climbed the Villeta di Negro, passing imitation grottos and cascades, to the peak where the Oriental Museum sits with a clear view over the old city and the sea. On the landward side, dark forested mountain ridges plunge down, crushing the city against the water. Genoa tilts downhill and grips the valleys with long, brick-red tentacles, like an octopus with its back to the sea. With no sign of a fertile hinterland, it leaves the impression of an inelegant city which has had to struggle to survive. But, as the city was heavily bombarded by the French in 1684, suffered a terrible siege from the Austrians in 1800 and was bombed and shelled in the Second World War, I have perhaps judged it too harshly.

At the Bristol Palace I borrowed the telephone directory with the idea of contacting a Colombo, a possible descendant of Columbus's Uncle Antonio. I counted a hundred and ninety-two Colombos. What should I do, start with the only Cristoforo? It seemed a hopeless task. But, while I had the book, and with the historian's curiosity, I looked up Caboto, for though John Cabot was a Venetian citizen, he was born here in Genoa. There were no Cabotos in the Genoese phone directory. With that useless piece of information, I went up to my room for a rest before dinner.

The morning was bright and sunny and warmer and the grey stone face of Genoa smiled as best it could. According to my unreliable *Guide to Genoa*, Columbus was baptized nearby. I climbed two flights of steps and emerged at a platform. The church of Santo Stefano is a solid, round 11th-century Romanesque structure with a square bell-tower, extended upward two floors, so to speak, when Doric columns became a popular ornament in the 17th Century. It squats near the viaduct I had driven over two days earlier. Actually there's no record of Columbus's baptism, and I walked on up to the viaduct and came across this extraordinary plaque:

In 1879 the prominent merchant Giulio Cesare Drago contributed with his own money to the arched bridge which links the route from the Sottoporto District to the facing hill and which was bordered by an iron railing. He fell from the bridge to meet a voluntary or fortuitous death.

A *fortuitous death* when it was bordered by an iron railing? He had fallen a good twenty metres to the Via XX Settembre below, not far from the entrance to the Bristol Palace. I walked on to the Palazzo Reale, a red and ochre palace, remarkable for its tall conservatory-like windows framed in white, once home to the kings of Savoy.

I was the only visitor in the Palazzo Reale's gallery and had the honour of being accompanied by a short woman with a shock of auburn hair, the custodian of the gallery. In the second salon, on the right, I stood before a large eighteenth-century canvas, *La Battaglia de la Isola delle Correnti*, painted by Ludolf Bahujsan. Ships burn, are dismasted and, amid the chaos, fire cannon at point blank range. In the foreground an officer – his red tunic is buttoned to the throat and a white tricorn sits perfectly on his periwig – bobs effortlessly to shore with the aid of a ladder. We know little of Columbus's early life at sea, but Fernando, in the *History of the Admiral*, described his arrival in Portugal after a naval battle.

The ships met off Cape St. Vincent, in Portugal, where they fought fiercely and in such a way that both sides grappled with great hatred, wounding one-another without compassion with swords, lances, cauldrons of burning oil and firearms. After fighting from morning to sunset, with many dead and wounded on both sides, fire broke out on the large enemy ship and the Admiral's ship. The two were held together with hooks and iron chains, used by seamen for this purpose. Owing to the grappling irons and the terror of the fire, which spread rapidly, neither ship could be saved. The only hope was to jump into the water, better to die by drowning than to endure the flames. The Admiral was a strong swimmer and being about two leagues [six miles] from shore, he grabbed a sweep which was floating in the water; sometimes resting on the oar and sometimes swimming, he prayed to God, who watched over him for greater things, to give him the strength to reach land. When he did, he was so exhausted and sodden from sea-water that he took many days to recover.

There was a sea battle off Cape St. Vincent in the summer of 1476, when five Genoese merchantmen were attacked by corsairs flying the French ensign. The assumption that Columbus sailed with the Genoese fleet is weakened by his own testimony that he had once fought as a corsair for René of Anjou. Also his name was not on the crew list of the Genoese ships, nor did he regroup with the Genoese survivors in Cadiz. Perhaps he sailed with the French.[6]

Fernando reported him to have landed at Lagos, some miles east of Cape St. Vincent, a coast I know well. The skeleton of Lagos has changed little in the last five centuries. A long open beach curves away from the fort and town walls to the east, and a wind often blows in from the southwest with long rollers breaking on the gently sloping beach, carrying flotsam, seaweed and Columbus clutching his sweep. The old slave market, a hundred yards from the old port, is now a gallery and flea market specializing in African artifacts, T-shirts and semiprecious gemstones. As chance — or God — would have it, a southwesterly wind washed Columbus up at the first port of discovery in Europe. From here, Henry the Navigator saw off the discovery fleets that set out to explore the islands and coastline of West Africa. After Henry's death and sixteen years before Columbus's arrival, King John moved the centre of navigation from Sagres and Lagos to

Lisbon. Columbus was twenty-five years old. This chance landing on the coast of Portugal marked a turning point in his life: by settling on the Atlantic coast his orientation turned to the west and the seemingly limitless Ocean Sea.

I left the Palazzo Reale, picked up my luggage from the foyer of the Bristol Palace and retrieved the Renault. I had one last obligation in Genoa and that entailed a visit to the Staglieno Cemetery, perched up on one of the hills which soar up from the sea to the Appenines. I was to look for the grave of a friend's grandfather, once Ottoman Ambassador to Bulgaria, who was taken ill aboard a ship bound for Marseille and landed at Genoa where he died.

With some difficulty I navigated my way out of the city and up the valley leading to the cemetery. I parked near a row of flower shops and passed under the welcoming arch to the Information Centre. At the counter a cheerful-looking woman took my request with interest and passed on the information to an elderly man in a tweed jacket and grey flannels, evidently her boss. Soon he had all five clerks at his disposal searching through two-foot tall brown leather tomes dated 1918, 1919 and 1920. 'A plentiful period,' he remarked, 'because of the influenza epidemic.' But Mehmet's grandfather wasn't in the Staglieno Cemetery and had probably been buried in one of the other cemeteries in the city proper. The supervisor took this failure to find my Turk to heart and, eager to please, pressed me to see the English section of his cemetery. To please him I allowed him to lead me outside and up the hill, giving me instructions on how to find my compatriots.

Once dead, the Genoese lead a blissful life. Their sumptuous mausoleums are well spaced on terraces with a stunning view over the city to the sea. The grass and abundant herbaceous borders are immaculately maintained, plentiful pines, cedars and chestnuts providing shade in the summer. The sense of tranquility is heightened by the absence of cars. Shiny marble, black, rose or white is the preferred material, and one is surrounded by more sculptures than can be found in all the rest of Genoa. The English section of the cemetery is simple by comparison. Rows of crosses and gravestones line three small terraces, one above the other. The lower terrace is dedicated to servicemen who lost their lives in the First World War, the upper to those who were killed in the Second (mainly aviators bombing Italian targets) and civilians occupy the middle. I wondered what we had done with the German aviators killed over Britain – I was sure we would never have allowed them to be honoured on one of the finest positions in our cemeteries. Within a week I was back in Madrid and wouldn't leave for Portugal, where Columbus married and lived for eight years, until the summer.

2

PORTUGAL

We stayed at the Estalgem Moleiro outside Estoi, twelve kilometres inland from the port of Faro. From our bedroom window
vineyards fell away before us to a dark smudge on the horizon –
the summer haze limits visibility – where the coast merges with
the sea.

A slow drive along the coastal road brought me to Lagos,
where Columbus was washed up in August 1476. For a nation
so famous for its nautical prowess, Portugal is awfully short of
ports. From Lisbon all the way down to Cape St. Vincent and
around to Lagos there is but one harbour, and that is at Setúbal,
near Lisbon. This is one-third of Portugal's entire coastline,
which Morison describes as an 'iron coast'. After Lagos things
improve, with four more ports until the possibilities end at the
frontier with Spain. Even Lagos's harbour – I do not refer to the
modern port – would be better termed a good anchorage, since it
offers protection from the prevailing southwesterlies but little
else. A sea wall, with a square fort pointing out into the sea,
offers further protection from southerly and easterly winds.
However Lagos is the closest thing to a harbour from Sagres and
that's why Henry The Navigator (a purely English misnomer
since Henry never navigated a ship or travelled further than
Ceuta) chose it to launch his expeditions down the west coast of
Africa. Why then did Henry choose to live in Sagres?

I drove an inland route, along lanes often no wider than my
car, to avoid the permanent traffic jam on the coastal road to
Sagres. Distances are misleading. 36 kilometres separate Sagres
from Lagos, but it took me over an hour, and I was forced off the
road into the edge of a field by an oncoming van, which preferred a head-on collision to giving way to a car with Spanish
plates.

From the landward end the fortress's wall is intact, but this
initial promise is just that. I leant into a strong southwesterly
breeze, passing through the unvigilated gate to a cluster of brick
and rendered buildings – a Victorian house, a new auditorium

and various outbuildings – and a huge stone compass rose which, unaccountably, some guide books have difficulty identifying. A tiny chapel in the shape of a bunker and a small stone watch-tower still stand, the latter used as an unofficial pissoir. The craggy headland juts out into the Atlantic a good two hundred feet above the incoming swell which smashes on to the rocks below, the hounding westerly wind blowing the spray, with the consistency of soap suds, up the cliff face. Off to the right, north-westwards, is Cape St. Vincent, the southwesterly extremity of the European mainland, and a near copy of Sagres Point.

Here, with an open westerly and southerly view of the Ocean Sea, barren save for an anaemic-white trumpet of a flower sprouting from crevices in the bare rock, and miles from the nearest village, Henry established his centre for discovery. Seated on the edge of the compass-rose, I looked at this forlorn point where wind and breaking seas dominate the senses. There is no escape from the roar of the elements, and the air is filled with a saline scent carried in by the wind. I realized why it all seemed so familiar – it was the closest one could get on land to being at sea. That, and its vantage point for sighting vessels returning from the African voyages were, I was sure, the reasons Henry chose Sagres.

Only a visit to this barren end of Europe, a week's horse-ride from the civilized life of Lisbon, enables one to appreciate the determination Henry applied to his venture. Every spring he gathered a hotchpotch of fishermen, merchants and knight adventurers and sent them out to seek new lands. The general objective of Henry and John II was to round the southern point of Africa and sail across the eastern arm of the Ocean Sea to reach the spice islands of the orient. Circumnavigating Africa had only been successfully attempted 1,900 years earlier by Phoenician sailors sent by King Neco of Egypt, after abandoning an attempt to build a canal betwen the Mediterranean and Red seas. They had set out from the Red Sea and returned through the Straits of Gibralter, twice interrupting their voyage to land, sew and reap a harvest before re-embarking. Herodotus reports another attempt, this time by Satespes (a nephew of Darius), on the orders of Xerxes, commuting the punishment of impalement for raping a girl. Satespes took a Carthaginian crew, passed through the Straits of Gibralter and sailed months south, before being forced to put about. Unwisely, Satespes returned and Xerxes imposed the original punishment and had him impaled.

Portuguese progress was slow, in part because seamen lost heart when they reached Cape Bojadar, a mere pimple on the Western Sahara's coast, returning year after year with stories of boiling seas, infernal heat and wild winds. Sixty years of systematic exploration from 1418 yielded the discovery of Madeira (meaning 'wood' and soon after its discovery the Portuguese started a fire which burned for seven years), the Azores, the Cape Verde Islands, and the coast of Africa as far south as the River Zaire. They were still far from their objective when Columbus was swept ashore at Lagos.

Fernando wrote that Columbus travelled to Lisbon *where he knew he would find many other Genoese and knowing him, they made him so welcome that he made the city his home...*

How had Lisbon struck Columbus? Standing on one of a labyrinth of walls, all that remains of John II's palace, I looked out over the medieval districts of the Alfama and Santa Cruz to the Tagus estuary, dwarfing the orange ferries that link its southern shore with the city. Camoes described Lisbon as *The Princess of the world before whom even the ocean bows,* not much of a description, but such is the epic style. King John II, residing in the Royal Palace inside the heavy ochre stone walls of St. George's Castle, was the undisputed centre of power. Walking down the twisting, narrow streets that fall away steeply to the Tagus, the estuary spread before me *like a field of gold in the afternoon sun,* to quote a local guide book, quite believable as it spreads away to the west, and an improvement on Camoes. Entering the Alfama proper, its narrow street plan reminds one of a souk though only the occasional house or wall dates from its Arab period. One alley, running parallel with the Tagus, is the fish market, whose high smell is retained in its confined space, augmented by the water and fish guts stall owners sluice over its cobblestones. Dropping further down, I emerged at a small courtyard overshadowed by a section of the huge Arab wall above me. Standing with my back to the wall, the triangular square recovered its proportions, and I focused on a conch-shaped fountain set into a smaller wall through which an arabesque portal leads directly to the Tagus. This was the gate to the Jewish quarter, through which Columbus used to pass with such frequency that he would leave half a silver mark to its gate-keeper a quarter of a century later.

A prevailing westerly, fresh and moist, brings regular rain that washes away the city's filth. After the brigandry, factional wars, invasions, poverty and pestilent claustrophobia of Genoa, Lisbon must have seemed a paradise to Columbus. He settled down, *and married*, according to Fernando. *Because he was of noble bearing, handsome and couldn't be separated from all that was honourable, it happened that a lady of noble blood, Doña Felipa Muñiz, who lived in the Convent of All Saints, where the Admiral usually went to mass, took such pleasure in his conversation and friendship that they married.*

There is no record of the year of the marriage, but Felipa gave birth to a son, Diego, in 1480. Columbus's younger brother, Bartolomé, joined him. Bartolomé, with God and Isabella of Castile, was the most important figure in Columbus's life. Some ten years his junior, of similar physique – tallish, powerful, blond and blue-eyed – Bartolomé became, like Columbus, a fine sea-man and map-maker, but with two qualities that would become invaluable to Columbus: he was fearless in battle without the reflective, imaginative elements that steered Columbus away from such direct confrontations, and he was wholly trustworthy as a second-in-command. Las Casas knew Bartolomé and described him as: *A very sensible, energetic man, more circumspect and astute than he seemed and less candid than Columbus. He understood the affairs of men and was notably wise and practiced in matters of the sea. I believe he was not much less learned than his brother in cosmography and in the making of charts and globes, and in some of this he exceeded him, since he had to learn it to make a living. He was above average height and had an honourable and authoritative bearing, though not in the same degree as the Admiral.*

Felipa's family owned Porto Santo, a small, barren (overrun by rabbits imported by Columbus's father-in-law), thinly-popu-lated island near Madeira, which Columbus soon abandoned for Funchal. By 1483, they were back in Lisbon. Both ports were bases for Columbus who rarely left the sea, trading sugar, and perhaps gold, slaves and other items for the Genoese merchant houses of Centurione and Di Negro. Information is scarce because there is no official record of Columbus in Portugal for the eight or nine years (1476 to 1484/5) he lived there, and the circumstantial evidence is sparse.[7]

A mile down the estuary from the Castle, just out of my view, lay the port of Restelo. From there, each spring, caravels, with the maroon cross of the Knights of Christ emblazoned on their sails, embarked on the southern voyages of discovery. Columbus was at the seat of such endeavour.

When a destitute Genoese sea-captain defies the scholars of the day to persuade merchants, foreign courtiers and kings to support him in a venture which seems doomed to fail, one wonders what were the conditions which made it possible. And some insight is required into a period when man suddenly became interested in *the secrets of this world* (to quote Columbus) to the extent that he would risk his life trying to discover them. Phoenicians (circumnavigating Africa in the 5th Century B.C.), Arabs (the great Ibn Majid piloted Vasco da Gama's fleet across the Indian Ocean), Ming Chinese (sailing around the rim of the Indian Ocean, 1405-33, under the direction of the Grand Eunuch, Cheng Ho) and Portuguese made long sea voyages, but ships and men were gathered on the orders of their rulers who had clear objectives – to seek new trading routes or tribute from an extended empire. Even the Vikings only discovered Iceland, Greenland and Vinland by chance, storms driving ships off-course from known routes. Thus around 860 AD Nadd-Odd was blown off course on the way to the Faroe Islands and discovered Iceland (which might have already been colonized by Irish monks) which he called Snowland. About the year 900 Gunnbjörn was sailing from Norway to Iceland when he was blown off course and discovered a new land he called Gunnbjörn's Skerry. It wasn't until 985 that Eric the Red, exiled to the western extremity of Iceland for murdering a man, colonized the new land which he renamed Greenland. A year later Bjarni Herjolfson, sailing from Iceland to Greenland, lost his course too, sighting to the west three new islands, whose discovery was followed up six years later by Leif Ericsson, calling them Helluland (Baffin Island?), Markland (Labrador?) and Vinland (Newfoundland). To the contrary, Columbus had to persuade a foreign Prince to sponsor him, accept his particular view of the world and thereby satisfy his longing to discover its secrets. It was an extraordinarily individual enterprise, but this was a time of extraordinary individuals.

One inspiration was God. Columbus frequently wrote of God choosing him for this venture, and God was always at hand to inspire and help him *when everything seemed lost*. In an age when, as Oswald Spengler noted, the emphasis was on the individual, this elevation enabled Columbus to solicit support from the Courts of Portugal and Spain, reaching such a level of familiarity with their Princes that King John II of Portugal would address him as 'my special friend in Seville' and Isabella and Ferdinand would consent to a treaty between the Crown and this destitute foreigner, all on the basis of an unrealized project.

The virus of adventure was in the air and the Portuguese had perfected the means of discovery: they developed the lateen-rigged caravel, a small, fast vessel that pointed well to windward and was of low draught; a school of cosmographers designed new charts with a grid – latitude and longitude – and painted in prevailing winds and new landfalls to help navigation; navigators borrowed the astrolabe from the Arabs, who had acquired it from the Greeks, and they designed seamless tanks for preserving water and wine in the difficult conditions of an oceangoing vessel. Columbus breathed this air and, thanks to his marriage to Felipa, had access to John II.

Sometime during 1484, Columbus proposed to King John II a voyage by the western route to Asia. Why did he think Asia was within navigable distance? How did he think he would get back? Why did he believe he could conquer the Sea of Darkness where others had died in the attempt?

The cerebral Madariaga cites Columbus's numerous notes to Pope Pius II's *Description of Asia*, D'Ailly's *Imago Mundi* and his Ptolemy as the fundamental source of inspiration. Morison, rightly in my opinion, pooh-poohs this argument with the comment that 'scholars find it difficult to imagine ideas coming in any other way.' So Morison, while discussing the legends and driftwood which might have inspired him, suggests the idea might have come to him in childhood as he pondered the story of his namesake (a French corsair), or in youth, or in manhood... Taviani gets closer to the man when he writes that the inspiration came from *the impressions, deductions and considerations prompted by personal experience.* Then he waxes lyrical about his imagination of genius, *forging reality from dreams,* as if Columbus somehow had guessed the presence of America. Fernández-Armesto, while discarding none of the theories, favours three possible destinations (Asia, the Antipodes and as yet undiscovered islands) which Columbus chose indiscriminately depending on the preference of his audience. Fernández-Armesto, by proposing that any objective was a good objective provided some Prince supplied Columbus the necessary ships, succours the revisionist theory that Columbus headed out into the Ocean Sea without any definite objective in mind. This, I am sure, is a mistake.

Let Columbus have his say. He explained to Queen Isabella and King Ferdinand that *From a very early age I went to sea sailing and I have continued up to today. Whoever follows this profession is inclined to want to know the secrets of this world. I have been more than forty years in this. I have sailed everywhere where one can sail. I have talked with and met men of letters, ecclesiastical and secular, Latin and Greek, Jews and Moors and many other sects. Our Lord has favoured me in this and He gave me an intelligent mind. He made me capable of seamanship with sufficient skills in astronomy, geometry and arithmetic, and the hands to draw the sphere and in it the cities, rivers, mountains, islands and ports all in their correct place.*

I have sailed everywhere where one can sail is a big claim, and in other letters and postils Columbus was more specific. In a letter to Isabella and Ferdinand, he wrote undiplomatically that he had captained a corsair from Marseilles to Tunis (1472) to attack a Catalan vessel. As a merchant, presumably, he sailed to Chios (1474-5) in the Dodecanese (only five miles from Anatolia), then a Genoese colony and famous for mastic, from which perfume was made. In another letter, he informed a no-doubt bemused Isabella and Ferdinand of the best route between Cadiz and Naples in summer and winter. But it was after his arrival in Portugal that he set out on his long, oceangoing voyages: in February 1477, just seven months after his fortuitous shipwreck off Lagos, to England, Ireland and *a hundred leagues beyond Iceland.* As this was beyond the normal trading range of Genoa,

Columbus showed an early interest in lands on the extremity of the Ocean Sea.[8] In a note in the margin of D'Ailly's *Imago Mundi*, he reported frequent voyages to El Mina on the Guinea Coast, where he must have traded the products most appreciated by his Genoese employers – gold and slaves. Elsewhere he wrote of his experiences in the Cape Verde Islands and the Azores.

Except for the relative backwater of the North Sea and the cul-de-sacs of the Black Sea and Baltic, Columbus had sailed *everywhere where one can sail.* He picked up information from older mariners and islanders, encouraging him to believe there was land not that far to the west. This brings me to the second influence on his thinking, which comes clearly through the mouthpiece of his son, Fernando. Driftwood – carved wood, American pines, canes *so thick that, from one knot to the next, there was room inside for nine pipes of wine* – were found by seamen and islanders from the Azores to Porto Santo, meaning there was land to the west, and presumably not too distant. And, reports Fernando, *Some Portuguese included this in their charts with the name of Antilla [legendary remains of Atlantis], never more than two hundred leagues to the west, opposite the Canary Islands and the Azores.*

The pines, canes and carved wooden pieces surely did come from America. An Azore Islander gave Morison a *favo do mar*, an American sea-bean, which had been washed up. And a certain Floridian, Robert Morgan, has been dropping bottles into the Gulf Stream at the rate of two a week for a quarter of a century, receiving replies from Britain to Morocco. The latest recipient found a bottle on a beach in Brittany a year and a half after Morgan launched it. These sightings encouraged Columbus in his belief that land – islands, mainlands, Asia – was not far to the west.

Then his frequent references to Marco Polo, Ezra and Alfraganus help to explain his idea of the relative position of Asia to Europe: Marco Polo reported that Cipangu (Japan) was 1,500 miles off the coast of China and so a stepping stone in that direction, and he wrote of the great wealth he found in China and believed existed in Japan (solid gold roofs and so forth); the prophet Ezra asserted that five-sixths of the earth was land and only one-sixth water, thereby limiting the possible dimension of the Ocean Sea; and the Arab mathematician Alfraganus calculated the earth's circumference at 20,400 miles, in Arab miles within five percent of the real distance. In the Roman miles Columbus used this meant our planet was relatively small – about seven-tenths of its actual circumference.

But for all these authorities, voyages and driftwood, I was sure that Columbus's determination to *discover the east by going to the west* had another, more potent explanation. But what?

While the children played in a small pool at the bottom of the garden, I sat on my sister-in-law's terrace which has a view over the Tagus estuary. It's a wonderful sweep of water, broad, well protected from storms at sea, though with a racing current when the tide floods to fill and partially empty the huge tidal basin which is Lisbon Harbour. All classes of vessel use it, from block-long tankers to small sailing craft and fishing vessels, insignificant even here, within hailing distance of land. Years earlier, I had sailed down this coast in a 35-foot catamaran without putting in to any Portuguese port. Though it was July, mist obscured the coast until we reached Cape St. Vincent, where ships line up in preparation for the run through the Straits of Gibraltar. For navigation we relied on RDF fixes on console stations, now made obsolete by satellite navigation, and we knew that to the east was Oporto and the entrance to the River Douro, the landmark which is the Rock of Sintra... And then it occurred to me. Columbus was a practical sea-captain, not a wild adventurer, so something very persuasive had convinced him to seek the East by going to the West. Columbus was a map-maker, a fine navigator and he reported using a chart on board the *Santa Maria* on the First Voyage of Discovery. What better to decide your course than a map? If you take a map aboard a discovery vessel, you intend to use it to find your destination. Once we have Columbus's map, we have his destination. All the indications point to the map the Florentine mathematician Toscanelli[9] described sending to King John. This map was lost, but we have a very good description of it in Toscanelli's letter, carefully copied and saved by Columbus:

Florence, 21st June 1474.

To Canon Fernando Martins of Lisbon, the cosmographer Paolo Toscanelli sends his greetings. I was pleased to hear of your health, your good favour and relationship with the King, the most noble and generous Prince. On another occasion I spoke to you about a maritime route to the land of spices which is shorter than the route via Guinea. The most serene King now asks for a report, or rather a clear exposition, so that even the moderately well informed will understand this route. Although I know this can be shown by using a spherical image, like the world, I have decided to show the route on a navigational chart, as this is more easily understood and more easily made.

The famous map! Passing over his explanation of sailing west to reach the east, descriptions of Zaiton with its hundred ships filled with pepper, and a Chinese emissary's tales of gold, silver, gems and spices, I arrived at the last paragraph where he describes his map:

From Lisbon westward in a straight line there are twenty-six spans, each of 250 miles, marked on the map to the very notable and grand city of Quinsay [Hangzhou] The distance is nearly one-third of the globe. This city is in the province of Mango [South East China], bordering on the province of Katay [North East China], seat of the Royal Palace. But from the island of Antilla [imaginary], which you know, to the famous island of Cipango [Japan] are ten spaces; and this is the richest island in gold, pearls and gems and they cover their temples and palaces with solid gold; – exactly what Columbus and Pinzón promised potential crew members for the First Voyage – *so one has to cross not too large a space of sea by the new route. Perhaps one should explain these matters with greater clarity, but a thoughtful man interested in this should, from this information, be able to understand the rest. Farewell my friend.*

I opened my atlas's map at the Atlantic and marked Toscanelli's distances from the longitude of Lisbon to Antilla, Cipangu and Mangi, but at a latitude just south of the Canaries to take account of Columbus's westward and southwestward course from La Gomera. This, filled in with the help of Martin Behaim's Globe of 1492, is what I found: (see Map 1).

It fitted. Cipangu fell just short of Hispaniola, and Mangi coincided with the Gulf Coast of Mexico. No wonder no one could shake Columbus's faith that Hispaniola was Cipangu-Japan and that his brother, Bartolomé, called the Central American mountain range, which blocked their route to India, the Chinese Mountains.

Map 1 – Columbus's 'map' superimposed on the genuine map of the Americas

Everything pointed to Toscanelli's letter (and map), which Columbus had so carefully preserved, as being the inspiration for his westward voyage. As he bound it into his copy of Pius II's *Description of Asia*, together with a calculation of the age of the world (5,241 years) in 1481, he must have read it at least three years before proposing his voyage to King John. The planisphere Columbus drew and kept with the Toscanelli letter is the first document we have where he was thinking in world terms; and it was almost identical to the planisphere bound into the back of *The Book of Privileges* he had sent to Genoa fourteen years later. It was as if these planispheres he painted, illustrating the gap between Europe and Asia represented by the Ocean Sea, were his proof of copyright, and Toscanelli's geographic concept of the world was identical to Columbus's as he explained it in later years. If that wasn't enough of a clue, both Las Casas and Fernando Colón recorded Columbus corresponding with Toscanelli shortly before he died in May 1482. The correspondence is controversial, but what was important was the importance Fernando, Columbus's mouthpiece, gave it.[10]

According to Toscanelli, and translating the Roman miles to nautical miles, the distance from Lisbon was 1,600 miles to Antilla, 3,680 to Japan and 5,200 to China, in hops of 1,600, 2,080 and 1,520 nautical miles respectively; hardly daunting to a man who had sailed to El Mina, 3,500 miles from Lisbon, and Iceland, 1,600 miles distant. With contrary winds these were still formidable, impossible distances, but Columbus had a secret which he didn't divulge for at least eight years (1484 to 1492): when stopping at the Canary Islands on the First Voyage of Discovery, *I rerigged the* Pinta *square because she was lateen-rigged* (the other two ships were already square-rigged). Though it was easier to sail downwind square-rigged, with no danger of gybing, the lateen was better for beating against the wind and so the preferred rig of the Portuguese discoverers. As Morison first pointed out, there is only one satisfactory explanation for rigging square. By 1484, Columbus had noted the prevailing northeasterly winds, between the latitude of the Canaries and the Cape Verde Islands, *and the prevailing westerlies*, from the latitude of the Azores to Britain. I stress the westerlies because he would need them to return to Iberia.[11] Columbus had no intention of beating across the Sea of Darkness (see Map 2).

So what was his objective? In Portugal he was said to have offered to sail to Cipangu, Japan; Columbus's agreement with the Crown of Spain was to discover *islands and mainlands*; he wrote in the Prologue to the First Voyage that he would go to the Indies, meaning Asia, and *the prince who is called the Great Khan*, then thought to be residing in China; en route to the Indies he thought he passed islands in the Sargasso Sea; when he approached the Bahamas he wrote that he'd press on to Mangi (China), leaving Cipangu for later. It seems confusing until one puts them in context: all these destinations are consistent with Toscanelli's map. Columbus's objective, as becomes patently obvious in his Journal, was Japan and China, but he believed he would find other islands before reaching them.

Map 2 – The Atlantic wind systems and places Columbus had visited on the edge of the Atlantic

This leaves another mystery: why does Columbus never mention Toscanelli elsewhere, beyond the privacy of his copy of the *Description of Asia*? He frequently cites Marco Polo, Ptolemy, Ezra, Isaiah, D'Ailly, Pope Pius II, Pliny, St. Augustine, Alfraganus, Josep Vizinho and others as authorities. But not once does he mention Toscanelli. Madariaga's inescapable conclusion is that by copying Toscanelli's letter he had broken the trust of John II. Fear of exposure explains Columbus's silence. At this point I feel obliged to return to Yale University's Vinland Map whose authenticity has recently been reasserted in a new edition (1996) of *The Vinland Map and Tartar Relation*. I would refer the reader to Morison's convincing argument that the Vinland-Greenland sections have been falsified (*The European Discovery of America, the Northern Voyages*, pages 69-72). By now, it must be obvious that Columbus's objective had nothing to do with Vinland, which he never mentions and which is 1,800 miles north of his outward course.

The Jeronymite Monastery, begun within Columbus's lifetime but after he left Lisbon, miraculously resisted the Great Earthquake of 1755. Walking around its exterior, I admired the long line of delicate Gothic windows, carved as finely as ivory in the Manueline style, overlooking simple green gardens of lawn, boxwood and bedding plants to the Tagus. Buttresses and fluted towers flow parallel to the river, filling the view with their isolated majesty. But to one side stands a mammoth stone bunker, a memorial to Portugal's Presidency of the European Union, and beyond the square rundown redbrick warehouses and terraces show a blank face to the rutted street and the commuter railway, whose poles and overhead cables spoil the view of the estuary.

Inside the Monastery, in the west wing, behind the Manueline plateresque façade, is the Museu da Marinha. At its entrance a huge map of the world fills one wall. The map-maker painted the Portuguese royal emblem, a blue cross on a white background framed in ermine and surmounted by a gold crown, over most of the world: Quebec, Brazil, Africa and India. Seven-foot modern bronzes of 15th-century discoverers – Nuno Tristâo, Pedro de Sintra, Gonçalvez Zarco, Gil Eanes, Diego Câo, Gaspar Corte-Real and Vasco da Gama – line the walls, monuments to the energy and perseverance of a century of discovery. Rock inscriptions brought back from Africa (Lelala, Cape Cross, Cape Santa Maria), a fragment of a cross retrieved from Anjedira in the East Indies and mementos of the fortresses of El Mina, Diu, Calicut and Goa, now abandoned and in ruins, are sad reminders of a brilliant past.

I stood before a glass case of beautifully crafted, but obsolete navigational instruments – a universal astronomical ring, a diptych sundial, planispheric astrolabes, quadrants and sextants, of cedar, bronze and brass – and breathed in the musty air of the monastery-museum. Contemplation of the achievements of our forefathers – and the seven-foot mariners – enervated any will to emulate them. Freud's concept of being 'wrecked by success' was wrought to the scale of a nation.

In 15th-century Portugal two strong men, the Infante Henry and King John of Portugal, lured men into new waters with the promise of rewards, of islands or estates, that were not always kept. Columbus had to deal with King John II, a man who pops up at crucial moments in Columbus's life.

This is what the official chronicler, Ruy de Pina, had to say about his master :

The King Dom João was a man of largish build, with a rather ugly face, well-proportioned limbs and a suitably thick beard. His hair was brown and smooth, and at the age of thirty-seven neither his head of hair nor his beard were very grey, which pleased him greatly; but with age his hair grew grey. He had perfect vision and, at times, when he was angry, he showed the whites of his eyes afflicted with blood, and when he was like that, he had a terrifying appearance. In times of glory or pleasure, he was very merry and royal and of excellent humour; his nose was a bit snub and bent without being ugly. He was very pale except his face which was good and ruddy. He was a Prince of marvellous ingenuity and sudden wit. He had a very sharp and trained memory and clear and profound judgement. His sayings and stories he invented and told were always coloured with truths, wit and authority rather than sweetness or elegance of language, which he pronounced loosely and intoned through such a thicket of nasal hairs that it was amusing.

The Portuguese remember King John II as the Perfect King for his decisive consolidation of power in the Crown, including the destruction of the House of Bragança, having its patriarch, the Duke, tried and executed and the family's estates confiscated. In 1484, the year Columbus proposed his westward voyage to Asia, the Perfect King summoned the Duke of Viseu to his chamber and thrust a dagger into his breast, killing him on the spot. He suspected the young Duke, his brother-in-law, of conspiring against him. War – with Castile – and the threat of conspiracy had ridden beside John since he has a child. The experienced diplomat Machiavelli wrote that all people expect of a ruler is excellence in the art of war. Proximity to such a Prince could be dangerous, as Machiavelli, tortured and imprisoned by the Medici, would testify. But John, entrusted with the Africa trade by his father at the age of nineteen, promoted discovery fleets for the rest of his life; an ideal Prince to sponsor Columbus's venture of the Indies.

Columbus was thirty-three when he proposed his voyage to John II. Fernando described his father:

The Admiral was a well-built man, neither fat nor thin, of above average height with a long face and high cheeks. He had an aquiline nose, was blue-eyed and pale complexioned, tending to vivid red. In youth his hair was blond, though by the time he was thirty it had turned grey. In eating and drinking and the adornment of his person, he was always temperate and modest. Among strangers his conversation was affable and with members of his household very agreeable, with modest and pleasing dignity. He was so observant of religious matters, of praying and fasting, that he could have been taken for a member of a religious order. He was so great an enemy of cursing and swearing that I swear I never heard him utter any oath other than 'By San Fernando', and when he was most angry, his reprimand was, 'May God take you, why did you do this or say that?'

King John II and Columbus shared an obsession with discovery and each was to disappoint the other. Beyond the contents of the Toscanelli letter, familiar to both men, there is little additional information on Columbus's proposal. Forty-five years later, Joâo de Barros gave the official version for the rejection of Columbus's venture:

The King gave little credit to what this Christovem Colom said because he was such a talker and gloried in showing his cleverness and, what is more, was full of fantasies, believing in his island Cypango. However, on the strength of his persistence, he was sent to Dom Diego Ortiz, Bishop of Ceuta, Master Rodrigo and Master Josep, who were responsible for matters of cosmography and discovery. All listened to Christovam Colom's pointless proposals which were all founded on the invention of the island Cypango of Marco Polo. The commission thought Marco Polo's book was a tall tale and discarded Cipangu-Japan as an imaginary island, though they were happy to pepper the Ocean Sea with other unknown islands – Brasil, Brendan and Antilla were the most common.

Fernando Colón offers a different, but not necessarily conflicting, explanation.

The King, advised by Dr. Calçadilla, whom he trusted greatly, decided to send a caravel secretly to try to do what the Admiral had offered, since, by discovering the new lands this way, he would not be obliged to give such a large reward as the Admiral had asked for his discovery. Quickly, and in complete secrecy, he prepared a caravel, pretending to send it with supplies to the Cape Verde Islands. However, he ordered it to follow the direction which the Admiral had offered to go. But, as the officers did not have the knowledge, persistence or character of the Admiral, after sailing for many days they returned to the Cape Verde Islands, mocking such a venture and saying it was impossible to find land on those seas.

Knowing the demands Columbus made in Castile and the secrecy and impatience of the King to find a route to Asia, Fernando's report, which can only have come from his father or Uncle Bartolomé, is well substantiated. It is known that Fernâo Dulmo and Joâo Estreito set out from Terceira in the Azores in 1485 to seek, officially, Antilla, though as Morison points out this could well have been the first step to Cipango. Of course they ran into headwinds and found nothing. Fernando continues:

When the Admiral got to hear of this voyage, he took a great dislike to Lisbon and Portugal, and with his wife now dead, he decided to leave for Castile with his small son Diego Colón... At the end of 1484 the Admiral, with his son Don Diego, secretly left Portugal, fearing that the King would detain him. Not an unfounded fear, since King John would not want Columbus's services offered elsewhere, especially to his old enemy in Castile, Columbus's destination. However, there was another reason for the secret flight from Portugal. Three years later, poor and humbled in Castile, he wrote to King John (the letter is lost) offering, again, his services and requesting immunity from prosecution. Prosecution from what? One possible explanation is the debts he left with three Genoese merchants in Lisbon recognized, with a curious legacy to *a Jew who lived at the gate of the Judería in Lisbon,* in his will twenty-two years later (and perhaps – this is a long shot – the Jewish gatekeeper loaned Columbus half a silver mark to help him pay his way to Spain; this would explain the exactitude of Columbus's legacy and its peculiar destinantion). The King summoned him in what was to be a postscript to his eight or nine years in that country.

To Xpouam Collon, our special friend in Seville.

Xpoual Colon. We, Dom Joham… send you our greetings. We saw the letter you wrote us and greatly appreciate the goodwill and affection you show in your desire to serve us; both for what you mention and for other matters, where your perseverance and ingenuity will be most needed, we can assure you that it will be done to your satisfaction. As you might distrust our justice for some obligations you might have, with this letter we guarantee that during your stay here you will not be arrested, held, accused, tried or held responsible for any civil or penal matter. With this letter we order all our justices to abide by this decree. So we ask you, and would consider it a great favour, if you would come immediately.

Written in Avis on the 20th March 1488. The King.

By March 1488, Portuguese sailors had neither rounded the horn of Africa nor had discovered lands to the west. Sitting in Lisbon, progress towards discovering a sea route to the Indies was agonizingly slow and King John was not noted for his patience. Why not give this Genoese boaster some vessels in the off chance that he would discover a western route? In Postil 23b of D'Ailly's *Ymago Mundi*, Columbus recorded this visit to Portugal, where he met Bartolomeu Dias who *returned to Lisbon this month of December 1488; and he informed the King that he had sailed into unknown waters 600 leagues, i.e., 450 southward and 250 [Columbus is out by 100 leagues] to the south of a promontory he [actually the King] has named the Cape of Good Hope [Dias had named it the Cape of Storms], which we believe to be in Agesimba. He says that according to his astrolabe this place is forty-five degrees south of the Equator [it is 35°S.] so remote that it is 3,100 leagues from Lisbon. He related his voyage and drew it league by league on a navigational chart to show it to the very eyes of the most serene King, and I took part in all this. It confirms that everywhere the sea is navigable and that this is not hindered by excessive heat.*

As Columbus's arrival coincided with the return of Bartolomeu Dias from rounding the southern point of Africa, King John changed his mind. He decided to concentrate his efforts on the African route to India, and Columbus returned, disappointed, to Spain. The next time the two would meet, it was in very strained circumstances.

Returning to late 1484 or early 1485, Columbus left Lisbon in debt, a widower with a five-year-old son, believing that he'd been betrayed by the King. He arrived in Castile poor and unknown. He had to begin again. For the next seven years, Columbus was land-bound in my adopted country.

3

SPAIN

After crossing the Portuguese-Spanish border at the River
Guadiana by the new suspension bridge, I could have turned off
for Ayamonte, the first port on the Spanish side. But Columbus,
travelling by sea, carried on to the next major estuary where the
ports of Huelva, Palos and Moguer sit on the two rivers which
conflux before meandering lazily into the Atlantic. Why did
Columbus choose Castile and, specifically, these minor ports
instead of Cadiz or Seville? Madariaga, ever consistent, claims
that this Sephardic Jew was returning to his homeland – in which
case one might wonder why he waited until 1485. Taviani suggests that Columbus went to 'the larger and more powerful
neighbour' and to Huelva to leave his son with Felipa Moniz's
sister and her family. Fernández-Armesto paints the broad historical setting to explain Castile's competition 'at all levels' with
Portugal and, striking a stronger note, her possession of the
Canary Islands as good reasons for Columbus's election of
Castile, without mentioning his historically unimportant selection of Palos as his port of entry.

This choice of Castile can't be fully understood without
answering another question: why did Columbus stay on in Iberia
for a further seven years? Why didn't he move to France,
England or even the larger seafaring states of Italy, such as
Venice and Genoa, when his venture was rejected by the Spanish
Crown? The traditional explanation, that he stayed because
Isabella had promised to eventually sponsor his venture, doesn't
fit his restless energy and ambition or even the facts. For some
very good, but unexplained reason, Columbus stayed in Castile.
I will come to that later.

Fernando Colón reported his arrival in Castile in the winter of
1484/5, *Leaving his boy in a Monastery in Palos, called La Rábida.*
Palos, with Moguer, are the minor ports (Palos's is now silted
up) on the left bank of the Rio Tinto, close to Huelva on the left
bank of the Rio Odiel. As a first step, Columbus's choice of
Palos was necessary regardless of his next destination. He had to

leave his small son, Diego, with his sister-in-law, Violeta Moniz, and her family who lived in Huelva on the other side of the estuary – and she was later rewarded by Columbus and Diego who each gave her an annuity of 10,000 maravedis. By chance he stayed in the Monastery of La Rábida, less than a kilometre from Palos, where he met Fray Antonio de Marchena. Much later, Columbus wrote to Ferdinand and Isabella, *Never did I find help from anyone except Fray Antonio de Marchena.* Cosmographer and head of the Franciscan Order at La Rábida, with good connections at court, Marchena was to be his mentor for many years. And in La Rábida, Columbus was always reminded of the sea.

I turned off the main Huelva-Seville road for Palos, now asleep in the midday heat, and drove the last kilometre along the road Columbus and Diego had walked 510 years earlier to La Rábida. A short walk through the gardens, the plants chosen for their striking orange and red tones, takes you to the monastery's door. Perched on a small hill, La Rábida overlooks the Rio Tinto to the west, where ships returned from slave raids to Africa, fishing boats rolled in laden down with their catch from the continental shelf off Morocco, and trading vessels returned from England, Flanders, France and the Italian states. To the south there is an open view over the bar of Saltes and marshland, where a distant blue streak marks the edge of the Ocean Sea.

Today the monastery, a compact building dressed in the ochre stone of the region, has become a shrine to Columbus; on the payment of a small entrance fee you can follow his exploits via the modern frescos adorning its interior and view the room Columbus supposedly occupied. If Columbus did little for Palos in his lifetime, the former port is making up for it now. They are building a big Visitors' Centre down by the water, at the foot of the monastery, which will not only commemorate his departure from here for the First Voyage, but will include a theme park, a café and replicas of the *Niña*, the *Pinta* and the *Santa María*, moored in the river and ready to be tugged into a small harbour being built for the purpose. As replicas they have none of the oceangoing qualities of the original ships, the *Santa María* actually capsizing when it was launched in 1992. Also, the traditional opinion that she was a three-master has recently been proven wrong; apparently, she had four masts, two on her forecastle.

As Columbus was not worthy of chronicling until 1492 and his writings and correspondence began with the *Journal* of the First Voyage, the evidence of these seven years is mainly circumstantial. In general, I intend to follow the Spanish historian J. Manzano Manzano's well-documented study of Columbus's whereabouts in the seven years prior to his First Voyage. Fernando Colón wrote that Columbus went to Court where *he became friends with those who were most receptive to his proposal and were in a position to persuade Isabella and Ferdinand to accept it.* Though Fernando refers to an appearance at Court at Córdoba in 1485, his first Royal Audience took place in 1486 in Alcalá de Henares, twenty miles east of Madrid, where he sought support for his venture of sailing to the west to discover the east. As he depended on Isabella and Ferdinand for his well-being, even his life, until his death twenty-one years later, his relationship with them has been extensively analyzed. So what were they like?

Hernando de Pulgar wrote that Queen Isabella *was of average height and well composed in her person and in the proportion of her limbs. She was very pale, her hair was blond and her blue-green eyes had a pleasing and honest expression. Her good-featured face was lovely and happy. Her movements were dignified; she never drank wine; she was an excellent woman who liked to surround herself with trustworthy older women of noble lineage [to prevent scandalous rumours].*

She loved the King, her husband, and watched over him beyond the call of duty. She had a keen mind and yet was most discreet, which is a rare combination; she spoke well and was so clever that in spite of being occupied with the complex business of governing her kingdoms, she decided to learn Latin. After a year she understood both spoken and written Latin. She was a devout Catholic, secretly giving alms to the right causes; she honoured houses of worship and liked to visit monasteries and other religious houses, especially those which maintained an honest life: she endowed them munificently. She abhorred sorcerers, fortune-tellers and people with similar tricks and fabrications.

She enjoyed the conversation of the clergy who led honest lives and often received their advice; and though she often appeared to listen to them and to other scholars who were close to her, she usually decided what to do herself. She seemed to have fortune on her side in all the affairs she undertook. She was most inclined to dispense justice, so much so that it was believed she preferred severity to mercy; but she did this to stamp out the great crime and corruption she found in the Kingdom on succeeding to the throne. She wanted her letters and commands to be executed with dispatch.

This was the Queen who extirpated from the Kingdoms of Castile and Aragon the heresy of some Christians of Jewish lineage who had reverted to Jewish rites while pretending to live as good Christians.

She was a woman of great heart and concealed her anger; and those who knew her, be they Grandees of the Kingdom or others, feared her indignation. She was a hard worker as will be seen later in this Chronicle. She was firm in her objectives which could only be retracted with great difficulty.

The hard side of Isabella was forged in her early twenties, when Grandees used her to usurp the throne from Juana, the daughter of King Henry, her half-brother. One historian has described Henry as 'despicable', yet this redheaded, long-limbed man who avoided bloodshed and confrontation and loved long, solitary forest walks, music and melancholy songs, has my sympathy. He was eccentric, physically odd among his shorter, darker subjects and disliked war, a grave handicap in this period of warrior kings. He found it easier to slice off an estate or grant a pension to a troublemaker, who would continue to be his subject, than go to war and risk defeat. Generosity merely inspired ridicule, including an extraordinary ceremony in Avila (1465) where the Carillo faction despoiled his efigy. First the Archbishop of Toledo, Carillo, removed its crown, then the Marqués de Villena seized its sceptre and, one by one, the aristocracy of Castile tore all the ornaments from Henry's efigy, before it was thrown to the ground. Immediately afterwards they proclaimed the 11-year-old Infante, Isabella's brother, Alfonso King, but he died three years later of bubonic plague. Castile might have been left virtually ungovernable after twenty years of appeasement and anarchy might have ruled in parts of his Kingdom, but it had not suffered the twelve years of civil war in neighbouring Aragon.

Near the end of his reign, the Grandees bullied Henry into disinheriting Juana whom, they thought, was the natural daughter of Beltrán de la Cueva; and they feared Beltrán would exercise real power in her name. Since Henry's second wife and Queen, Juana, was notoriously promiscuous, Beltrán, or someone else, probably was the father. On one occasion, when Henry returned after an absence of nearly a year, as she was seven months pregnant, Juana escaped him by shinnying down a rope out of a window of their castle, only returning to Court once she had given birth to her child. Also, as Henry had annulled his first marriage to Blanca of Navarre on the grounds that it had never been consummated, he was rumoured to be impotent, even homosexual. So insistent were the rumours that he had several women testify that, from personal experience, they knew he wasn't. Voltaire summed up the procedure: 'Archbishop Carrillo and his party declared the King impotent when he was surrounded by lovers and, via an unheard of procedure in any State, pronounced his daughter Juana a bastard, adulterous and incapable of reigning.' This left Isabella, now married to Ferdinand, to fight Juana's Portuguese (including John and his father King Alfonso) and Castilian supporters for the throne. Six years of war ended in 1480, five years before Columbus's arrival.

Columbus is constant in his praise of Isabella. When he writes to her on any matter not purely informative, often his syntax becomes convoluted, his language abstruse. They were the same age, of similar colouring, both handsome and well spoken, and this has encouraged speculation about a special, almost amorous, relationship between Columbus and his Queen. Although he adored her uncritically, she didn't reciprocate his warm feelings until he returned from the discovery of the Indies, with all the proof that he had achieved what her scientific advisors had claimed was impossible. Until then he was another hanger-on, albeit handsome and well spoken, one of many men in search of Court favours. After Portugal, Castile, with its conquest of the Canary Islands (still incomplete), promised the next best reception for Columbus's venture to *discover the east by sailing to the west*.

Columbus's relations with Ferdinand were altogether colder and more difficult, but then Ferdinand, the model for Machiavelli's *The Prince*, was a trickier and less generous character:

The King was a man of medium height, well-proportioned limbs, regular facial features, smiling eyes and had a full head of dark hair. He was a self-controlled man and spoke in a steady manner, neither fast nor slow. He had a good mind and was moderate in food and drink and in the movements of his person; neither anger nor pleasure changed him. He rode sidesaddle very well, using a woman's saddle; he jousted with such skill that no one in his Kingdoms could do it better. He was a great hunter of birds, a man of considerable strength and indefatigable in matters of war. Naturally inclined to dispense justice, he was devout and sympathized with the wretched who were in distress. He was unusually graceful and so very friendly that whoever spoke to him came to love him and want to serve him. Likewise he sought out advice, especially from the Queen, his wife, whom he knew to be very competent; from childhood he was brought up with war, hard work and personal danger. As he spent all his income on military matters, we cannot say that he was generous.

He liked to play all sorts of games, such as pelota, chess and draughts and he spent more time on them than he should have. Although he loved the Queen, his wife, he was very taken with other women. Uncontrollably so, frequently found kissing Court Ladies in hallways and siring a flock of illegitimate children, two of them sisters who shared the same name (María de Aragon) and one a future Archbishop of Zaragoza. Isabella was intensely jealous.

Machiavelli wrote that had Ferdinand been renowned for his generosity, he would not have started and successfully concluded so many enterprises. Parsimonious at heart, ambitious beyond the means of his kingdom, Ferdinand procrastinated and prevaricated rather than pay what he owed. Columbus correctly sensed it would be Isabella, and not Ferdinand, who would see that he was rewarded for his discoveries. Also, Ferdinand's Aragon looked to Italy, Sardinia, Sicily and points east (with consulates in Alexandria and Famagusta) for commercial and territorial expansion.

Rarely has the destiny of a country been so marked by its sovereigns, as Isabella and Ferdinand remade Spain. The reign of the Catholic Sovereigns was extraordinary for the energy they channelled into the unification and organization of the state. No wonder Fernando Colón believed (wrongly) they were too busy with wars and conquests to consider Columbus's proposal. Spain was a crystal smashed into dozens of pieces and Isabella and Ferdinand devoted their lives to fusing it into a whole, to realize the cry, *España! Una, grande, libre* which Franco would make his own. Within Iberia there were five states (Castile, Portugal, Navarra, Granada and Aragon, itself divided into the autonomous nations of Aragon, Valencia, Catalonia and Majorca), class interests (Grandees, Clergy, Cortes, Religious-Military orders) and religious groupings (Christian, Jewish and Moslem) all more or less independent of the central authority, the Crown, all more or less financially autonomous. To unify Spain Isabella and Ferdinand had to be ruthless, but the means they used were sometimes despotic and cruel. A passage from the decree expelling the Jews illustrates their thinking:

And when any serious and detestable crime is committed by some persons of a college or university, it is right that such college or univer-sity should be dissolved and annihilated, and the lesser suffer for the greater, and one be punished for the other; and those that disturb the welfare and proper living of cities and towns, that by contagion may injure others, should be expelled therefrom...

Without this principle that *the lesser suffer for the greater* Isabella and Ferdinand would never have unified Spain. Unification meant a protracted war against Moslem Granada, requiring huge new taxes both to support a Royal army and to offset the loss of Granada's tribute, and direct control over dissident groups, which could only be achieved by imposing new powers for the Crown. Ferdinand and Isabella convoked the Cortes in 1476 and again in 1480 to establish regular taxation, but once the Cortes had voted the moneys, they ignored it for eighteen years. Needing still larger sums, they imposed a Crusade Tax on the Church, increasing the state's revenue fourfold between 1474 and 1510; though the Reconquest was over, they continued to levy the tax, rather as Income Tax is a residue of first the Napoleonic and then the Crimean Wars. Fresh from victory over Juana's forces, they reduced the nobles' state pensions, saving the treasury precious funds while reducing their potential rivals' wealth.

Simultaneously, Ferdinand and Isabella organized the state to bring all its main elements into their power, giving life to the Santa Hermandad (Holy Brotherhood), a national police force which had been created in the early years of Henry's reign and allowed to languish. To seize direct control of the cities, they appointed *Corrigedores* directly responsible to the Crown. To strengthen central, royal government, they gave new powers to the Royal Council, the Finance Council and the Chancelleries, incidently increasing the prestige of the judicial system and so encouraging greater respect for the law. To usurp the power of the Church, Ferdinand had himself appointed leader of the religious-military orders and negotiated, with the judicious use of bribes, the accession of a Spanish Pope. Alexander VI, a Borgia, was a dreadful choice from an ecclesiastical viewpoint. Renowned for his debaucheries and string of natural children, as Pope he legitimized four of them by the Roman noblewoman Vanozza Catanei, appointing one of them Cardinal (Cesare soon gave it up in favour of a good marriage to a cousin of Louis XII, exchanging his soutane for a sword). Nevertheless, Alexander served Spain's interests well. To ensure that Jewish and Moslem converts to Christianity remained loyal to their new faith, Ferdinand and Isabella established the Holy Office of the Inquisition, an office first authorized by Henry IV who, out of sloth or wisdom, never gave it any practical powers. To rid Spain of nonconforming and potentially perfidious Jews and Moslems, they expelled all those who wouldn't convert to Christianity. And to make certain that the new apparatus of the state was run loyally and efficiently, they established a new class of functionary, the *Letrados*, university graduates drawn mainly from the lower ranks of the nobility. Columbus arrived when Isabella and Ferdinand's work was far from complete.

In this first audience at Alcalá, Columbus showed Isabella and Ferdinand a world map – surely taken from Toscanelli's – with his Cipangu a mere 750 leagues (2250 miles) from the Canaries and beyond that the lands of the Great Khan. This map and his eloquent speech, backed up a month later by Fray Marchena's audience, piqued the Sovereigns' interest. Ferdinand acquired Ptolemy's *Geography* and they set up a commission (June, 1486) of *specialists in cosmography to inform them fully and give an opinion.*

Meanwhile, Columbus trailed along with the Court as it made a thousand kilometre sweep through Old Castile before descending to the summer heat of the Guadalquivir valley and Córdoba, where it paused for nearly three months. It was here, argues Manzano, that Columbus met his mistress Beatriz Enriquez. By July, now in the blazing heat of an Andalusian summer, the Court moved eastward to Linares before swinging north, like an army lost in unknown territory, up the sides of the spectacular Despeñaperros Gorge on to the meseta and La Mancha, a withering burnt plain in the height of summer. The Court pressed forward to the cool mountain resort of Guadarrama, 50 kilometres north of Madrid, now famous as a Civil War battlefield. From there it northwested over the 1,500 metre Guadarrama pass between the sierra whose peaks reach 2,600 metres, before dropping down into the present province of Segovia, where the air cools in anticipation of the misty green hills of Galicia. At Santiago de Compostela, the end of the great pilgrimage route, they halted for two weeks. The itinerant Court soon packed up and was back on the road, heading due north to meet the Atlantic Ocean at La Coruña. Leaving the coast, the Court marched southeast across the green hills of Galicia until the land turned hard and brown as it penetrated, once again, the flat and undulating plains of Castile. They arrived at Salamanca on 7th November where they wintered. In fifteen weeks the Court had marched 1,600 kilometres from Cordoba, taking in an immense loop through northwest Spain.

According to Manzano, the Commission pronounced its judgement on Columbus's proposal here in Salamanca sometime between November 1486 and April 1487. *They judged the venture as vain and impossible, and that it was not right that such serious and high-minded Princes should act on such weak information,* reports Fernando. Columbus, in a 1498 letter to the King and Queen, summarized his opinion of the commissioners: *Your Highnesses already know that for seven years I followed your court, importuning you for this. Never, in all that time, did one find a pilot, seamen, philosopher or anyone of any other science who did not say my venture was false.* This coincides with Rodrigo Maldonado, a former Professor of Law at the University of Salamanca and member of the Commission who recalled: *All agreed that what the Admiral was saying could not possibly be true, and against their opinion the Admiral was determined to go on that voyage.*

Despite this rejection, Columbus stuck to the Court, following its meanderings through the iron-hard mesetas and sierras of a Castilian winter until it emerged again in the pleasant warmth of Córdoba (the winter quarters in Salamanca had lasted a mere two months). There seemed no end to the importuning; every halt in a new town or village meant a search for a roof to sleep under and, without an income, he had to rely on the generosity of villagers, monks or courtiers to keep him from starving. Midwinter in Castile in inadequate accommodation can be bone-chilling – the second most bitter winter I have lived was in a house in Pozuelo, 15 kilometres north of Madrid, when the swimming pool froze and the feeble electric heaters wouldn't raise the temperature of the drafty house above 53° Fahrenheit.

When the court moved, should he move with it? Columbus never knew when an important official, Juan Cabrero, the King's Chamberlain, or even the King or Queen might summon him. Circumstances – a fresh report on new discoveries from Portugal, a temporary surplus from the Crusade Tax, a new report from the Commission of scholars, a decisive move by Cardinal Mendoza – might, quite suddenly, favour his venture. Gnawing away at his optimism was the thought that some sea-captain would set out with the northeasterly trade winds behind him and discover his route to the Indies.

In May 1487 he followed the Court to Malaga and received a first-recorded payment of 3,000 maravedis, to be followed by three further payments, totalling 11,000 maravedis, in all about the pay of an able seaman. It is supposed it was here that Isabella promised him his venture would be undertaken once she had won Granada. Though it fits neatly with the timing of events – she accepted his venture directly after Granada's fall – and Fernando's history, there is no evidence that either Isabella or Ferdinand had any serious interest in his venture at this time. After October 1487 he seems to have been forgotten. Manzano has him in Seville and Cordoba making and selling maps and trading in books imported from Italy and Germany but there is no definite information as to his whereabouts, though, as his son Fernando was born in August 1488, it is reasonable to assume that he was with Beatriz Enriquez in Córdoba the previous December. Then, in what must have been a desperate moment in the early months of 1488, he wrote to King John pleading for an audience.

Columbus is known to have been at Court in Murcia (450 kilometres from Cordoba) in June 1488, for he received a further 3,000 maravedis from the Royal Treasury. Fernando was born in August in Córdoba and later, in October perhaps, he travelled to Lisbon for the frustrating interview with John II and the bitter news that a Portuguese Captain had rounded the southern point of Africa. Manzano thinks he returned from Portugal before Bartolomeu Dias's December arrival from rounding the Cape of Good Hope. It must be said that Manzano's reasoning – Columbus would compare the torrential rains in Hispaniola to *Castile in winter* and that winter had to be 1488 when there were reports of heavy flooding – to be, at the least, tendentious, as he unhelpfully adds that 'I have no idea what Columbus was doing in Portugal'. Certainly by May 1489, Columbus was living with his patron the Duke of Medinaceli in El Puerto de Santa María, near Cadiz. A plaque (to 'the Glory of Genius!') on the castle of San Marco claims he resided here from 1484 to 1486. While we would dispute the dates, Columbus certainly lived in this small but elegant castle, whose chapel is a mosque converted with just a whiff of Christianity. Looking from the battlements over the neighbouring town to the Bay of Cadiz and the port at the mouth of the River Guadalete, Columbus could watch ships sailing in and out of Castile's main harbour: a source of frustration more than inspiration.

1489 promised well: in May, Isabella, surely at the suggestion of one of her courtiers, gave the order that all inns in Andalusia must maintain Columbus and that summer he had another audience with Isabella and Cardinal Mendoza in Jaen, where his evident poverty prompted Ferdinand's Chief Accountant, Alfonso de Quintanilla, to feed him. Manzano suggests he followed the Court in its autumnal meanderings through the cooling cauldron of Andalusia, via Baeza and Almeria in a long sweep to Guadix, just 55 kilometres from the Catholic Kings ultimate objective of Granada. Then Columbus drops out of the picture for almost two years.

Fernando explains the Sovereign's procrastination with the excuse that they were too busy *with wars and conquests* to support his father's venture. We have to attribute Fernando's description of events, which took place before he was born or when he was an infant, to his father or Court gossip many years later. On the fringes of Court and almost demented by delays and uncertainties, Columbus was not in a good position to judge events. What were Isabella's intentions?

Isabella and Ferdinand often authorized expeditions: to conquer the Canary Islands from the Guanches, pirate Portuguese treasure ships from Guinea, capture a Berber port or go on a slave raid, but they were always at the expense of the sponsors. If we believe the Duke of Medinaceli, Columbus had a sponsor: *I would furnish him three or four well-fitted caravels, since he asked no more than that,* but the Duke said he retracted because it was a matter for the Crown. If the Sovereigns had any interest in Columbus's project, the cost of three caravels was a pittance to the Treasury. As they were far too decisive to put off a decision for seven years because *they were busy with conquests,* there had to be another reason for keeping Columbus's waiting. The simplest explanation is that the Sovereigns, after the Commission's unfavourable report, were no longer interested in his venture.

Columbus had taken to wearing the habit of a Franciscan friar, something which caused him some ridicule at Court. At first he surely wore the habit out of necessity – he was living on charity – rather than choice. Later, the Franciscan habit became a symbol of friendship with the men whose faith in him never wavered and a reminder of *these seven years importuning,* as he put it, in Castile.

In 1491, Columbus was forty years old, an age to take stock of his life. He had abandoned the sea, where he could have become wealthy as a merchant, for a country which provided him no living, where promises were easily given and broken, and where men were proving themselves in battle against the Moor to be rewarded with lands and the privileges of the nobility. His venture, rejected by a traitorous King John in Portugal, rejected by Henry VII in England (Bartolomé Colón had travelled to London), prospering badly in France, where Bartolomé was at Court, was diabolically in limbo in Spain. On a personal level, his marriage into the aristocracy of Portugal meant nothing in Spain. Yet he could not marry Beatriz Enriquez without renouncing his ambitions of founding a family of Grandees and prejudicing his position at court with Isabella.

Columbus's refuge from the rejection and humiliation he suffered as a mendicant at Court and at El Puerto de Santa María was Beatriz Enriquez, his sons and the friars at La Rábida. Beatriz Enriquez, though a country girl, could read and write. She is a shadowy figure, never mentioned by her son, Fernando, and only twice by Columbus. In a 1501 letter to Diego, he wrote, before setting out on his last voyage, *For your love of me, I entrust you with Beatriz Enriquez to look after her as if she were your own mother; give her ten thousand maravedis every year in addition to her income from the slaughterhouse of Córdoba.* In his will, also addressed to Diego, he wrote, *I entrust you with Beatriz Enriquez, mother of Don Fernando, my son, to look after her that she may live honestly, since she is a person to whom I am in debt. And this is done to discharge my conscience, because this weighs heavily on my soul. It is not right to write here the reason.* The mere fact that Columbus sought to look after her, probably thirteen years after their relationship ended, is as much a tribute to her constancy and good nature as to Columbus's loyalty. Both of his sons were intelligent and loyal to their father, a heartening thought for a man so eager to see them raised to the highest rank of society. The friars at La Rábida, Antonio de Marchena and Juan Peréz, provided an intellectual balm for his wounds. Marchena, a highly regarded cosmographer, and Peréz, one of the Queen's confessors, were also of practical help. Finally, the Genoese looked after their own, and the important communities in Seville and Cadiz must have been open to him.

Hope, life, resided in an ambulatory court. Isabella and Ferdinand, glimpsed from a distance, were always surrounded by courtiers. This *importuning* was heartbreaking and Columbus would never forgive them. Information, filtered through courtiers, was unreliable and contradictory. Why, oh why did he stay?

Fernando reported that an old pilot, a friend of Columbus's, had told Columbus that, when discovering the westernmost island of the Azores, they *were guided by many land birds.* This was *more than a hundred and fifty leagues to the southwest,* meaning that the birds were flying from a land southwest of the Azores, where Toscanelli had marked Cipangu and Mangi. Why hadn't I made the connection before? The birds were flying with the trade winds, at this latitude contrary to Columbus's route westward. With his knowledge of the wind systems and the latitude of lands reported by D'Ailly and Toscanelli, the jumping off points to his Indies had to be the islands of Madeira, the Canaries or the Cape Verde Islands; for only in this zone could he pick up a following wind, the northeasterly trades. France, England, Genoa and Venice were all too distant from his objective. This explained why he never left Iberia, though he let his brother Bartolomé negotiate with England and France to put pressure on the Iberians to accept his venture. Columbus had to set out from one of the Iberian-controlled ports and that was why he stayed for seven years in Castile. He left ample clues in his postils in his copy of Cardinal D'Ailly's *Ymago Mundi,* which he had read by 1489:

The mass of sea-water runs from one pole to the other and extends from the end of Spain to the beginning of India in a not great width.

There is no great distance between the end of Spain and the beginning of India; indeed it is close and it is proven that the sea is navigable in a few days with a favourable wind.

Aristotle: Between the end of Spain and the beginning of India is a stretch of sea, short and navigable in a few days.

Always Spain! Fixated on embarking from one of the Iberian possessions, his mission to Lisbon a failure, Columbus had no alternative but to press on with his project in Castile.

Then, in October 1491, Fray Peréz wrote to the Sovereigns saying that Columbus was with him in Palos and was on the point of leaving Spain. Would they see him? They invited Columbus to Granada and sent him money to buy clothes for the Royal Audience. They also permitted him to ride a mule (to encourage horse breeding, only women, clergymen and the infirm were permitted to ride mules, an easier ride than a horse) for the 400 kilometre journey from Palos. This is the first indication that he suffered from arthritis, an infirmity which was to pursue him, ever more intensely, to his death.

Evidently Isabella and Ferdinand did not just invite Columbus because one of their favourite confessors had suggested it. So who really supported Columbus? He was clear: if he wrote that *only Fray Antonio de Marchena* had supported him, he later wrote to his son Diego, *One must go with haste to the Bishop of Palencia [Diego Deza, Converso and future Inquisitor General and Archbishop of Seville] who was the reason I stayed in Castile and their Highnesses had the Indies.* But failure is an orphan and success breeds a thousand fathers. The Duke of Medinaceli boasted years later, 'Through my doing and through keeping him in my house for two years, an enterprise as great as this could be fulfilled.' Las Casas wrote, *In a letter written in his own hand, Columbus said to the King that the Archbishop of Seville, Fray Diego Deza, and Juan Cabrero [Converso and Chamberlain to the King], had been the main reasons by which the sovereigns had been able to become rulers of the Indies.* Fernando Colón cites Luis de Santángel (another Converso) who, with Francesco Pinello, would loan the Sovereigns their share of the costs of the venture; Genoese and Florentine merchants – including Juanoto Berardi, his future agent in Seville – provided Columbus's share.

There are many other claimants. As Fernández-Armesto suggests, little by little, Columbus and his supporters convinced a sufficient weight of courtiers to push his venture with the Sovereigns, and Isabella, followed by Ferdinand, found it easier to concede than to resist. Finally, the merit rests exclusively with Columbus: it was he who had the idea, he who had the perseverance to importune for seven years, he who chose the route and navigated the Sea of Darkness, he who discovered the Indies and he who found the way back.

Columbus's moment coincided with the capitulation of Granada. Isabella offered to support his venture of the Indies and Columbus accepted, but with conditions which shocked Isabella and her court to such a degree that they rejected them. Columbus left the city thinking, according to his son, that he would travel to France and then to England. But this was only bluster: he had to convince one of the Iberian monarchs or forgo the venture.

Forty years old and poorer than a friar, after eight years in Portugal and seven years importuning in Castile, how could he leave without reducing his demands to a degree which would be acceptable to the Spanish Court? The most convincing answer offered up to now (first proposed by Las Casas and enthusiastically supported by Madariaga and Morison) is his pride, *orgullo*, which reaches its ultimate majesty in the Spanish *pundonor*, pride in honour, and *soberbia*, pride in arrogance. These seven years of importuning and humiliation had to be appeased. Princes and courtiers had toyed with him and now, if they wanted his services, they would only have them on his impossible conditions; grant him these impossible conditions and he would be their servant. The miraculous happened, the Sovereigns had second thoughts, called him back from the road from Granada, and submitted to his demands.

But I am not a believer in miracles and I find this argument inadequate: for one, no one mentions any negotiation between the parties; Columbus merely stated his conditions and Isabella, after a hearing of the Royal Council whose 'opinions were divided' (so reported the Papal Nuncio), rejected them without further discussion. Columbus never allowed disappointment or pique to interfere with his objectives. Rather, he was renowned for his dogged persistence, and would hardly have left the Court with nothing. As we are in the realm of speculation, I would speculate as follows: Columbus's backers at Court knew he was not the best man to negotiate with Isabella, for he would adopt a hectoring air when advocating his venture, regardless of the rank of his audience. They told him to leave Santa Fé, promising him that the Queen could be persuaded to accept his terms. And so it happened. The fact that the Crown would not have to disburse one maravedi – Luis Santángel, Ferdinand's Keeper of the Privy Purse, loaned the Crown's share – surely must have oiled the deal. For the record, Manzano has made the closest estimate of the expenses of the First Voyage and who financed what:

	Maravedis
The Crown's share financed by Santángel	1,140,000
Provided by the port of Palos, paying off a debt to the Crown	360,000
Columbus's share financed by four Italian merchants and syndicated by the Florentine Juanoto Bernardi	500,000
	2,000,000

For those who have made such a fuss over the expense of Columbus's venture and the Crown's empty purse, I mention one of the gems unearthed by Manzano: Isabella and Ferdinand laid out 16,400,000 maravedis to buy half of Palos from the Silva brothers 24th June 1492 – just five weeks before Columbus's fleet sailed.

The agreement between Columbus and Isabella and Ferdinand is known as the Capitulations of Santa Fé, the siege city near Granada. It was legally documented and witnessed, becoming binding on both parties. Once he had discovered new land, he was to be called Don, a title only granted to Grandees and, over a century later, to tutors and heads of English colleges; he was to be titled Admiral of the Ocean Sea with the same privileges as that Grandee, the Admiral of Castile; he was to be Viceroy and Governor of all the lands he conquered with all the prerogatives these titles implied (and they were spelled out); a tenth of the profit from trade would be his, free of tax, and a fifth the Crown's; if he invested an eighth of the cost of the trade, a further eighth of the profit was his, with the tenth a greater proportion than the Crown's. All the conditions and titles were hereditary 'for all time'.

These amazing concessions by the Crown are usually explained by a desire to preempt Columbus's services which would otherwise be offered to John II, Charles VIII and Henry VII, and the support of Columbus's backers who were keen to finance the voyage. These might have been sufficient to persuade Isabella but not, I am sure, Ferdinand. Ferdinand's Machiavellian character and his later breaching of all the important clauses of the Capitulations point to a stronger motive: outrageous conditions could be negotiated, agreed and even settled in a legally binding document, but later, thanks to the absolute power of the Monarchy, ignored.

Columbus summarized these events in the Prologue of his *Journal* of the First Voyage of Discovery, addressed to Isabella and Ferdinand later that year:

My Lords, in this year of 1492, after your Highnesses had ended the war with the Moors who reigned in Europe and finished the war in the very great city of Granada where I was present on the 2nd January, I saw the royal banners of your Highnesses placed by force of arms on the towers of the Alhambra, the fortress of that city. I saw the Moorish king leave the gates of the city and kiss the royal hands of your Highnesses and of the Prince, my Lord. And later, in the same month, after giving you the information about the lands of India and of a prince who is called the Great Khan... you thought to send me, Cristóbal Colón, to those regions of India... And you ordered that I should not go by land to the east, the customary route, but by the western route, which we can be sure no one has gone. For this, you granted me great favours and ennobled me, so that from now on I am called Don, and I am Senior Admiral of the Ocean Sea, Viceroy and perpetual Governor of all the islands and mainlands that I discover and win, from now on, of everything that is discovered and won in the Ocean Sea; and so will my eldest son succeed me and so on from generation to generation for all time.

The sight of *the very great city of Granada* must have confirmed his dreams, nurtured on Marco Polo and Toscanelli, of the wealth of the orient. Besides its olive groves, orchards, vinyards and wheat fields, Granada was renowned for its paper, ceramics and silk – mulberry trees and the silkworm being imported to the Alpujarra by the Moors in the 11th Century – while fruit exports were monopolized by the Genoese trading house of Spinola, employers of Columbus.

Driving to Granada from the north is a dispiriting experience. The road leaves the great olive groves of Jaen behind as it climbs gradually through barren hillsides, though a view of a valley, green with tall stalks of maize and decorated with poplars which follow the gentle curves of a river hidden from view, briefly raise ones hopes of rich farmland ahead. But it might as well be a mirage, for you leave it behind and are once more surrounded by tough brown earth and barren scarps until the first, scrappy buildings which litter the outskirts of so many Spanish towns – rundown repair shops, petrol stations, bars where *tapas* sit sweating under glass, blank warehouses before which a rusting cemetery of farm implements mix with lumps of concrete and reinforcing wire – mark the beginning of Granada. The road bends and climbs and a park to the right and a glimpse of the Cartuja to the left promises better things. And quite suddenly you enter the city proper with the picture-postcard Alhambra high up ahead, its crenellated battlements dominating the lower city against the skyline of the Sierra Nevada.

The elegant living of the Albayacín, the lower city, is still apparent today. The reconstructed Silk Market is a delight of colour (thanks to the much-maligned leather, clothing, pottery, silver, metalwork and souvenir shops, which could equally be part of the souks from Istanbul to Marrakech) and brickwork with the characteristic Islamic horseshoe arches (actually first constructed by the Visigoths). In Columbus's time it was just a corner of the city's souk spreading out at the base of the main mosque, a foreign maze of markets and artisans as impenetrable to the 15th-Century Spaniard as Fez's souk is to the Western visitor today. On the way to the residential quarter are the Arab baths, with the same system of frigidarium, tepidarium and calidarium as the Roman baths from which they were copied. But bathing in communal baths was somehow alien to Christians and the baths, which had been functioning in perfect order for four centuries, were allowed to deteriorate. They have now been rebuilt as a minor tourist attraction, though without the water they are pretty uninteresting. Stretching back from a narrow, foul river, which separates the rock of the Alhambra from the Albayacin, are the elegant houses of the main town hidden behind slender walls from narrow, cobblestone streets. Their tiled roofs glitter in the sun around interior patios shaded by orange trees, cedars and Spanish oak. This lower city still appeals to the senses.

Sweet-scented myrtle and orange trees and refreshing fountains accompanied the walk up the steps of the long hill to the Alhambra (largely built by Christian slaves) and the Generalife. There, palaces – each Emir built a new palace – gardens, pools and fountains, all interconnected, each setting off the other, are reminders of the exquisite nature of Islamic architecture. Post-Moorish additions have merely degraded the architectural pinnacle of Islam which was Granada. Charles V, the Flemish grandson of Isabella and Ferdinand, destroyed the town in the Alhambra to build a rude, Castilian palace which sits like a hairy wart between the wondrous filigreed arches, reflecting pools and ornamental patios of the Alcalzaba and the sweet Partal gardens preceding the climb to the cool seclusion of the Generalife. The myrtle and orange trees separating the higher city from the lower were allowed to wither and die so that three centuries later Wellington, taking pity on the barren hillside, had a shipload of English elms delivered and planted. Churches were built on the sites of Mosques with none of the architectural flair that blended Córdoba's Mezquita into the city's cathedral. Ferdinand's war of attrition – he virtually strangled Granada to death – included the destruction of Granada's olive groves, wheat fields, vineyards, cotton trees and orchards of apricots, oranges and peaches. But Columbus, seeing even the remnants of Granada's glorious wealth, could dream of the riches he would bring back from the east, from the cities of Cipango and Mangi.

I stood on the far side of the Rio Genil from the city, beside a *rabita*, a squat octagonal whitewashed building now dedicated to St. Sebastian, formerly a Moorish hermitage. Here, on Friday, 2nd January 1492 at 3 p.m., Columbus witnessed the last Emir of Granada, Boabdil, after kissing their hands, hand over the keys of the city to Ferdinand and Isabella. Tearfully, Boabdil and his courtiers headed south for the Alpujarra before finally seeking exile in Morocco, where he seems to have been poisoned. Thus ended 781 years of Islamic rule in Spain. For Spaniards, this was the great event of 1492.

On the terrace of the Hotel Alhambra Palace, sipping a *fino* among the tourists whose culture-bucks have decidedly contributed to the maintenance of the Alhambra (and for that I surreptitiously toasted them) I reread Columbus's Prologue to the First Voyage. I suddenly realized that Columbus hadn't mentioned gold or riches, or even his share of the profits, and if he wrote of his mission to find *the way to enable the conversion of them to our Holy Faith*, his fleet carried not a single priest. Riches and the conversion of the Great Khan's people to the Holy Faith were merely promised as rewards for the outlay of his backers, incidental to his main objective. I pictured Columbus on the sterncastle of the Santa María, the scent of the sea in his nostrils and a fair breeze on his cheek setting out on the voyage of his dreams – to *discover the secrets of this world*, as he put it.

4

DISCOVERY

Much has been made of the fact that Columbus set sail from Palos on the same day all Jews had to be out of Spain. Was it a coincidence or did Columbus deliberately time his departure to coincide with a boatload of Jews? Columbus, on the Jewish question, is a bundle of inconsistencies, sometimes condemning Judaism and Conversos, other times exalting Conversos, occasionally defending Judaism, always exalting God, and he was unquestionably a pious Christian. Aware of his Jewish roots, afraid of their discovery, loyal to his Catholic faith, friends with many Conversos, the religious politics of the day could only leave him with a sense of despair.

Columbus, as a Catholic-Jew, had lost his sense of community and he wandered, rootless, at sea and on land virtually all his life. He lived through one of the tragic moments in Jewish history and I wondered how, as a Converso, he had sympathized with their plight – to convert or leave Spain. Madariaga is surprisingly vague, alluding to Columbus's 'fiery imagination and prophetic sense of mission' which must have been inflamed before the 'providential coincidence which made Israel smash into smithereens at the moment he was raised towards the summit of victory'. This describes an Historical Figure, a God or a Saint, not a man. Morison places the expulsion of the Jews in the context of yet another obstacle for Columbus (they blocked roads and made demands on ships and men) while these 'Jew-bearing ships' caused him to sail in 'unwanted company'. Very unsatisfactory.

Jews are thought to have come to Spain in the wake of the Roman conquest (214-133 BC) and Brenan (in *South From Granada*) noted the earliest Jewish epigraphs, on the tombstones of two children at Adra, date from the reign of Augustus (27 BC to 14 AD). The Moslem community, beginning with the Eighth century invaders, was soon outnumbered by converts from Christianity who adopted Arab names, language and customs. Conversion to one's rulers' religion was a common practice, based not on theology but done with the knowledge that life for oneself and one's family would be that much less complicated. By 1100 three-quarters of all Spanish Christians had converted to Islam, but by 1614 every last Moslem had converted to Christianity or left the country.[12] So it is not surprising that a majority of Spanish Jews converted to Christianity when the wind blew strongly from that quarter. Of course conversion, being dictated by practical considerations, was often a half-hearted affair and former Christians, Jews and Moslems were liable to continue their family's customs, even if they no longer attended church, synagogue or mosque.

The mixture of religions bred its own perjorative language: Christians converted to Islam and living in Moslem territory were 'Renegades' (*Elches* from the Arabic 'ilý = renegade); Moslems converted to Christianity and living in Castile were 'Turncoats' (*Tornalizos*); unconverted Moslems living in Christian territory were 'Vassals' *(Mudejares* from the Arabic mudaýýan = vassal); Moslems forced to convert to Christianity after the fall of Granada were 'Blackamoors' (*Moriscos*); Jews who converted to Christianity were 'Converts' *(Conversos)* or New Christians; Conversos who secretly practiced Judaism were 'Swine' (*Marranos)*; and Christians of Christian families were Old Christians. Alliances were confusing. The Converso, Hernando de Talavera, who had presided over the commission that rejected Columbus's proposal, became the first Archbishop of Granada, protecting Moriscos from the Inquisition. Another Converso, Fray Diego Deza, who encouraged Columbus in his venture, became Inquisitor General.

As part of their drive to unify the Peninsula, the issue of religion reached its peak in the reign of the Catholic Monarchs. Isabella and Ferdinand's clear vision of an organized, centrally controlled state required social policing that was new to Spain. In 1480, they established the Holy Office of the Inquisition and ordered the concentration of Jews into *juderías*. Three years later, they expelled the Jews from Andalusia and reinforced an odious dress code (until then ignored by both Jews and Moors) to identify nonconforming elements of society. Priests' concubines had to wear a strip of red cloth three fingers wide, Moslems a blue half moon on their left shoulder and Jews a red wheel on their clothing. After the surrender of Granada in January 1492, Isabella and Ferdinand decided to expel those Jews who would not convert to Christianity. They announced it in a long decree, dated 30th March 1492, which began:

Being informed that in these our kingdoms there were some bad Christians [Marranos] who judaized and apostatized from our holy Catholic faith, the chief cause of which was the communication of Jews with Christians [Conversos]... Between Conversos (about 300,000) and practicing Jews (about 200,000), the Sephardim numbered ten percent of Spain's population. I believe the Sovereigns were sincere in their belief that they could never be sure of their Conversos – who included important advisors at Court – while a large practicing Jewish community lived in their midst. Indeed, the century preceding their expulsion is littered with edicts and laws, whose purpose was to somehow control the movement and influence of Jewish and Muslim subjects.

The decree gave the Jews until 31st July, later extended to 2nd August, to settle their affairs and leave Spain. Between 50,000 and 150,000 of the 200,000 Jews chose exile over conversion. They left under the most tragic circumstances. Andrés Bernáldez, Columbus's friend, recorded:

They offered their many, many farms, fine houses and property to the Christians for little money and begged them to take it and, not finding anyone to buy it, they gave a house in exchange for an ass, a vineyard for some cloth or linen, because they could not obtain either gold or silver [neither could be legally exported]. Yet it is true that they secretly took out an infinite amount of gold and silver; they bent many cruzados and ducats with their teeth and swallowed and carried them in their bellies; the women swallowed most at the crossings where they would be searched and in the mountain passes and ports, and it is said that a person could swallow thirty ducats at one go.

Youths and adults, the elderly and small children, left the land of their birth and set out on the long road on foot, on other beasts and in wagons, and the gentlemen on horseback. They continued their journey to the port they had to go to. They went by roads and fields in great hardship, some falling, other rising, some dying, others being born, some becoming ill. There wasn't a Christian who didn't suffer for them. Always, wherever they went, they were invited to be baptized and some, with grief, converted and remained behind, but very

*few. The rabbis pushed them on making the women and young men
sing and sound tambourines and carracas to cheer up the people.*

*When these men and women, large and small, went to embark at
the Puerto de Santa María and they saw the sea, they screamed and
shouted, in their prayers begging for the mercy of God. They thought
God would miraculously open a way between the seas, but after many
days and seeing they would have no such fortune, some wished they
had never been born.*

This new exodus was, for all the suffering it caused, a mild
measure when compared to the pogroms, the Holocaust or even
the relatively modest persecution of the Conversos by the Holy
Office of the Inquisition. Also, from Isabella and Ferdinand's
perspective, the expulsion was voluntary – for anyone could
escape it by simply renouncing his Hebrew faith and adopting
Christianity. Some Jews, who had taken refuge in Portugal and
Navarre, converted to Catholicism and returned to Spain, and
Isabella and Ferdinand welcolmed their conversion and ordered
their officials to treat them well. One Spanish historian has ven-
tured the opinion that, if the Jews had not left Spain, he would
have feared for their lives in the intolerant centuries which followed the Reformation, when families strived to prove their
'purity of blood', the absence of a Converso ancestor. Indeed,
provoked by the Church, the Jewish community in Spain had
been frequently under attack. These ranged from King Sisebut's
orders (fortunately ineffective) in 633, inspired by his tutor San
Isodoro, author of the first anti-Jewish treatise in the West, to
have all Jewish children taken from their families, to the killings
in 1391 and the anti-Jewish riots (causing Pope Eugene IV to
protest in a 1436 Papal Bull) which punctuated, with terrible
regularity, the decades preceding their expulsion. It was the common people of Spain who were anti-Jewish, egged on by the
Church's lesson that they had killed Christ, by the (sometimes
justified) belief that, in the great battle with the Moor, the Jews
sympathized and even aided the enemy, and by the dislike for a
people who preferred their own way of life to the Christian's, an
intolerance which is as easy to understand as to condemn.
Massacres of Jews were, sadly, not limited to Christians. In 1066
the faqih Abu Ishaq raised a pogrom against the Jews of
Granada, on the grounds of their wealth, their power over

Muslims and their hateful tax-collecting sinecures. Most were put to the sword.

Amazingly, a few of their synagogues – in Toledo and Cordoba – have remained intact and the *juderías* of Seville and Cordoba are still among the most interesting quarters of these cities. But the Catholic Sovereigns' ousting of Jew and Moslem from Spain has left a permanent mark on Spaniards, which only now with *la democracia* is fading from public and private life. Until recently births could only be registered if the first name corresponded to a Saint, to speak in *cristiano* is to speak in clear, straightforward Spanish, while *moro* is still a widely used disrespectful term for dark-skinned foreigners.

Columbus's only direct allusion to the expulsion of the Jews, in the Prologue of the Journal of the First Voyage, is not entirely neutral:

Your Royal Highnesses, as Christian Catholics and Princes, lover and promoters of the Holy Christian Faith, enemies of the Muhammadan Sect and all idolatries and heresies, thought to send me, Cristóbal Colón, to those regions of India to the said Princes, peoples and lands to see if they are disposed to, and the best way that they may be converted to our Holy Faith... And so, after throwing out all the Jews from your Kingdoms and Domains, in the same month of January, your Royal Highnesses sent me with a sufficient fleet to the said India. Did he deliberately omit the Jews from the enemies of Christian Catholics and Princes? Was he aware that his choice of words ('aver hechado') to describe their expulsion implied a certain distaste for the proceedings?

After the fratricidal bloodlettings in Genoa, after the enslavement of the population of Malaga, after the Christian conquest and the departure of Boabdil and his court he had witnessed in Granada, Columbus was hardened to tragic events, of which the expulsion of the Jews was just another. Also the expulsion of the Jews was not a novelty: England expelled them in 1290, France in 1306 (though in both cases the numbers were far smaller) and Isabella and Ferdinand had expelled them from Andalusia two years before Columbus's arrival. King John II, who admitted Jews expelled from Spain, charged them a hundred cruzados a head before expelling them eight months later. Columbus's closest friends, the Genoese community in Andalusia, the friars at La

Rábida, Conversos and Christians at Court, included no practicing Jews. Coming from a Converso family, he had reason to receive the news of the expulsion with relief, for it promised, incorrectly as it turned out, to remove the pressure of the Inquisition from earlier Conversos.[13]

As the expulsion of the Jews was not something anyone, especially a Converso, could criticize openly for fear of reprisal, doubts as to Columbus's true feelings remain. The closest we can get to Columbus's opinion is recorded in a bold letter he wrote to Isabella and Ferdinand in 1501. *I am saying the Holy Spirit works in Christians, Jews, Moors and in all others of all other sects.* Having shipped with Latins, Greeks, Moors and Jews and living half his adult life as a foreigner in Portugal and Castile, he had the breadth of experience and the intelligence to abhor the indiscriminate punishment of a whole people. This enlightened cosmopolitanism of Columbus is frequently lost on his biographers, but it goes to explain his genuine interest in the Taino Indians he met in the Caribbean.

The expulsion of the Jews would confirm that only the sea provided a haven from the unpredictable, evil doings of Princes. He would sail from Castile the day after all Jews had to be beyond the frontiers of Spain; but first he had to find the ships and the men.

It was only in the comparatively new Western culture, with its exaltation of the individual, that Sovereigns with the ostensible power of Isabella and Ferdinand would leave a venture such as Columbus's in his hands alone. After all, he was a foreigner, a pleb and a pauper. They gave him the means, but he had to recruit the men he needed without recourse to coercion. How did he recruit men for such a dangerous venture? What sort of men did he sail with?

On the 22nd May 1492, Christopher Columbus arrived at Palos de la Frontera with a letter from Isabella and Ferdinand. This instructed the town's authority to provide him with two caravels, fully provisioned, at the town's expense, to commute a fine imposed for an unspecified past 'disservice'. The same letter authorized him to charter a third caravel. All within the impossible period of ten days. Columbus also carried a letter authorizing him to purchase provisions at the expense of the Crown, and a third letter authorizing him to enlist certain classes of convicted criminals for his crew. Wisely, he only made use of this last letter to enlist a man imprisoned for killing a man in a brawl and three others who had helped him escape. The Niebla region, including the ports of Palos, Moguer, Gibraleón and Huelva on the Rio Tinto and Rio Saltes (now Odiel), was a good source of seamen. As fishermen and corsairs and crews of vessels trading as far away as England, the Canaries and Italy, they were experienced in ocean sailing. Unfortunately, Columbus was not respected as a seaman in Palos, his venture was dangerous and men wouldn't trust him. Twenty-three years later, seamen testified in the lawsuit between the Crown and the Colón family:

Juan Rodriguez Cabezado: *Many people mocked the Admiral for wanting to undertake the venture of going to the Indies. They taunted the Admiral in public and considered the venture foolish.*

Diego Fernández Colmenero: *When the Admiral Don Cristóbal Colón came to the city of Palos he had no men with him because his voyage was dangerous.*

Juan Rodriguez de Mafra: *I was in Palos when the Admiral fitted out the ships, but I did not want to go with him on that first voyage because I considered it a figment of his imagination and did not believe they would find land; I knew the King of Portugal had fitted out a fleet once or twice and it had come back without finding lands.*

Taunted and ridiculed, with only the support of the friars at La Rábida and an old seaman who encouraged younger men to sign up, Columbus despaired of ever leading a fleet westward. He never forgot these taunting seamen, lumping them with pilots, philosophers and other men of science, not one of whom *did not say that my venture was false.*

In June, Columbus met a local shipowner and sea-captain as eager as he to make the western voyage to discover the East. This man was Martín Alonso Pinzón. Many years later, Francisco Medel testified:

Martín Alonso Pinzón decided to go and make the discovery in the company of Don Cristóbal Colón and he took his brothers and many relatives and friends with him on his ships. If Martín Alonso had not decided to make this voyage and had not taken part in it personally, no one would have dared to go, for many of those who went thought they were going to their death and had little hope of returning. Pinzón appealed to their fortune-hunting instincts. Fernán Yañez de Montiel depositioned that Pinzón said, *Friends who go there so pitifully, come here and join us for this voyage. With the help of God we are going to discover a land famed for its gold-tiled houses and everyone will return rich.*

Pinzón, who was in his late forties – Columbus was then forty-one – had sailed the Mediterranean and the Atlantic and took to Columbus's proposal with gusto. Four of the Pinzónes signed up: Martín Alonso as Captain of the *Pinta*, Francisco Martín as her master, Diego as seaman and Vicente Yañez – later an explorer in his own right – as Captain of the *Niña*. Juan de la Cosa, who would paint, eight years later, the first world map to include the West Indies, captained the *Santa María*, the largest of the three (a *nao*, from the Catalan *nau* for 'ship' to distinguish it from the smaller caravels) and Columbus's flagship. Four foreigners, other than Columbus, enlisted, one each from Portugal, Genoa, Calabria and Venice. In all, they were ninety men. The only man whom we know owed personal allegiance to Columbus was the Marshal of the Fleet, Diego de Arana, Beatriz Enriquez's cousin from Córdoba.

Three monuments commemorate three departure points of Columbus's fleet. The first is at Palos, beyond the edge of the town at a sad little point on the banks of the Rio Tinto. After mass at St. George's Church, still standing neat and prim in a picturesque square by the oak that is said to be the tree where men enlisted for the Voyage, the townsmen accompanied the seamen to the ships lying at the dock – now silted up and nearly a mile from the Rio Tinto – to give them a rousing sendoff. On the 2nd August 1492, the two caravels and the *nao*, in the company of a ship bearing Jews out of Spain, slipped down the river and anchored by what is now known as the Queen's Pier, at the foot of the Monastery of La Rábida. Here, not a hundred metres from the new Visitor's Centre, is an obelisk, commemorating the departure of Columbus's fleet and the first flight from the Old World (Spanish Morocco) to the New (Brazil), piloted in 1926 by Ramón Franco, brother of the *Caudillo*, and his crew of three.

An hour before sunrise on the following morning, the three ships sailed out of the Rio Saltes with the ebb tide and set a course for the Canary Islands. On the approximate latitude of

Marco Polo's Cipango and China, the Canaries offered a last point for taking aboard provisions before picking up the north-easterly trade winds to carry the ships across the Ocean Sea. At Grand Canary he had the *Niña's* lateen rig rerigged to square. Here, after at least eight years of secrecy, he revealed his knowledge of the wind system.

The third memorial for his departure point is at the tiny port of San Sebastian on La Gomera where he stayed to take on cheese, water and firewood. Here he met the Lady of La Gomera, the widow Doña Beatriz de Bobadilla.

This Beatriz was beautiful, amorous – she had become King Ferdinand's mistress and Isabella had arranged her departure from the Court – and was still young, with the strong character and energy of a *conquistadora*. She had subdued the island after her husband's death, killed by Guanches after raping a girl, and had the cold-blooded nerve to have a man hung for gossiping about her sex life. Columbus, if he hadn't known her, had seen her at court and knew of her reputation. She was a flaming comet in the black ether of Gomera and Columbus fell in love with her.

He spent a month in the Canaries, most of it at La Gomera with this extraordinary woman who, isolated a thousand miles from Castile with a small band of followers outnumbered by recently subdued Guanches, was ripe for love. This extended stay in the Canaries – whose motive goes uncommented – saved the discovery fleet from arriving in the Caribbean in the hurricane season.

Spaniards were still fighting the Guanches, a Stone-age Berber-related people, for Tenerife and La Palma. The conquerors sold Guanches in the markets of Cadiz and Seville and indentured labourers to work in the new, highly profitable, sugar plantations. Columbus visited the heavily-wooded Western group[14] where a screen of boisterous black-green plants punctuated by brilliant flashes of red, purple and orange flourished in the black volcanic soil. On the same latitude as Florida, the Western Group share damp, balmy winters and drier, warmer summers, cooled by the afternoon sea breeze. Blessed with deep valleys, sudden mountains – the cone of the Teide is, at 3,718 metres, the highest point in Spain, frequently piercing the clouds over Tenerife – blond and brunette beaches, no disturbing insects or beasts, adequate rainfall and a warm climate, Columbus could anticipate the discovery of similar islands on his route to China. His passing the Canaries has justified the establishment of a small museum in the Casa de Colón, a 16th-Century Governor's house in Las Palmas. Needless to say, Columbus never even saw the house which was constructed after his last visit to the island.

Columbus gave the order to set sail from La Gomera on the 6th September. The three ships were small, with an overall length of between sixty and a hundred feet, their decks packed with water casks and firewood. Only the captains and Columbus had regular covered accommodation, the rest of the crew living and sleeping where they could find a space on the open deck.

Ocean sailing in the latitude of the Canaries – their compass course was due west – is the most pleasurable experience I know. The rhythm of the Atlantic swell raises and lowers the horizon, carrying the vessel forward in surges, a nautical pulse slowing the tempo, interrupted by the four-hourly change of watch and the gentle rise and fall of the sun. These are salad days of reading, chess and unhurried conversation interspersed with the minor tasks of boat maintenance. The smooth pinions of the ship's wheel tug in response to the swell, and the helmsman has only to follow a compass course and keep a weather eye open for fickle changes in the wind. Suddenly a school of dolphins race alongside, top fins dancing in the translucent water, intelligent black points for eyes and long smiling faces saluting the ship's hull. Or flying fish, wings aloft, skim from crest to crest, occasionally landing on deck. When the wind drops, it's time to drop the sails and dive overboard to freshen up in the endless sea. This is the pleasure of ocean sailing, provided you know where you're going and you've prepared for the hazards described in the Pilot's Guide.

In uncharted waters, the gentle pace of the day breeds doubt and fear. In the poor visibility of a cloudy night, thoughts turn to obstacles ahead, rocks or the silhouette of a lee shore; suddenly the following wind is an enemy as men tighten sail and claw off the coast until daylight when the search begins for a harbour or cape offering shelter and a good anchorage. One, two, three weeks with a following wind and the mind calculates the thousands of miles from a known port. Against sea and wind this is a voyage of months, impossible perhaps in a fifteenth-century caravel. I sympathize with Columbus and his men. They lived in dread of running out of fresh water and provisions spoiling; they feared that tackle, canvas and timber wouldn't hold up to beating for months against wind and sea on the return voyage. And what if the ship approaches an area of tempests, sea spouts, tidal waves? Stories of lost caravels, of ships found with the crew dead from thirst, sailors mad from drinking sea-water, begin to circulate. Tales of mountainous waves tossing ships poop over prow, black storms and sea monsters gain credence and nightmarishly interrupt sleep. With little else to occupy the mind, fears have a life of their own and the instinct is always the same: turn back now, before it's too late.

Columbus's *Journal* only obliquely touches these fears, for it is a daily record of distance travelled and observations on the weather and marine life they encounter. But it is full of hope, with Columbus taking every new bird, fish, weed or cloud sighted as a proof that land was just over the horizon, as if t h e Ocean Sea was a barren desert of water, nourished only by its contact with the shore. As the hope of a landfall goes unrealized, anxiety accumulates, popping up with increasing frequency.

Nine days out from the Canaries, Columbus spotted a ringtail and a tern, meaning they were *within twenty-five leagues (seventy-five miles) of land*. On the tenth day, they sailed into the seaweed of the Sargasso Sea, another sign of land. The seaweed thickened on the eleventh and twelfth day, they sighted another ringtail, found tiny crabs in the seaweed. Land, at least an island must be close by. Terns flew by on the twelfth day, small birds *that could not fly far from land* flew past on the fourteenth, and Columbus was sure there were islands to the north and south. On the fifteenth day, they saw a whale, according to Columbus *a sign they were near land, because they always swim close by*. A contrary wind blew up on the sixteenth day, Columbus wrote in his Journal, *which I needed sorely, because my men were restless, thinking there were no winds in these seas to take them back to Spain*. Mutiny stirred in the small fleet, men talking of throwing him overboard. On the nineteenth day, Martín Alonso Pinzón announced that he had sighted land and all the men fell to their knees to give thanks to Our Lord. The next morning they discovered *the land was sky*, cloud formations. Twenty-three days out they spotted a frigate bird which *never leaves land more than twenty leagues*. They sailed into withered weed, a weed-bearing fruit, on the twenty-seventh day and saw no more birds; Columbus believed he had passed the islands marked on his chart. Two more days and Martín Alonso Pinzón wanted to change course from due west to south-west by west to find Cipango-Japan. But Columbus ruled that they press ahead to the mainland (China), since Cipango could be left for the return voyage. This discord between the Captains encouraged the first mutiny on the *Santa María*, which Columbus was only able to bring under control with the help of Martín Alonso. The following day the *Niña* raised a pennant and fired a lombard, the agreed signal that they had sighted land, but by the afternoon land had disappeared. A flight of birds coming from the southwest convinced Columbus to change course in that direction.

Thirty-four days out from the Canaries the men mutinied for a second time, demanding to head about and return to Spain. The Captains met and the Pinzóns, Captains of the *Niña* and the *Pinta*, gave Columbus three more days; if they did not sight land, the three ships would head about for Spain. He wrote in his *Journal: I told the men it was useless to complain, for I had started out to find the Indies and would continue until, with the help of our Lord, I had reached them.* This was pure bravado. The men were with the Pinzóns, who had become arbiters between them and the Captain of the Fleet.

At ten o'clock in the evening of the thirty-fifth day out of port, Columbus spotted a moving light he thought came from land, but the light, if it was a light, disappeared. They were sailing southwestward at over seven knots when, at about two in the morning of the thirty-sixth day, Juan Rodriguez Bermejo sighted the shadow of land from the crow's nest of the *Pinta*. It was the 12th October 1492 by the Julian Calendar, 21st October by our Gregorian Calendar. Columbus gave the order to stand off the coast until sunrise.

The Sovereigns had promised an annuity of 10,000 maravedis for the man who first sighted land. Columbus argued that the moving light was the first sighting of land and claimed the annuity, ceding it to his mistress and mother of Fernando, Beatriz Enriquez de Arana. Columbus's ungenerous claim is understandable, since it represented his final triumph over the doubters at Court, in Palos and among his own mutinous crew who, if they'd had their way, would have put about and returned to Spain. It is just that the first benefit from discovering the Indies went to Beatriz, the one person who had helped him survive the seven years importuning in Castile. But what had he discovered?

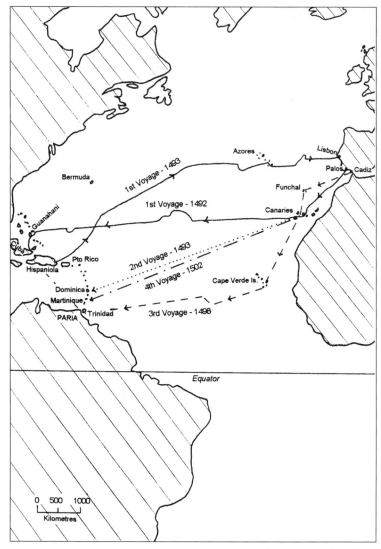

Map 3 – Columbus's four crossings of the Atlantic

5

THE TAINOS

It is a favourite hobby of naval officers and sailors of leisure with an interest in Columbus to choose an island between the Florida coast and Hispaniola and prove it is Guanahaní, as the Taino Indians called the island where Columbus made his landfall. The only safe statement is that no one can identify with certainty Columbus's landfall. This is because the only source for Columbus's ship's log is Las Casas, and Las Casas reports a digest of a copy of the original *Journal*, transcribed by someone who mixed up miles and leagues and possibly course markings as well. For the enthusiast, these uncertainties only add to the excitement. The most probable Guanahaní is the island of San Salvador (formerly Watling Island), authoritatively supported by Morison. San Salvador and its nearest competitors[15] are in the south east quarter of the Bahamas. The British choice of Watling Island (from the eponymous corsair) to name this tiny island in the Bahamas led Madariaga (1940) and the Madrid daily *El País* (1992) to protest at our insensitivity towards Columbus's landfall. The editors of *El País* will be glad to hear that the Bahamian government rectified this error in 1926.

Still the confusion over the Landfall is understandable immediately you look at a large-scale map of the region. Islands, cays and rocks are strewn about the ocean as if God had lobbed every size of rock and stone from a great height and they had settled where they fell to the bottom. Overflying the Bahamas (and Turks & Caicos which are geologically inseparable) adds another understanding to the problem. These coral islands are all low-lying, merging at times into the ocean on shallows from which a sandbank or reef might surface, sometimes almost colliding, like weirdly-shaped ships, into other equally odd-shaped islands. Tiny islets, reefs and sandbanks appear where the map shows nothing. Mapmakers have struggled to put order where there is none. A string of dozens of cays, spread like a daisy-chain over 200 kilometres of the ocean, are lumped together as Exuma Cays. Further south a semi-circle of rocks and cays are gathered together as the Ragged Island Range. In the region of Andros, the largest 'island', the mapmaker finally called it quits, lumping the main island, subsidiary islands, cays and rocks under the one generic name. The lack of identifying features – the coast of each island has the same beach behind which lies the same green scrub – makes identification from sea level virtually impossible from only visual observation. First as a pirate hideaway, frequently as wreckers and then as a drop point for smuggling contraband into the United States, Post-Columbian residents have made their living from this huge shipping hazard which is the sea-maze of the Bahamas. After the abolition of the slave trade, it served as a base for smuggling in illegal slaves; during the Civil War it was used as a refuge for blockade runners, during Prohibition it was liquor and more recently drugs – the source of 11% of America's consumption. Morison wondered why Juan de la Cosa, whom Columbus sent on a caravel to survey the islands in 1494, did such a poor job of charting them. I'm amazed he didn't founder in the attempt.

Archaeologists have dug up pottery shards all over the Caribbean, from whose distinctive styles they have pieced together the various migrations of peoples from Florida and Venezuela to the islands Columbus discovered. The earliest inhabitants were neolithic cave-dwellers, known as the Ciboneyes, hunter-gatherers who had navigated the straits between Florida and Cuba and Cuba and Hispaniola, arriving between 3,000 and 2,000 BC. By the time Columbus arrived, they had been driven to the western extremities of the two islands by the encroaching Arawak-speaking people known as the Tainos.

By dating shards of Taino pottery, archaeologists have established that the Tainos moved into the Lesser Antilles, closest to the Venezuelan coast, in the 1st Century BC. By the 1st Century AD they had advanced to Puerto Rico where they developed farming techniques over a period of centuries. By the 600's Tainos had spread to Hispaniola, which was to become the richest and most populous island in the Caribbean, with groups migrating to Jamaica in the 7th Century and to Cuba and the Bahamas in the 8th. At some time another linguistic group, known as the Macorixes, occupied North Central Hispaniola and Central Cuba, while a fourth group, the Ciguayos, occupied North East Hispaniola. Macorixes and Ciguayos absorbed the Taino's culture and farming techniques and played a full role in the varying alliances of tribal groups within the island.

In the Taino's wake came their mortal enemies, the Caribs, also from Venezuela, conquering all the Taino islands, except Trinidad, from Tobago to Guadaloupe, enslaving the women and eating the Taino men they captured. By Columbus's time, all the islands between Guadalupe and Puerto Rico were uninhabited, a sort of buffer zone between the two warring peoples, which may have been raided out by Carib canoe-borne war parties.

Nothing has remained of the Taino Indians Columbus met other than some ceramic, stone, wood, shell and bone artifacts, zemis and stone belt moulds used in the ballgame, *batey*, and words which have seeped through from Spanish. We have to rely on the accounts of the first discoverers, colonizers and especially missionaries to fill in where the archaeologists' work ends. The first accounts are those of Columbus and his ethnologist-missionary, Fr. Ramón Pané.

Books about Columbus usually ignore the people who inhabited the islands Columbus won for the Spanish Crown unless they rebelled, were enslaved, died in large numbers or impinge directly on Columbus's life. In other words, they are unimportant to the story save as a reflection on Columbus and the Spaniards' alleged cruelty. But the Indians were important to Columbus on several levels – as potential allies or enemies, as pilots and interpreters, as a people to be won over to Christianity, to be economically exploited via trade or as cheap labour and as a new phenomenon to be understood.

There is something pathetic and revealing about the origin of their name: the first Indians Columbus met ran out to meet the Spaniards shouting *'Taino, taino'*, meaning 'Good, good' in Arawak. Columbus recorded in his *Journal* his first encounter with the people on Guanahaní. Though his first impressions have been published, more or less completely, in other books, I make no apology in repeating them (in a new translation) now, for they are precious:

We arrived at an island… called in the Indian language Guanahaní *[land of Iguana]. Many Guanahani islanders came to see us. I gave some of them red caps and glass beads, which they hung around their necks, and many other things of little value – giving them such pleasure it was a wonder – because they were friendly. I judged these people would be better converted to our Holy Faith by love than by force. Later, they came swimming out to our ships to bring us parrots, balls of cotton thread, spears and many other things they exchanged for our truck, such as little glass beads and hawks-bells. They seemed to me to be poor in everything. They are quite as naked as the day they were born, the women too, though I saw no more than one girl. All the men I saw were young, none more than thirty years old, all well built, handsome of body and face, their hair as thick and smooth as a horse's mane and cut short. They keep their hair above the level of the eyebrow, except some who let it grow long at the back. Like the Canary Islanders [Guanches], they are neither black nor white, and some paint their faces, others all their body, while others paint only the eyes or nose black, or white, or red, or whatever colour they find.*

They do not bear arms or know of them because when we showed them swords, out of ignorance they grabbed them by the blade and cut themselves. They have no iron and their spears are sticks, some with a fish tooth or something else incrusted in the point. Some had scars on their body. I made signs to ask them what they were, and they showed me how other people came from nearby islands to capture them and how they defended themselves. I believed they came from the mainland to capture them for servants. As they are very quick to do what they are told, they must make good servants. I believe they will easily become Christian, since it seems they have no sect. If Our Lord pleases, when I leave, I will bring six of them to your Royal Highnesses to learn our language. I saw no beast of any kind, except parrots, on the island.

They all have wide foreheads, more so than I have seen in any other people [they strapped a flat stone to the newborn's forehead], and their eyes are handsome and not at all small. Their legs are very straight and none have a paunch. They came to the ships in dugouts, like long boats, made from the bark of a single tree. These are beautifully worked, some large enough for forty or forty-five men, others smaller, and some just big enough for a single man. They row very rapidly with a stick like a baker's peel and, if it capsizes, they all swim and right the boat, bailing out with gourds they carry for this purpose.

I tried to find out if there was gold. I saw how some of them wore a small piece hanging from a hole in their nose. By signs I could understand that further south there was a king who had great vases of gold.

I saw two or three villages and the people came to the beach calling and giving thanks to God. Some brought us fresh water, others food, and when they saw we were not going to land, they came swimming out to us. We understood that they asked if we had come from Heaven. An old man came out in a small boat and others, men and women, cried out, 'Come and see the men come from the sky, bring them food and drink'. Many men and women came out, each with something, giving thanks to God, throwing themselves on the ground, raising their hands to the Heavens and then calling on us to land; but I was afraid of a great shoal of rocks which encircled the island.

These people are very unskilled in arms, as your Royal Highnesses will see from the seven I have taken to bring to Castile and learn our language. I will return them, unless your Royal Highnesses order that they all be brought to Castile or keep them all captive in their own island, for with fifty men you can subdue them all and do what you want with them.

On the 15th October, Columbus landed at Santa María de la Concepción (Rum Cay, Bahamas). *I went ashore and the islanders, the same as San Salvador, were completely naked and they let us wander around the island and they gave us what we asked for.*

Just as I was about to board the ship, one of the men from San Salvador Island jumped into the sea and climbed into a large dugout, lying alongside the caravel Niña, and escaped in it. In the middle of last night, another man from San Salvador jumped into the sea and escaped in a dugout we could not catch, because it was so far away.

In the same journal entry Columbus mentions dry leaves, tobacco, *which they value highly.* Two days later he was on Fernandina (Long Island, Bahamas).

Those who went for water told me how they came to their houses, which are well swept and clean, and of their hanging beds [hammocks, derived from the Taino-Spanish hamaca*], like cotton nets. Their houses are very high tents with good fireplaces.*

On 19th October they anchored off Isabela (Crooked Island, Bahamas). *My eyes will never tire of seeing such beautiful greenery, so different to ours, and I still believe there are many herbs and trees worth a lot in Spain in dyes, medicinal spices, more than I know of, which is a great shame. Arriving at the Cape [Fortune Island, Bahamas], there wafted towards us a scent, so fresh and sweet of flowers and trees, it was the sweetest thing in the world.*

Two weeks later they were on Juana (Cuba).

The two men [with a San Salvador islander who had learned enough Spanish to act as interpreter] I had sent to the interior [to parley with the Great Khan, one being a Converso who spoke 'some Hebrew, Arabic and Chaldean'(?)] returned. They told me how they had walked twelve leagues to a village of fifty houses and a thousand villagers, since many people live in a single house. They were received with great solemnity, according to their customs, and all of the Indians, both men and women, came to see them and lodged them in their best houses; the people touched and kissed their hands and feet wonderingly, believing they had come from heaven.

On Christmas Day 1492, now on Hispaniola (Haiti-Santo Domingo), and after the grounding of the *Santa María*, Columbus wrote: *He [the* Cacique *or Chief Guacanagarí of the nearest village] and all his people wept, for they are people of love without the slightest greed and accommodating in everything. I can guarantee your Royal Highnesses that there is not a better people, nor a better land, in all the world; they love their neighbours as themselves, speak sweetly, are gentle and always laughing. Men and women walk naked as their mothers bore them and among themselves, your Royal Highnesses, they have fine customs. Their king is of a wonderful rank and with such a bearing that it is a pleasure to watch him [Guacanagarí remained a staunch ally of the Spaniards]. They want to see everything, always asking, 'What is this and what is it for?' and memorize everything.*

Columbus had one of the Indians baptized 'Diego Colón' in Castile, after his son, and took him back to the Indies as interpreter. While Columbus had every interest in magnifying the glory of his discovery, his enthusiasm for the Taino Indians is spontaneous and convincing. From the first day in the Indies he had Indians aboard – and as two escaped, they must have had free run of the ships – and eleven years later, on his last voyage, he still carried Indians with him, not as slaves but as pilots and interpreters. It says a lot for Columbus that, though he must have been bitterly disappointed by his failure to find a civilized nation with which to trade, he never complained about the Tainos.

At first the Tainos enchanted him with their simple, friendly nature. Three years later, after the murder of the men he had left on Hispaniola and the inevitable confrontations over gold, land and forced labour, he could still write with enthusiasm of the Tainos. Though some historians doubt his sincerity, on the grounds that he was 'marketing' the Indies, I find his detailed study of their habits convincing. He wrote of the Tainos on Hispaniola (1495):

The cold does not affect the Indians, save to prove that the land pardons no one. I saw them so robust, well disposed and handsome it is a wonder; they are the cleverest people with their hands and their workmanship is a witness to it. They are wonderfully great hunters and trackers; I have seen some of them walk thirty leagues. They eat very little unless they are given food by others and then they will eat for three of us. Their food is very light and easily digested and theirs is the best water that exists beneath the sky, though they drink very little. Likewise, it is a wonder how the women work: they plant peppers and yucca, from which they make bread, and harvest them and cultivate the plants. Hunting, fishing and turning the soil for sowing is the business of the men. The women do everything else, except those of the Cacique who are more pampered and rested than the daughters of Christian Dukes; they will not make good domestic slaves, but they know how to work cotton beautifully.

Eager to learn more about their customs, on the Second Voyage Columbus brought a friar of the Order of St. Jerome with him to report on their traditions and mythology. Fr. Ramón Pané lived with two Caciques, Guarionex and Mabiatua, on Hispaniola for several years, establishing a precedent which later missionaries, by learning the languages and customs of native Americans, would follow. Fr. Ramón, as Las Casas recognized, was the only Christian to conscientiously study the Macorix and Tainos on Hispaniola. Fernando Colón thought his report of sufficient importance to include it in *The History of the Admiral*. As the first systematic study of the Indians Columbus encountered,

I find it a fascinating insight into an extinct people and the mind of the first priest in America:

On the Creation, Fr. Ramon Pané reported: *From the Canibajagua grotto came most of the people who populated the island. It happened that one of them, Guahayona, told Yahuceba to collect a herb called* digo *with which they clean their body when they go to bathe. He went ahead of the others and the sun snatched him away and changed him into a bird that sings in the morning, like a nightingale... Guahayona, indignant that those who had been sent to collect the* digo *to bathe with hadn't returned, told the women, 'Leave your husbands and let us go to another land, leave your children and bring only some of that herb, and later we will return for them'. Gauhoyana left with all the women and arrived at Matininó [a legendary island of Amazons, whose whereabouts teased the curiosity of European sailors for decades] where, much later, he left the women and travelled to another region called Guanín.*

They had left the small children next to a stream. When the small children became hungry and the men could not console them, they called for their mothers, crying Mummy, undoubtedly wanting the breast. Crying and begging for the breast, saying tou, tou *as one would beg something of great desire, they were transformed into little animals, like frogs, they call* tona, *because of their pleading for the breast. And this way the men were left without women.*

One day the men went to bathe and, while they were in the water, it rained dew and they had a great desire for women. They saw people falling from the branches of trees who were neither man nor woman, since they had not the sex of either. They tried to catch them, but they were as slippery as eels. So the Cacique sent two or three men to find a man who had caracaracol, *an illness like scabies, because their hands were so rough they could hold them firmly. After they had caught them, they discussed how they were going to change them into women.*

They looked for a bird called inriri *that makes holes in the trees, what we call a woodpecker. They took the sexless people, tied them by their hands and feet, and lashed the woodpecker to their body; and the woodpecker, believing it was wood, began picking away at the place where women normally have their sex. According to the old Indians, this was the way that they had women.*

After recording their belief on the origin of syphilis and the cures of the shamans (medicinal herbs, diet, hallucinatory drugs and by suggestion. If the patient died, the shaman risked having his eyes and testicles torn from his body), Columbus's ethnologist wrote on God and the afterlife:

They believe there is an immortal being in Heaven, who cannot be seen, and he has a mother but that there is no other beginning. They believe the dead appear on the paths when someone is alone because, when they go together, they do not present themselves. Their ancestors have made them believe this, because they know not how to write or count beyond ten.

They believe there is a place the dead go... at the very end of the island. They say during the day the dead are confined, but at night they leave to enjoy themselves, eating a certain fruit called guayaba *[guava] with the flavour of quince, and join the living. To discover the dead, they touch their belly with their hand and if they do not find a navel, they say it is* operito, *meaning dead, since they say the dead do not have navels.*

While someone lives, they call his soul Goeiza *and after he is dead* Opía. *They say there have been many men brave enough to fight the Goeiza and, trying to embrace it, it disappeared and the men thrust their arms out towards the trees and they were left hanging. The dead do not appear during the day but only at night; because of this an Indian only goes out at night with great fear.*

All, or nearly all, the Indians of the island of Hispaniola have many zemis [idols – Fr. Ramón describes several] of different sects. Some contain the bones of their father, mother, cousins and other ancestors; these are made of stone or wood, and there are many of both. Some talk, some give birth to things to eat, some make rain and others the winds. These simple, ignorant people believe the idols do all of this; or, better said, the devil as they know nothing of our Holy Faith.

In the recently discovered *Libro Copiador*, Columbus further describes the zemis and their use by the caciques – all this for the eyes of Ferdinand and Isabella.

All their kings have a house separated from the village, in which there is nothing more than carved wooden images they call zemis. In this house nothing is done that is not at the service of the zemis, with ceremony and prayer rather like our churches. In this house they have a round, carved table like a chopping block, in which there is a powder they ceremoniously place in the head of the zemi; afterwards, they sniff the powder through a two-branched cane they insert in their nose. With this powder they become mad, raving like drunks. The caciques and people boast that theirs is the best zemi. When they are in the house of the zemis, they guard them from the Christians and do not let us enter and, if they suspect we are coming, they grab the zemis and hide them in the woods, fearing we will take them away. One has to laugh, because they are accustomed to rob zemis from one another. It once happened that, distrusting us, they entered with the Christians in this house and suddenly the zemi shouted loudly and spoke in their language. We discovered beneath the hollow zemi a type of trumpet, hidden by the foliage, leading to the dark side of the house where a man spoke whatever the cacique wanted. As we suspected what it might be, we pushed the zemi aside and found what I have told you. The cacique, seeing we had discovered it, pleaded with us not to say anything to the Indians, his vassals, nor to anyone else since, with this guile, he kept them all obedient.

Fr. Ramón Pané described the Taino's prophecy of doom, which coincided with the arrival of the Spaniards and similar prophecies in other pre-Columbian cultures.

The great Lord, who lives in the sky, sent Caicihu to fast, as they commonly do, when they are confined for six or seven days without eating anything at all, except the juice of the herbs they wash with. While they are fasting and, due to the weakness they feel in body and head, they say they see some things... They say the Cacique Caicihu had spoken to Yucahuguana, who announced that those living after his death would enjoy little of his power, because clothed people would arrive and dominate and kill them, and they would die of hunger. They thought these would be the cannibals [Caribs]; but later, considering they did no more than steal and leave, they believed the zemi spoke of other people. That is why they now believe them to be the Admiral and the men he brought with him.

These, the first impressions of men seeing, with an untutored eye, a people without any link to 15th-century European civilization are both precious and incomplete. Reading about the Taino's customs in the airy reading room of the Museum of America's library in Madrid, I thought of the Samoans as described by Margaret Mead. They shared the same tropical climate with its easy growing of crops and the same warm waters, plentiful with fish, and seemed to have resolved their life much as the Tainos of Hispaniola.

Like the Samoans, the Taino's basic loyalty was to the village, which with a few surrounding hamlets might number a thousand people. Their daily life was leisurely, at least for the men, whose duties of cultivating the land, fishing, canoe-making and hunting iguana (so valued for its meat that its consumption was limited to the caciques), small mammals and birds left them ample time for other pursuits. Men provided the shamans and took care of the spirits, their zemis, sculpted idols and beat out gold masks. Even then they had time to spend hours a day bathing in rivers or the sea, so that one conquistador noted that 'the men only fish and eat'.

Both sexes played a ball game, called *batey*, which, as described by Oviedo, was remarkably similar to one of the versions of the Mayan ballgame. Ten to twenty players played on each team in a rectangular field, using a hard, solid rubber ball. According to Oviedo, the players carried no protection whereas stone yokes, similar to those used to mould leather belts in Mesoamerica, have been found on Hispaniola. A player from one team threw the ball into the court and the players hit it towards their opponents, using only their heads, elbows, shoulders, buttocks and knees. Once the ball passed the territory of one of the teams it was recovered and the opposing team received a mark, or goal. Then it was the turn of the team that had lost the goal to put the ball into play. The Taino's ballgame had none of the macabre associations of the Mayan game, though their word for it, *batey*, is far too similar to the Mayan word for a ball game yoke (*baté*) to allow for a non-Mayan source; but does this prove that the Tainos traded with the Maya? Two Mayan products, beeswax and pottery, have been found on Cuba and yet there is no evidence that the Tainos ever knew of the existence of Yucatan or Central America or that the Maya knew of the existence of the Greater Antilles before the arrival of the Spaniards. As Las Casas reports finding the beeswax lying in the sand on the beach, it seems that this and the pottery were washed ashore in a Mayan canoe. Perhaps a few Maya survived the voyage and taught the Tainos the game. It remains an enigma.

Women, as in Samoa, were allocated the more time-consuming tasks. The daily preparation of cassava bread from yucca was a lengthy chore, as the tuber had to be peeled with sea-shells, grated with a stone *guayo*, dried and squeezed inside the sewn-leaf *cibucam* to extract its poisonous juices before baking and drying. The resulting cassava bread, *casabe*, has the crispness and bland flavour of dense white toast which has been left uneaten for a couple of days, with the virtue that it can be stored for months. Women also looked after the children and captive birds, collected herbs and plants, fetched water, made pottery, and wove cotton cloth, hammocks and baskets.

With no knowledge of smelting, the Tainos used stone implements to carve wood, with such skill that many Spaniards commented on it. They used nets for fishing, stones as weights and wood blocks for floats, as well as hook and harpoon. Some of their hunting techniques were ingenious. In freshwater pools and streams they stunned the fish with narcotic powder ground from the *baygua* plant, and at night they used pine torches to attract and blind their marine prey. To catch wild duck they used a strange ploy. They floated pumpkins in the water until the ducks became accustomed to them and then the men slipped their head inside a split and scooped-out pumpkin in which they had drilled a small peephole. Moving through the water, with only their pumpkin-disguised head above the surface, they approached the ducks and when they found one at a short distance from the rest, they grabbed it and held it under water until it drowned. Probably their most important source of protein was the flesh of the manatee, a large, harmless vegetarian mammal which likes shallow coastal waters where the Tainos hunted it with harpoon and even bows and their short, dart-like arrows.

The Taino's most organized activity was the cultivation of maize, tubers, beans, peppers, tobacco and cotton, and this included the use of irrigation canals in parts of the drier south-west side of the island. As cassava bread was the basic diet – maize, sweet potatoes, potatoes and guáyiga were cultivated in small quantities – yucca was the main harvest. They had developed a system the Spaniards called 'montón', individual mounds each with a diameter of twelve feet, in which they planted about nine yucca plants, fertilizing it with ash, excrement and seaweed and turning over the soil with a wooden spade. It has been calculated that each Taino required 73 mounds of yucca to provide him with his daily cassava bread and that their yield per acre was about double the present yield of farming yucca in fields. In all, tubers accounted for 90% of the Taino's food arising from cultivation, 60% alone from yucca. It is hard to imagine today's Antillean diet without the produce imported from the Old World – bananas, sugar cane, rice, pigs, chickens, cattle and citrus fruits among them and helps us understand the Spaniard's despair at the Taino fare, even if it was relieved by occasional seafood (the lambi conch, a chunky seafood with the colour, consistency and flavour of scallops), fish, dog-meat with the flavour of kid, fruit collected in the forest and three varieties of pineapple imported from neighbouring Puerto Rico. Curiously, the Tainos seemed to have disliked some of the fruits which we most appreciate – papaya, passion fruit and avocado pear among them.

Michele de Cuneo, Columbus's Ligurian friend, reported that the men practiced sodomy 'not knowing that they were doing well or evil', but notes that their libido was generally low, speculating that this must be a result of the near absence of meat from their diet. Columbus is far too prim to comment on such matters, but their lax sexual customs are also reminiscent of Samoa where Mead found a high incidence of homosexual practice among both men and women. De Cuneo coincides with other conquistadors on the beauty of the Indian women, no doubt accentuated after months at sea and inspired by their nudity – only married women wore a loincloth. De Cuneo adds that 'the Indians live little' since he had seen no one over the age of fifty.

Village society, like the Samoans, was structured by families with a cacique at the head, followed by *nitaino* sub-chiefs and *naborias*, or servants, at the bottom. The shamans (*behiques*) formed another subgroup within the village, responsible for the zemi cult as well as curing villagers of illness, using a variety of herbs and exhortations. When Columbus arrived at Hispaniola, the island was divided between five loose Taino tribal confederations each led by a cacique with some lesser caciques at his command, and other caciques who could be counted upon as allies in time of war. On Puerto Rico the entire island was united under the Cacique Hagueibana, reflecting the increasing pressure of Carib raiding parties and the need for a united defence.

It is all too easy to think that the Tainos lived in Arcadia, forgetting the universal condition of man's character which denies him permanent felicity. The Tainos feared Carib raids, feared the power of the *opia* so that they would not venture out of their village at night, and hunger too, for crop failures and droughts frequented the islands. Burying alive the favourite wives of a cacique at his funeral can hardly have been a pleasant experience for the women concerned, nor for other women who had been bought by other caciques. And the infirm, if not from the cacique and nitaino classes, were often left unattended in the forest with a small ration of food and water, which would have to succour them until they expired from their illness or from hunger and thirst. The caciques were men to be feared, for their authority was formidable, to the degree that they organized gladiatorial contests for visiting caciques where many men were killed. Las Casas described a fiesta in Xaragua witnessed by Bartolomé Colón and his men, at the invitation of the Cacique Behechío:

Suddenly two squads of men, armed with bows and arrows and entirely naked, came out and began to skirmish and play among themselves like in Spain where they play at sticks. Little by little the event warmed up. As if they were fighting against their fiercest enemy, they fought so hard that in a short space of time four of them fell dead and many more injured. This was done with all the rejoicing, pleasure and happiness in the world, not bothering about the dead and wounded, as if they had given them nothing more than a slap on the face. This mockery would have lasted longer and many more would have been killed, if the Cacique Behechío had not ordered it stopped at the entreaty of Don Bartolomé Colón and the Christians.

However the general picture the first Europeans have left us is of a happy, easygoing people living in small communities without the pressure for land or even the internal rivalry which caused such bloody battles – and practices – as on the American mainland. With their needs met from the abundant fruits and waters of their tropical islands, like the Samoans they had little incentive to seek better ways of making war or improving crop yields to create a tradable surplus, those great motors of what we have learned to understand as civilization. Nevertheless, the Tainos' Neolithic civilization was flowering – in terms of embryonic crop irrigation, ceramic, cotton and gold work, inter-island trade, and religious beliefs moving away from animism – when it was suddenly truncated by the arrival of the Spanish ships.

Such a culture was ripe to be consumed at pleasure by a more aggressive and technically advanced civilization. The Tainos might have had an inkling of their vulnerability when they first saw the 'men from the Heavens' and ran out to welcome them, rather as a dog rolls over and shows his belly at the arrival of a more aggressive, powerful beast.

After seven years 'importuning', Columbus realized his dream of discovering new lands. Although he didn't forget his search for gold, he chose to send lengthy reports to Isabella and Ferdinand on the customs of the natives, their zemis, their laughter and gentle manners. What sort of a conquistador is this? In his Prologue to the First Voyage, he'd set out to discover *islands and mainlands* with no reference to trade or riches. These are reports from a man delighted at discovering *the secrets of this world* – and this explains the presence of Fr. Ramón, charged with reporting *the beliefs and idolatries of the Indians.* Evangelization, trade and gold were important but subsidiary objectives.

Columbus was the first of a new breed of men – the explorers. This romantic element in Columbus's soul is usually overlooked. Indeed in the Revised Version, Fernández-Armesto weaves impressions and suppositions together with Columbus's occasional biblical references to argue that his solitary position as leader (and a foreigner to boot) of the expedition, combined with the strange people, fauna and flora of the Caribbean, somehow unhinged him, making him 'ready for the most acute and profound religious experiences he had yet recorded'. However, as the *Journal* of the First Voyage is the first surviving document Columbus wrote, we have no insight into his mind before 1492. Unquestionably, only a tremendous faith in his venture, which in the 15th Century would be accompanied by the belief that God works through an individual, would have sustained Columbus during his seven years *importuning* in Castile. Now that he was proven to be right, against the opinion of all the experts of the day, his belief that God had inspired him and chosen him for this task was merely confirmed.

Remembering the importuning at the Spanish Court and the ridicule he had suffered from scholars, courtiers and seamen, this welcoming, simple, uncritical people, living so contentedly in their lovely islands appealed to his heart. And, according to his contract with the Crown, they were virtually his. Of course, he could never forget the reality, the quest for gold and other riches, the hoped-for encounter with the Great Khan – though, unknown to Columbus and the Courts of Europe, the last Great Khan had fled from China in 1368. Columbus dreamed, as romantics will and, only when the reality ousted his dreams, would he have to confront the unpleasant demands and decisions testing his skills as Viceroy and Governor of the Indies, arbiter between native and conquistador.

6

CANNIBALS AND CHRISTIANS

Toynbee observed that whenever civilization comes into contact with primitive societies, the latter commonly meet their end through violence. Columbus could never have stopped the extinction of the Tainos, and it is senseless to make moral judgements as if he could have. What matters are Columbus's observations, intentions and deeds. On his first day in the Indies, he wrote that he gave natives gifts because he judged that *the people would be better converted to our Holy Faith by love than by force.* Such enlightenment was uncommon to the conquistador, though not to Isabella who shared his intelligence and sensibility and his (sporadic in his case) enthusiasm for evangelism.

If America was discovered by men greedy for riches and conquered with the steel blade, gunpowder and the crossbow, the symbol of conquest was the cross Columbus and subsequent explorer-conquistadores mounted at every landing and village they encountered. After purifying Spain of Judaism and Islam, Isabella and Ferdinand wanted to bring Catholicism to the Indies.

Around the year 1007, Norsemen in Greenland baptized two American Indian boys captured by Karlsefini and his men in *Markland.* Five centuries later, in April 1493, six Tainos, who returned with Columbus to Castile, were baptized at Court with Ferdinand and the Infante, Don Juan, acting as godfathers. The King gave his name to one, Don Juan to a second and Columbus gave the name of his elder son, Diego Colón, to a third. 'Don Juan' lived for two years until his death at Court, where *he was well behaved and circumspect, as if he were the son of an important caballero.* There were many precedents in Spain for baptizing conquered subjects. Moorish lords and taifas and Guanche chieftens were sometimes baptized, given Christian names and elevated to the aristocracy to secure the surrender of their territory.

Columbus's ethnologist-missionary, Fr. Ramón Pané, baptized the first Indians in America. Living alone with naked

Indians in a palm-roofed hut, rubbing in herbal extracts to repel mosquitoes, sleeping in an unaccustomed hammock to keep crawling insects out of his bed and surviving on a diet of cassava bread, sweet potatoes, guava and the occasional hutia (large rodent) or, when by the coast, fish and seafood, for years Fr. Ramón bore the lonely charge of studying the Indians' customs and trying to convert them to the Holy Faith. Sadly, his first convert became the first Indian martyr in the New World. That Fr. Ramón survived to tell the tale is a tribute to the rapport and respect he elicited from Macorixes and Tainos – and their fear of the Spaniard's shaman.

Fr. Ramón's years in Hispaniola were deeply frustrating. At the beginning he had the satisfaction of converting his first Indian, Guaticaba, on St. Matthew's Day 1496, baptizing him 'Juan Mateo', *whom I had as a good son and brother*. Guaticaba was also useful as interpreter between Taino and the Macorix language which Fr. Ramón had learnt. He converted the Cacique Guarionex and his tribe, with whom he lived for two years, but two days after he left the village, Guarionex's men forced their way into the prayer-house and stole the images. They threw them to the ground, *covered them with earth and then urinated on them saying, 'Now your fruit will be good and great.'... and all this as an insult.* The Christianized Indians *ran screaming* to Bartolomé Colón who had the offenders burnt. Guarionex, incensed by the Spaniards seizure of land and goaded on by other caciques for his conversion to Christianity, plotted to kill both them and the Christian Indians. Though he was prevented from killing the Spaniards, they killed *Four men, Juan Mateo, the senior clerk, and his brother Anton, all of whom had received the Holy Baptism.* Fr. Ramón was now with another Cacique, Mahubiatibire *who after three years continues with the goodwill to be Christian, and he has no more than one wife, while usually they have two or three and the important men up to ten, fifteen or even twenty.*

Columbus's initial enthusiasm to convert the Indians to Christianity assumed that the Tainos, by nature, would be subservient to their Spanish rulers and the relations between the two peoples would be peaceful. Conquest was never so smooth, and in 1494 Isabella had to remind Columbus, occupied with both discovery and the governorship of Hispaniola, *to procure, as best he could, to bring them [inhabitants of the Indies] to our Holy Catholic Faith.* But, according to Fr. Ramón Pané, the first Indian was not baptized on Hispaniola until 1496. Neither Isabella nor Columbus abandoned their missionary duty, but other, more pressing issues dominated their time. Anyway conversion was a relative concept to the Indians. The Christians' zemis – Christ, the Virgin and the pantheon of Saints – were evidently powerful and worth acquiring to add to the traditional ones, while the finer points of the Holy Faith were entirely beyond their understanding. The Caribs would prove even worse material for the missionaries, with men wandering their island to be baptized at every opportunity to receive their christening gifts. Patrick Leigh Fermor, relying on Father Labat, reported that not only did the Carib language have no word for God, Soul or Spirit, but they had no word for Good either though they had a vague understanding aided by a word for Evil, which they occasionally worshipped as the more powerful of the two.

The Taino Indians Columbus encountered were surely among the most pacific in America. His evident pleasure at their customs and personal attributes was rarely shared by other discoverers; he always referred to them as 'people' or 'Indians', never the derogatory 'savages' of the French and English, the 'wretches' of the Vikings, or the unflattering *naturales* (natives) of later conquistadores. And, as one of the Tarragona documents of the *Libro Copiador* shows, Columbus's intentions, even after the massacre of his men at Navidad, were honourable. In May 1494 he wrote:

To avoid upsetting the Indians, I sent the Treasurer with hawksbells, beads and other things to purchase all the provisions they [his men in the fort of St. Thomas] needed… and in the presence of the Chief Accountant to trade for gold.

Later, in the same letter, he reported on the farming of crops and livestock brought over from Europe – vines, sugar cane, melons, cucumbers, wheat, chickpeas, beans, chickens, pigs, goats and sheep. Hardly the report of a plundering conquistador. Something else separated Columbus from most other discoverers: he carried no great burden of prejudice. As he said, he had learned by speaking with *Greeks and Latins, Jews and Moors and of all other sects.*

Then he encountered the man-eating Caribs, and here I encounter the wishful thinking of certain Americans academic circles. Kirpatrick Sale denied that the Caribs were either warlike or cannibals, assuming Columbus merely passed on ill-founded rumours and superstitions as facts. He cites *The Man-Eating Myth*, whose authors were 'Unable to uncover adequate documentation of cannibalism as a custom in any form in any society.' Sale reveals his pretence at objectivity by citing an isolated incident of cannibalism in Medieval Europe, the quite unfounded observations that Columbus couldn't converse with the Guadeloupe Islanders (he had two Taino interpreters aboard) and that the Surgeon-General of the Fleet, Dr. Chanca, couldn't recognize a human neck boiling in a stewpot when he saw one. Madariaga, Morison and Fernández-Armesto, the first two writing before the existence of cannibalism became questioned, make the natural assumption that if men reported cannibalism that is what they had seen.

Columbus was a precise chronicler who, when confronted with the unknown, could sometimes be led astray by his idea of the world. As at first he wouldn't believe the Tainos' fear of being eaten by the Caribs, Columbus can hardly stand accused of arriving at the Indies with the preconceived idea he would find cannibals.

He first learned of them by reputation on Cuba and recorded (26/XI/92):

Everyone I have met up to now talks of their great fear of the Caniba *[suggesting, of the* Can *(Khan)] saying they live in the island of Bohio [usually identified with Hispaniola, but they didn't] which must be very large. As they [the Cuban Indians] are very cowardly and know nothing of arms, they believe they [the Caribs] will take them to their land and houses; and this is why the Indians I brought do not live by the sea, because they are neighbours of the Caniba. As we head for this land, they are left speechless with fear of being eaten and we cannot get it out of their mind. They say these people have only one eye and the face of a dog. I believe they lie, and I suppose they must come from the* Gran Can *who captures them.*

A month later from Hispaniola:

Again they talk with great fear of the Caniba, whom here they call Cariba, *none other than the people of the Great Khan, who must live close by. They will have ships which come and capture them and, as they do not return, they believe they have been eaten.*

By the time he wrote his last three journal entries in the Indies and the letter announcing the discovery, the Indians had convinced Columbus that the Caribs ate human flesh. Far from inventing the cannibal legend, it took months of contact with the Tainos to persuade him that the Caribs were cannibals.

He first came upon the Caribs on his return when, taking a more southerly route across the Atlantic, he made a landfall in the Windward Islands. He wrote:

I arrived at this island which I named Santa María de Guadalupe [Guadeloupe]. It was a great pleasure to see the vegetable gardens, the fine setting of the houses and the many springs of the mountain at the edge of the sea. I sailed up the east coast of the island, without finding either port or anchorage, until I arrived at the north end where most of the people lived; there were many on land and I anchored with all the fleet [seventeen vessels]. I tried to talk to them [he had at least two Taino Indians aboard as interpreters], learning that all these islands belonged to the Canibales and are populated by these people, who are eaten by others...

We saw four men and took fewer; they all fled into the mountains and, due to the thickness of the trees, we could not take more than the women whom I am also sending to you with many other beauties they kept here. They [the 'kept women'] told me they had been brought from other islands and, to my way of thinking, were held in servitude as concubines. They also told me by words and signs how their husbands, sons and brothers had been eaten, and they had been forced to eat them. I also found some youths who had been taken, and all of them had their member cut off. I thought it must be because they were jealous of the women, but I learned this fattened them, as in Castile we do the capons to eat on a holiday. They never kill the women. I found baskets and large chests of human bones in their houses and heads hanging from every house. I found many of their canoas, as they call their longboats, which I had destroyed.

Dr. Diego Alvarez Chanca, Surgeon of the Fleet, gave further details to the City Council of Seville:

The Caribs raid the other islands and carry off the women they can take, especially the young and handsome. They keep them in service and as concubines, carrying off so many that in fifty houses no males were found, and of the captives, more than twenty were girls. These women also say they are treated with a cruelty which appears to be incredible, for they eat the male children whom they have from them, only rearing those they have from their own women. As for the men whom they are able to take, they bring the live ones to their houses to cut up for meat, and those who are dead, they eat at once. They say the flesh of man is so good there is nothing like it in the world, and it certainly seems to be so. From the bones which we found in their houses, they had gnawed everything which could be gnawed, so that nothing was left on them except what was too tough to be eaten. In one house there, a neck of a man was found boiling in a pot. They castrate the boys, whom they capture, and employ them as servants until they are fully grown. When they wish to make a feast, they kill and eat them, for they say the flesh of boys and women is not good to eat. Of these boys, three came fleeing to us and all three had been castrated.

Columbus and Chanca were not the only witnesses to report the horrific sight which met them on Guadalupe. The chronicler Peter Martyr quoted Melchor Maldonado's description that the Caribs first had a feast of the intestines and extremities, keeping the main members in salt, *as we do ham*; and *they took great care of the tibia and human arm bones to make the points of spears, which they made from bones because they had no iron.* Guillermo Coma, another doctor aboard the fleet, reported Pedro Margarit's experience when leading a landing party inland: The Caribs *toasted various Indians, roasting them on spits to satisfy their gluttony, while beside them lay piles of cadavers from which they had cut off their head and torn off their members. What is more, the cannibals do not deny it and publicly confess that they feed on men.* There are similar firsthand reports by Simon Verde, who spoke to a Carib brought back to Spain, Michele de Cuneo, aboard the fleet, and Juan De'Bardi, who had 12 Indians to send on to Ferdinand, *of whom three have been castrated, three are cannibals and three Indians.*

A hundred and fifty years later, De Rochefort described the Carib's method of preparing a man for cooking: while still alive the victim was sliced open at the back and sides and herbs and peppers inserted; clubbed to death he was trussed and placed on a spit (or *boucan*, the Taino word from which we derive buccaneer), basted and roasted until ready. Part of the flesh might be boiled and smoked to be preserved for times when meat was in short supply.

So extended was the use of Taino-speaking women as concubines, that Carib women adopted Taino as their language, while the men continued to speak Carib. Why would Columbus, Chanca and the rest invent reports of cannibalism? What had they to gain?

After Guadeloupe, Columbus's fleet sailed north. Fernando Colón wrote: *They arrived at the island of Montserrat, whose name he gave for its height, and he learned from the Indians that the island was depopulated by the Caribs who had eaten the islanders.* Was this an invention of the Indians?

On his Third Voyage to the South American mainland, Columbus wrote: *I tried hard to find out where they obtained their gold and they all pointed to a neighbouring land to theirs [Paria, Venezuela] to the west, which was higher, but not far; but they warned me not to go there, because over there they ate people. I then understood they were Canibales and would be like the rest.* Caribs occupied that part of the coast. Another invention? Were Columbus and his shipmates responsible for creating a man-eating myth in the Americas? If so, they were not alone, with cannibalism reported by mariners and priests from the River Plate to North America and a landing of cannibal Indians on the coast of Yucatan in the 14th Century is reported by one of the Mayan *Books of Chilam Balam.* Firsthand accounts include:

22 August 1501, the Portuguese Captain Gonçalo Coelho sent a handsome young man ashore to encourage communication with the Brazilian Indian women; after fingering him, they killed, cooked and ate him.

Amerigo Vespucci wrote in 1502 of the Guarani people of Brazil: *Those whom they capture they take home as slaves, and, if women, they sleep with them; if a man, they marry him to one of their girls, and at certain times, when a diabolic fury comes over them, they sacrifice the mother with all the children whom she has had. With certain ceremonies they kill and eat them, and the said slaves and the children who were born to them. This is true because we found much human flesh in their houses, placed in the smoke. We purchased from them ten creatures, male and female, who had been marked for the sacrifice which one might better call the crime... One of the men confessed to me that he had eaten the flesh of more than two hundred bodies.*

In mid-February 1516, on the coast of Uruguay, Peter Martyr described the natives' attack on a landing party of Spaniards. Observed from the Spanish ships, they killed them, cut them up and ate them. Among the eaten was Juan Díaz de Solís, discoverer of the River Plate.

Giovio recounted Giovanni Verrazzano's 1528 death in the West Indies, after he had captained an expedition which had discovered the eastern seaboard of America from Maine to Georgia. He was captured, killed and eaten by Caribs on an island Morison has identified as Guadeloupe.

In 1529, Sebastian Cabot returned from exploring the River Parana (Argentina) to his settlement at Santo Spiritus and reported finding his men dead and hideously mutilated. A captured Indian explained they had sampled their flesh, but found it too salty (according to De Rochefort, Frenchmen and Englishmen were the Caribs preferred European meat).

Las Casas quoted the letters from two Portuguese Jesuits (Pedro Manuel de Nóbrega, 11 August 1551, and Antonio Pires, 2 August 1551), resident in Brazil, who wrote about the difficulty of persuading the normally peaceful Indians to abandon cannibalism.

Cannibalism was, of course, frequently practiced in Mesoamerica, dating at least from the Olmecs, and still practiced by Aztec and Maya when the Spaniards arrived in the early decades of the 16th century. Limbs were reserved for the nobles.

In 1494, Columbus proposed a Carib policy to Isabella and Ferdinand: to capture as many as possible and send them back to Castile as slaves. This, as he pointed out, had several advantages: a good profit for himself and the Crown; in Castile, they would learn civilized customs, the Spanish language and be baptized; and the Crown *would win great credit* from the other Indians frightened out of their wits by just hearing them named. Isabella and Ferdinand encouraged the baptism of the Caribs, coldly informing Columbus that the slave trade *was suspended*. From now on Columbus ignored the Carib problem and avoided their base in the Windward Islands.

Finding cannibals encouraged Columbus in his belief that he was in Asia and not far from the Great Khan. Marco Polo reported cannibals on the islands in the China Sea and Sir John

Mandeville (his *Travels* were more widely read than Marco Polo's, even though Mandeville was *a nom de plume* and the author may have travelled no further than a library) wrote of naked men and women on Sumatra, in the 'Great Ocean Sea', who *will eat human flesh more gladly than any other*. But the Caribs must rank among the most voracious and rightly have given their name to describe man-eaters and, incidently, Shakespeare's Caliban.

I laid down my pen and thought of Lyall Watson describing (in 1995) cannibal rituals of the Asmat in Indonesian New Guinea and the Mundurucus of the Amazon. Ecological sense, is his judgement. What would the authors of *The Man-Eating Myth* make of that?

7

TRIUMPH

Columbus in the *Niña* and Martín Alonso Pinzón in the *Pinta* ran into a ferocious storm in mid-Atlantic on the return voyage from discovering America. The caravels rode high in the water and their ratlines, thick hemp tackle, heavy wooden masts and spars caught and held the wind. The *Niña* ran under bare poles and a heavily-reefed mainsail. Cross-seas threatened to overwhelm her and the *Pinta*, with Martín Alonso Pinzón aboard, disappeared. Columbus, fearing the worst, sealed a letter to Isabella and Ferdinand in a cask they threw overboard. All the men fell to their knees and prayed for salvation, promising before God that if they reached land, they would walk barefoot, in nothing more than their shirts, to the first chapel they encountered.

The *Niña* reached the most protected port of Santa María, in the Azores, and half the crew disembarked to fulfil their promise to walk barefoot to the island's church. Taking the Spanish seaman for possible pirates, the islanders captured the first men who went ashore, dressed only in their shirts. Columbus negotiated with the islanders, displaying a degree of courage which is rarely acknowledged. He showed them the Royal letters from the Sovereigns and, as that didn't work, threatened to return and take a hundred of them captive. To prove that his diminished crew could handle the caravel, he sailed out into the storm, taking refuge in another island before returning to Santa María. The islanders released his men and the unprovisioned *Niña* resumed her eastward course. The wind dropped but after a few days it strengthened again, splitting its sails on 3rd March. On 4th March, Columbus wrote in his Journal:

All night we suffered a terrible storm and I thought we were lost in the heavy cross-seas and the wind, which seemed to raise the caravel into the air, and the torrential rain from the sky and with lightning on all sides. I prayed to our Lord to keep us afloat, and we sailed like this until first watch when our Lord showed us land, which all the seamen saw. To stand off the coast until we could find a port to save ourselves, there was no alternative but to raise the mainsail [they were running under bare poles] and sail, with great danger, seaward. And thus God looked over us until daylight, but it was with infinite labour and fear. With daylight I recognized the Rock of Sintra at the mouth of the river of Lisbon where, as I could do nothing else, I decided to enter. So terrible was the storm that it was raging at Cascais, at the entrance to the river. The villagers told me they had prayed for us all that morning and, after we entered the harbour, people came to see us, marvelling at how we had escaped.

Columbus steered the *Niña* to the inner port of Restelo where, after a brief confrontation with Bartolomeu Dias, the sea-captain who had rounded the Cape of Good Hope in 1488, he agreed to give an account of his voyage to King John II. John's court was two days' journey inland. *I did not want to go,* he recorded, but he had no choice. Columbus wanted to continue his journey to Castile, fearing that Martín Alonso Pinzón, who had deserted him for Babeque and parted from him three weeks earlier off the Azores, would arrive first in Spain and claim the discovery of the route to the Indies. His fears were justified. Martín Alonso made the Galician port of Bayona a few days before Columbus's arrival in Lisbon, and from Bayona Pinzón wrote to Isabella and Ferdinand in Barcelona asking for an audience. They replied that they wanted to hear the news from the Admiral.

Columbus's audience with King John was difficult, though on the surface John treated him and his crew well, ordering the provisioning and refitting of the caravel at the expense of the Crown. Columbus reported: *He showed great pleasure that the voyage had ended well and it had been achieved; but he understood that, in the agreement between the Kings of Castile and Portugal, the conquest belonged to him.* Unknown to Columbus, John had ordered his men to capture the Spaniards should they land on Portuguese soil and, according to Las Casas, he had posted flotillas in the western approaches to capture the *Niña* and the *Pinta*. The King had feigned pleasure, and the Portuguese chronicler, Barros, gave a more candid picture of John's reaction:

The King received Columbus uneasily, very much saddened when he saw the people of the new land were not black with crinkly hair and the same build as those from Guinea, but more of an appearance, colour and hair like the people of India are said to be; and he had worked so hard in the venture of the Indies. Columbus spoke in the grandest terms and of unheard of things of the lands, and all in a flood of words, accusing and scolding the King for not having accepted his offer. Some noblemen present, indignant at his way of speaking and angered at seeing that the King had lost his enterprise, offered to kill him to stop him from going on to Castile.

The King, like the God-fearing Prince he was, did not accept the offers, which he forbade; but instead showed favour to Columbus and sent the people he had brought from the newly discovered lands to be grandly clothed.

John was furious. Nearly every year for sixty years he and his predecessors had sent ships down and around Africa to discover the eastern route to the Indies and now, in a single voyage, the Castilians had apparently found a short, western route. He quizzed the Indians, had first one Indian, then a second, chart with beans on a table the relative position of the islands. One of the Indians marked and named over a hundred. As the beans spread across the table, John realized this was no archipelago like the Cape Verde Islands or the Azores, but a host of islands, so great that he let slip – perhaps he had understood this from the Indians – his belief that there was a mainland to the south. His indignation at the injustice of it all and Columbus's intolerable arrogance fuelled evil thoughts.

In his *Journal* on 12th March, Columbus wrote, *Today, just as we were leaving Llandra for the caravel, a Royal page arrived, offering on the King's behalf that if we wished to go to Castile by land, he would accompany us and provide lodging, beasts for travel and anything else we might need. When I was leaving, the page ordered a mule for me and another for my pilot and, as I later discovered, he gave twenty gold coins to my pilot. I am telling you this so that the Sovereigns know what happened. That night we arrived at the caravel.*

Why did John suggest an overland route when the sea voyage was much faster? Why would he go to the expense of providing Columbus and his men with mules and lodging when he had a perfectly good caravel in Lisbon harbour? Why the twenty gold pieces for the pilot? Why did he feign *great pleasure that the voyage had ended well and that it had been achieved?* Unable to sleep, I worried over these questions in bed. Fernández-Armesto ignored the question and Madariaga made an allusion to a possible trap. Morison suggested John wanted to lull Columbus into a sense of security, entice him to make the overland voyage and then have a band of 'brigands' murder them all. Knowing nothing of the *Pinta*'s arrival at Bayona, John would annul the discovery of the Indies. Everything fitted but for the twenty gold pieces he gave to the *Niña's* pilot... and the supposed brigands. Everyone knew Columbus had landed at Lisbon, everyone would know he had set out on the overland voyage. How could John keep the knowledge that the brigands were his own men from Isabella and Ferdinand's spies at his Court? Surely that would be a *casus belli*. And who would sail the *Niña* back to Spain? Who would find the Indies?

I dozed off and woke in the death watch, jumped out of bed and almost shouted, Eureka! Only Columbus and his pilot had the navigational skills to find his islands. If his pilot received twenty gold coins, he had provided useful information to John. But John, who knew Columbus well, had addressed him as *our special friend in Seville* and asked him to return to Lisbon, would have first sought to entice the Genoese Captain, with little reason to be loyal to Castile, rather than his Spanish pilot. With a little artistry, the discovery of the Indies could be said to have been as much Columbus's as Spain's and if Columbus could be persuaded to place the Indies as a westward extension of the Azores, John would have a strong claim to them, just as Columbus reported in his *Journal*. John's plan was simple: win over Columbus, return the Spanish crew by the slow land route and keep the *Niña* in Lisbon harbour for further 'repairs' and, after a suitable delay, send it back to Castile. By the time Isabella and Ferdinand had learned of the discovery, Columbus, with a Portuguese fleet, would be on the high seas to the Indies. But Columbus rejected John's offer and, accurately suspecting that his Sovereigns would learn something about John's intentions, wrote his *Journal* entry, *I am telling you this so that the Sovereigns know what happened.*

Barros's account supports this interpretation: *The King Dom João, when he heard of the place where this Colom said he had discovered land, was most upset; and he truly believed the land which had been discovered belonged to him and so he gave to understand to his councillors... about which venture he received much advice. Later he resolved to ask Dom Francisco Dalmeyda, son of Dom Copo, the Count of Agrantes, to take a fleet to that land.* John never lived to witness Vasco da Gama's return from India or the Portuguese discovery of Brazil, and Dalmeyda never reached the Indies.

The *Niña* sailed out of Lisbon harbour on 13th March and crossed the Saltés bar two days later, a day ahead of Martín Alonso Pinzón in the *Pinta*. Even at the end of this historic voyage, Columbus couldn't forget the shame he had suffered importuning at the Court of Isabella and Ferdinand. He wrote in his last entry of the *Journal*: *In all the time I was in the Court of your Highnesses, this venture was opposed by so many important people of your house, all of whom were against me, saying it was a joke. As one can understand from this Journal, I recognize the many different miracles which have been manifested on this voyage and now I hope, with Our Lord's Grace, that this will be the greatest honour Christianity has ever seen.* Though he had lost a ship and was forced to leave thirty-nine men on Hispaniola, he had not lost a man on the voyage. All returned in good health – the ship's surgeon had proved superfluous – except Martín Alonso Pinzón, who died a few days after his arrival in Palos de la Frontera.

In a curious but understandable development, Spaniards have raised Pinzón to the podium of saint and martyr. It was Pinzón, they argue, who made the First Voyage possible, Pinzón who first suggested turning the helm southwest, Pinzón's vessel which first sighted land and Pinzón who first arrived back in Spain. The Crown, in its law suit with the Colón family, played up Pinzón's role and had men deposition that Columbus had not actually left his ship until he arrived at Cuba. Pinzón's son even claimed that his father had a map which had enabled the discovery of the Indies. From this concoction of half-truths and lies, a Pinzón legend grew – it was even said that he had died of a heart broken by Columbus's hogging of all the glory for himself.

Columbus seized the moment of his arrival to ask for a Cardinal's hat for his thirteen-year-old son, Diego (denied), and a confirmation of the Capitulations of Santa Fé. Yes, a Cardinal's hat. Why should Columbus have requested, of all things, a Cardinal's hat for Diego? There were good reasons not to.

Columbus had already designated Diego to inherit his titles of Admiral and Viceroy and so on, positions he'd have to renounce if he became Cardinal. Then, although Columbus pointed out that Lorenzo de Medici had his son (the future Leo X, one of the most promising popes, but who is remembered for excommunicating Luther) elected Cardinal at about Diego's age, the possibility of Isabella proposing a thirteen-year-old boy for the position was remote. So why the request? Puzzling over this with a mug of tea, it didn't take long to come up with an answer. The only answer. Again I thought as I imagined Columbus thought on his triumphal return from the Indies. He was on a roll. As he wrote in the *Libro Copiador*'s version of the letter to Isabella and Ferdinand, he had discovered the Indies which would provide the necessary riches to finance an army to reconquer Jerusalem, and he had found lands full of people who *with little work would turn to our Holy Faith. Oh Christian World, rejoice!* was his call. As he saw it, these were world-shaking events which justified a change to his plans. Fernando, the younger son, would inherit the lesser charges of Admiral, Grandee and Viceroy of the Indies. Diego was destined for a greater office – first Cardinal and then, thanks to his influence with Ferdinand and Isabella, who had already arranged the election of Alexander VI, the election of Diego to the Papacy.

Isabella and Ferdinand welcomed him back, promised him many favours, asked him to come as quickly as possible to Barcelona, urging him to assemble a fleet *in Seville or elsewhere* for a return voyage.

Columbus and his troupe set out on the 1,200-kilometre march to Barcelona like a travelling circus. When they approached a town, the Taino Indians donned their feathers and his men displayed brightly-plumed parrots, samples of gold work, cotton fabric and the flora and fauna which had survived the voyage, all led by the ringmaster, the Admiral of the Ocean Sea. A Spanish historian wrote: *There began the fame which flew over Castile, that he had discovered lands called the Indies and so many and such different peoples and all manner of new things. They found out that he brought these people with him and by which road he was coming. Not only did the people from the villages he passed through come to see him, but also villages far removed from his path emptied and filled the roads to receive him.*

He stopped at Córdoba to see his sons, Diego and Fernando, and Beatriz Enriquez, who was looking after them. He arrived in Barcelona, where all the town came out to meet him, in the third week of April. Isabella and Ferdinand, recovering from a sword wound in the neck and face from a would-be assassin – a thick gold necklace saved his life – received him with all the honours of a Grandee, seating him beside them and the Infante, Don Juan. Columbus, masterful and self-confident in his glory, spoke of his voyage and discoveries and presented his plumed Indians, gold work, parrots, tropical fruits, cotton bales and cloth, herbs, even the first rubber ball (the Venetian Ambassador noticed its bounce) to the Court. In an emotional moment, the entire court fell to their knees to give thanks to God. He rode through the streets of the city beside Ferdinand and the Infante, as the whole court accompanied him to his lodgings. He dined publicly with Cardinal Mendoza, who did him the honour of tasting his food and serving it from a covered silver platter. Some days later he received a letter from the Sovereigns:

And now, because it pleased Our Lord, you found many islands, and we hope that, with His help, you will find and discover other islands and territories in the Ocean Sea in that part of the Indies. You supplicated us to confirm the above mentioned letter, whereby you and your sons and descendants and successors one after another, and after your days, may have and will have the said office of Admiral and Viceroy and Governor of the said Ocean Sea and islands and mainlands, which you have found and discovered and will find and will discover, with all the powers and preeminence and prerogatives Admirals, Viceroys and Governors of our Kingdom of Castile and Leon enjoy... and we give you the possession of the said offices, of Admiral and Viceroy and Governor, for ever and ever...

The news of his discovery spread quickly in Europe. His letter of discovery was published in Barcelona in April, before his arrival there, and by the end of the year, ten Latin and vernacular editions were published in Antwerp, Basle, Paris and Italy.

While all was glory and triumph at Court, a hidden product of the Indies slipped into Spain. Dr. Ruy Diaz de Isla treated some of the first victims of syphilis in Barcelona in 1493; he believed the Indians infected Barcelona whores who, in turn, passed on the infection to seamen and residents.[16]

Isabella and Ferdinand wanted Columbus to undertake a second voyage immediately, to establish a much larger presence in the Indies and forestall John II's ambitions, reported by their Portuguese spies. Columbus proposed, and a papal bull from the Spanish Pope Alexander VI authorized, that all lands discovered to the west of a line drawn through both poles, one hundred leagues west of the Azores, belonged to Spain. This would leave Portugal Africa and all points east of this line. John rejected the papal bull and provoked a year of negotiations, ending in the 1494 Treaty of Tordesillas. This moved the papal line two hundred and seventy leagues further west. To identify the limits of the treaty, the Commission proposed that a ship from each country should sail 370 leagues due west of the Cape Verde Islands, and then turn south to reach land. As no one could accurately measure longitude on land, let alone at sea, and they could not accurately measure latitude at sea either, the proposal was never carried out. Each party interpreted the treaty as he wished – the Portuguese simply painted on their maps the new territories of Newfoundland and Brazil to the east of the line – and it was considered a resounding success. The treaty served both parties well until twenty years later the Portuguese, sailing east from India, met the Spaniards sailing west from Mexico in the spice-rich islands of the East Indies. Where did the line, extended over the Poles, divide their respective territories?

Before leaving for the Second Voyage of Discovery, Columbus received a warm, even affectionate letter from Isabella. He was *My Admiral of the Ocean Sea. We know increasingly, from day to day, the importance, greatness and substantial nature of the venture and you have served us well... We place great reliance on you and hope in God that beyond what we have promised, you will receive from us much more honour, grace and increase, as is right and your service and merits deserved.* She confided to him the present state of negotiations with John II and asked for a chart to settle the Spanish claim. To help him organize the new discovery fleet of seventeen vessels, she appointed Juan de Fonseca, Archdeacon of Seville and future Director of the Office of the Indies (literally, the Contracting Office), who would become a sturdy defender of the colonizers' rights over the Amerindians when these were questioned by the Dominicans, Las Casas and members of other holy orders. Fonseca had his virtues; he was a reliable and hard-working organizer of the discovery and provisioning fleets which left for the Indies and became, during his nearly thirty years at the head of the Office, the man who directed all 'American' affairs (for centuries, Spain continued to call the new continent *Las Indias*). His aristocratic origins, organizational skills and strict sense of justice rebelled at the upstart adventurers he had to deal with, and Columbus was but the first of many sea-Captains and conquistadors who would eventually find his obstruction to their plans to be unbearable.

In Barcelona, Columbus, handsome, charming and sur-rounded with an aura of success pleased Isabella and, for his part, he would always adore her, even in the most adverse moments. Were his feelings reciprocated? The consensus is they were, but I have my doubts. Columbus thought so, but who hasn't fallen in love without believing that his love is requited? For seven years Isabella virtually ignored him and his venture. When she was persuaded to approve it, Columbus, who was desperate for recognition, honours and riches, seized her approval as a sign of personal favour and interpreted her charm as a genuine sign of affection. He saw in her friendly messages and pleasing smile a warmth and depth of emotion which wasn't there. When he was no longer needed and became an encumbrance, she discarded him. When the expenses of his venture proved greater than the revenues, she did nothing to stop Ferdinand from withholding most of his income. Now at the height of his glory, he was one of her favourites, for he promised new conquests and great wealth for her kingdom, and she appointed his sons, Diego and Fernando, as Pages to the Court of Don Juan, her son. But Juan was not an inspiring prince; perhaps in reaction to his hardwork-ing, often absent parents, he was indolent and allowed to indulge himself in childish games and sweetmeats.

Columbus, with the euphoria of his grand reception in Barcelona still fresh in his memory, prepared for his Second Voyage. Fernando witnessed his father's departure:

In the month of June... the Admiral left Barcelona for Seville. When he arrived, he prepared the expedition of the fleet just as the Sovereigns had ordered. In a short time seventeen ships, between large and small, were ready and provided with the men and supplies judged necessary for those lands: craftsmen of all types, workmen and farmhands to cultivate the soil. With the fame of gold and other novelties, so many caballeros, hidalgos *and other noblemen presented themselves that he had to limit their number... and in all there were something less than 1,500, some of whom brought horses and other animals.*

My brother and I were present when, on Wednesday 25th September 1493, an hour before sunrise, the Admiral weighed anchor in the port of Cadiz, where the fleet had gathered. They set sail on a southwesterly course for the Canary Islands.

Columbus's youngest brother, Giacomo Colombo, soon to be known as Diego Colón, joined him, as well as an old friend, Michele de Cuneo, from Savona, on the Ligurian coast. Bartolomé de Las Casas described Diego Colón as *a virtuous person, discreet, peaceable and simple, and of a good disposition. He was neither artful nor mischievous and modestly dressed in a sort of clerical garb.* Diego was twenty-five-years old. His peaceable and simple qualities would not serve him well in the brutal frontier society of the West Indies.[17]

Columbus repeated his route to the Canaries, stopping again at La Gomera where he renewed his affair with Beatriz de Bobadilla. She received him with fireworks and salvos of cannon fire. *If I were to recount for you,* wrote Michele de Cuneo, *how many festivities, salvos and salutes we performed in that place, it would take too long. It was all for the sake of the Lady of Gomera, with whom our Admiral had fallen in love in other times.* He dallied a week with this beautiful woman. Significantly, in the recently discovered *Libro Copiador*, Columbus reported his departure from La Gomera a week earlier than the fleet had in fact departed, so cautious was he of his relations with Isabella, who knew Beatriz as her husband's former lover. Though he stopped for two days at La Gomera on his Third Voyage, he doesn't seem to have renewed his relationship with her and she married Alonso de Lugo, Governor General of Grand Canary.

Columbus's relationship with women is usually ignored. He was married in his mid-twenties, widowed by thirty-three, lived, off and on for six or seven years, with Beatriz Enriquez, punctuated by two short affairs with Beatriz de Bobadilla on La Gomera. Then, after 1493, there is not the slightest hint of a woman in the remaining thirteen years of his life. Indeed, he chose to live in a way that made any further love affair almost impossible: he refused to have women in his ships; he favoured the residences of monks or clergymen friends like Andrés Bernáldez (between the Second and Third voyages); he wore a monk's habit, surely a declaration of celibacy, and seemed to relish the monastic life. Yet he never forgot Beatriz Enriquez, mentioned in a letter to his son Diego nine years later and again in his will. Why did he suddenly lose interest in women, or, at least, exclude them from his official life?

His last known contact with Beatriz Enriquez was when she and his sons saw him off at Cadiz in September 1493. After that she was, in one sense, superfluous because his sons moved to court. The following month, at La Gomera, he overlooked a week he spent with Beatriz de Bobadilla when giving an account of his Second Voyage to the Queen. This year coincided with Isabella's great show of favour: seating him beside her in Barcelona, the warm letter to *my Admiral* offering him further honours and rewards, and the appointment of both sons as pages to Don Juan. And Columbus believed Isabella cherished him. How would she react if she heard about his affairs with the notorious Beatriz in Gomera or the other Beatriz in Córdoba? Columbus had great powers of self-control and an iron determination to accomplish what he set out to do. By 1493 he had achieved nearly everything he desired. Why risk it all for the sake of a woman who might prejudice his close relationship with Isabella? But it is hard to believe that Columbus, radiant in triumph and raised to the highest rank in the land, turned to celibacy.

Don Cristóbal Colón, Admiral of the Ocean Sea, Viceroy, Governor and Captain of a fleet of seventeen vessels, set a more southerly course than in the First Voyage, to find new islands and mainlands replete with gems, pearls, spices, but, above all, gold. Under the terms of the Capitulations of Santa Fé, *He shall take and keep a tenth of all gold, silver, pearls, gems, spices and other merchandise, produced or obtained by barter and mining, within the limits of these domains, free of all taxes.* And, *He is given the option of paying an eighth of the total expenses of any ships sailing to these new possessions, and taking an eighth of the profit.* Business matters, to make the whole venture of the Indies pay, would taint the pure pleasure of discovery and ultimately cost Columbus his reputation with Ferdinand and Isabella, bringing him and his brothers close to ruin.

8

GOLD IS BEST

The Banco de la República in Bogotá houses 25,000 pieces of Pre-Columbian gold ornaments and tools, the largest gold collection in the world. Walk in through the heavy gates of a modern grey façade, which could be in any city in any country, and one is led to a darkened room lit only by light reflected off a sample of gold pieces from the different regions of Colombia. In the first gallery is the most significant piece, a gold raft on which twelve men stand in preparation for the gold ceremony when the future Chief of the Chibchas, covered from head to toe in gold dust, would slip into the water of the lake of Guatavita to be cleansed. His people watched him from the lake-side and, when he emerged, they threw gold and emerald objects into the depths of the lake. From this custom came the legend that here was El Dorado.

I had visited the Laguna de Guatavita with my friend Fernando Plazas. We took a jeep and drove north on the road to Tunja out of the northern suburbs of Bogotá, passing luxury apartment blocks and the guarded entrances to large, opulent houses which, but for their high walls, intense colours of their gardens and sentry boxes, could have been sitting in Westchester County, New York. Even the rich north side of the city peters out in progressively poorer dwellings ending in a shanty town where perhaps a dead horse, once I even passed the body of a man, might be found near the roadside. Leaving the last bald-headed vultures perched on lampposts, brilliant green fields on either side of the road – the Savannah is rich in soil and water – and a range of dark mountains which tower up to the right, like a gargantuan wall, accompanied us with little variation for the 100 kilometres to the turnoff for Guatavita Nueva.

We left the manmade reservoir on the right and took an unpaved track up through low pines and bracken to the base of a volcanic cone. From there we had a short climb, up steps worn into the hillside by the use of centuries, to its peak and the still, emerald water, which fills its crater in an almost perfect circle of two-and-a-half miles, reflecting dark shrubs interspersed by blazing yellow madrigal daisies. From the lip of the crater 10,000 feet up in the Andes, I could imagine thousands of Chibchas, still ethnically a majority on Colombia's Savannah, a squat, walnut-brown people not given to smiling let alone laughter, observing the gold-cleansing ceremony in utter silence.

Treasure-seekers have probed the muddy bottom of the lake, a hundred and twenty feet below its surface, to try and retrieve the gold and emeralds launched by generations of Chibchas. But the soft mud has absorbed everything, though at least one lucky man found a gold pendant on the adjacent hillside. Fernando pointed to a ragged wedge which a giant seemed to have bitten off its lip. 'An Englishman tried to empty the lake. He dynamited the edge before he was stopped.'

Learning of the gold ceremony and finding lots of gold ornaments and implements, the first Spaniards searched fruitlessly for their gold mine. The Chibchas jealously guarded the secret of their wealth for over a century before their salt mine – a huge cavern, part of which has been consecrated as an underground cathedral – was discovered near the town of Zipaquirá. From here they traded salt for gold, by far the most widespread metal used in pre-Columbian America. They smelted gold with 15% copper to form a harder alloy, 'tumbaga', which they used to make chisels, needles, polishing tools, fish-hooks, files and tweezers. This same alloy, valued far more highly than pure gold by the Tainos, reached Hispaniola where it was known as *guanin*. In gold's pure form, 22 carats, they worked earrings, nose-rings, pectorals, pendants, bracelets, masks and a range of ceremonial objects such as staff-heads and lime containers which, when mixed with coca leaves, produces a narcotic effect.

Carrying on past the early galleries of the Gold Museum one arrives at a huge vault. Its heavy metal door swings open and the eye is dazzled by thousands of illuminated gold pieces, as if a piece of the Sun had mysteriously lodged itself there. This room was the dream of every conquistador, and for some the dream came true. From 1494 to 1600 35% of the world's gold came from Spanish and Portuguese America, most of it from Colombia. By the 17th Century the proportion had risen to 60%, peaking out in the 18th Century at 80% of the world's gold production. Technically, the goldsmiths of Peru and Colombia were the equal of their counterparts in Asia and Renaissance Europe. They knew every technique worth knowing: the lost-wax method, casting almost completely closed capsules to make a rattle, and gilding tumbaga by applying salt to the piece, producing copper oxide which, once removed, leaves a fine layer of gold. Clemencia Plazas, Fernando's sister, an expert on the subject, argues in *El Dorado* that the combination of techniques and early styles of Peruvian and Colombian gold-work imply an Asian, probably Dongan Chinese connection. The oldest piece we have comes from Peru, was made in the 8th century BC from hammered gold and has a Chinese-influenced design. Clemencia suggests that small Chinese colonies possibly settled in Peru, sailing across the Pacific in boats not that different to the Vikings' longships, only to be gradually absorbed by the Incas. Aware that she is walking an academic tightrope, she accepts that there are unsolved problems matching the chronology of gold techniques in America to possible migrations of Chinese, to which one can always add more. Why didn't the Chinese bring other useful techniques like the wheel, the sail and writing? As they must have come with the trade winds, they would first have had to sail as far south as New Zealand to catch the prevailing easterlies. This is not as impossible as it might seem, since Chinese-influenced art reached New Zealand as well.

It has taken an American historian to estimate that each maravedi invested by the Spanish Crown in Columbus's First Voyage of Discovery produced a return of 1,733,000 maravedis; and this includes only the gold and silver remitted to the Crown in the first century following the discovery. Columbus thought not in maravedis but in gold. When marooned for a year on Jamaica, he had ample time to contemplate it: *Genoese, Venetians and everyone who have pearls, precious stones and other goods of value, carry them to the end of the world to change and convert them into gold. Gold is best; from gold one creates wealth and, with it, whoever has it does what he wants in the world and if God, Our Lord, does not prohibit him, he arrives and rings the sunset bell in Paradise.*

For Columbus, gold was not only wealth and power but, in accord with his times, had Biblical connotations as well. In Panama he thought he had discovered King Solomon's mines:

They brought six hundred and sixty-six quintals of gold to Solomon, and from this gold he made two hundred lances, three hundred shields and the Tablet melted from spears, and he adorned it with precious gems. He made many other things of gold and many jewel-adorned cups for the Temple. Joseph in his Judaic Antiquities writes so. This is recounted in the Palipomenem and the Book of Kings.

Gold would provide the Spanish Crown with the necessary wealth to *send 5,000 horse and 50,000 infantry to capture Jerusalem.*

Gold is best. No wonder he littered his journals and letters with references to gold. The search for gold began with his 1492 land-fall at Guanahani. *I was observant and tried to find out if there were gold. I saw that some of them wore a piece hung from a hole in their nose. By signs I could understand that going south, or passing the islands on the south side, there was a king who had great urns of it, he had a huge amount.*

Two days later, on the south side of Santa María de la Concepción (Rum Cay), Columbus wrote: *I do not want to be delayed in my search for gold by exploring and sailing to many islands.* Another two days later, on Fernandina (Long Island), he thought he had discovered a gold coin. *Here they found someone whose nose had a piece of gold half the size of a castellano on which they saw letters. I rebuked them for not taking it and giving him whatever he asked, to see what sort of coin it was.* At the next island in the Bahamas, Isabela (Crooked), *I left to circumnavigate the island until I could talk to the king and see if there is gold, which I have heard he brings.* The next day, 22nd October: *All last night and today I was waiting for the king or other people to bring gold or other substantial things. I saw many of the people, similar to other islands, all naked and painted, some white, some red and some black… some of them brought gold nose plugs, which they happily exchanged for a hawks-bell and glass beads, but there is so little there is hardly anything.* The tinkle of hawks-bells delighted the Indians, who used them to accompany their dancing, and glass beads were a novelty, an adornment similar to polished stones which they strung and valued highly.

Abandoning Crooked Island, he set sail for Cuba. *At midnight I weighed anchor… to sail to the island of Cuba where I am told there are gold, spices, big ships and markets. From their speech, I under-*

stand that this is the island of Cipango [Japan] of which they tell wonders and, from the globes and world maps I have seen, it is in this area.

Four days later and still on Cuba, *The Indians told me that in this island there are gold mines and pearls.* A week later, *I showed them gold and pearls, and some old men replied that, in a place they call Bohio [Haiti-Hispaniola], there was an infinite amount that they hang round their neck, ears and on their arms and legs and pearls too. I understood more, they said there are big ships and markets, and all this is to the southeast.* Certain that he was on Cipango-Japan, Columbus decided to explore Cuba and remained a further four weeks. The Indians told them there was gold on the island of Babeque (Great Inagua), and Martín Alonso Pinzón deserted the Admiral in the *Pinta* to search for it there.

Convinced there were no gold mines on Cuba, and Cuba was not Cipango but the mainland, he sailed on to Hispaniola. Columbus was hopeful: *This woman had a gold nose plug, a sign there is gold on this island.* Five days later, *The Cacique showed me a great favour. Later the canoe left and they told me that, on the island of Tortuga [north of Hispaniola], there was more gold than on Hispaniola, because it is closer to Babeque.* By the time he was in sight of Tortuga, he didn't bother landing because, *I did not believe there were gold mines in the island of Hispaniola or in Tortuga, but they bring the gold from Babeque.* A dismal conclusion as he had heard nothing from the *Pinta* since she had deserted him for Babeque.

On 23rd December, two and a half months after landing on Guanahaní, Columbus showed signs of frustration. *They [two of the Indians he had brought from the Bahamas] returned with an Indian nobleman to the ship, with the news that there was a great amount of gold in the island of Hispaniola, and people come from other regions to buy it and they would make however much we wanted. I believe there must be a lot, because, in the three days we have been in this port, we have found good pieces of gold and I could not believe it had been brought from another land. Our Lord who guides us, for your mercy, let me find this gold, I mean their mine, for I am so wearied by what they say they know.* On Christmas Eve he received further information: *He [an Indian] brought another companion or family member with him and, among the places where there was gold, they named Cipango which they call* Cibao *[the gold-pro-ducing region in the interior of Hispaniola]. They affirmed that there was a great quantity of gold and the Cacique brings sheets of gold leaf, but this place is very far to the east.*

On Christmas Day the *Santa María* grounded and broke up on a sandbank. Columbus, busy organizing the rescue of its stores and equipment and the building of a fortress to house the thirty-nine men he would leave behind, had no time to explore further. The *Pinta* had returned with small quantities of gold. Both it and the *Niña* were leaking badly from the perforations of teredos (a mollusc which bores through ships' timbers), provisions were low and he decided to return to Spain.

A year later, after he had returned to Hispaniola, Columbus reported the discovery of the 'mines' to Isabella and Ferdinand.

People have come here who, while walking extensively through Cibao, have found gold nuggets in the beds of streams, meaning gold is born in the land and not water. A nephew of Juan de Luscán arrived yesterday from the east of Cibao… He found great quantities of gold in these streams and rivers, more so than these others and, according to him, he was told that sometimes they have found gold nuggets the size of a human head. There is nothing more to say about this gold, save there is not as much on the other side of the world and, before fifty years are up, we will have brought back so much it will be a wonder. Send us, your Royal Highnesses, Masters of Mines, for in your king-doms there are many places with the experience of mining different metals [the following year they sent the Master Gold Sifter Pablo Belvís to the Indies]. I am sure there is more gold here than iron in Vizcaya, and, as an afterthought, *this people, with a little work, will become Christian.*

He was discouraged by the Indians' casual method of collecting gold. *They have no cleverer method to collect gold than what is washed up in the river, and they only take nuggets within reach of their fingers. They collect just enough for their face masks which, until now, they neither sell nor barter. Also, when it rains heavily, large nuggets are found on the rivers' edge, washed up by the water.*

Of the twenty-six items he discussed in his business memorandum to the Sovereigns, the first four addressed the subject of gold. The problem was how to extract the great quantity of gold he had promised Isabella and Ferdinand: his own men were ill or building the new town of Isabela and the fort of St. Thomas; the Indians only picked out the nuggets *within reach of their fingers*; though they exchanged gold for hawks-bells and glass beads, they had a limited use for bells and beads; they didn't trade gold and, unlike the Africans at El Mina, they had no need of any Old World products and barely traded with one another.

With no one to trade with and no means of paying or encouraging the Indians to mine the gold, which anyway they had neither the knowledge nor tools to do, what was he to do? Not only his personal wealth, but the success of the whole venture in the Indies depended on transferring the gold in the river beds and mountains of Hispaniola to the royal coffers in Castile. Only coercion remained and Columbus settled on the Gold Tax, which he 'negotiated' with Guarionex and Caonaboa, the caciques who controlled the gold-producing rivers of Cibao and Vega Real. Every Indian over the age of fourteen was supposed to pay a hawks-bell of gold dust every quarter and the Caciques a much larger sum, the total to sum 60,000 pesos in three installments. Indians living away from the gold deposits paid a tax of twenty-five pounds of cotton instead. The Gold and Cotton taxes proved impossible to collect and Columbus reduced the quantities by half, but even half was beyond the Indians' willingness and ability to pay. Certain writers have made a big issue of the Gold Tax, imagining millions of Indians lining up at the tax-collectors' tables with the gold they'd accumulated over centuries. Nothing like this happened: the 1494 gold tribute sent to Seville amounted to a derisory 200 pesos – less than 90,000 maravedis.

Tolstoy once said, 'From the child of five to myself is but a step. But from the newborn baby to the child of five is an appalling distance.' This was the distance between the Taino Indian, living in a Stone Age culture with no sense of time or wealth, and the Christian conquistador. They took the natural course of flight, into the forests and mountains, and the gold tribute was never collected. Ruthless logic governed Columbus's reaction: the tax was an obligation to the Crown, and tax evaders had to be caught and punished. The island was larger than Sicily, mountainous, densely forested, with a population of perhaps 300,000 Indians, impossible to control from one point on the coast. Columbus had forts built and manned inland, from where his men hunted the Indian 'renegades'. The Spaniards' hounds terrified the Indians, whose only experience with canines were a race of small mute dogs, useful for hunting out small mammals.

Some Indians were killed and in retaliation the Indians attacked and killed their persecutors. When a Christian was murdered, he was revenged, *what the Christians called punishment*, reported Bartolomé de Las Casas, *not only the murderers but as many as might be in that village or regions were punished with execution and torture.* Las Casas arrived at Hispaniola after Columbus had departed, but it is generally assumed that Columbus used similar methods. I have my doubts. When confronted with the murder of the first settlers on Hispaniola – of which more later – his reaction was prudent, judicious and bloodless. If his men took revenge on the Indians, it was without his authority. Columbus avoided all mention of the subject, proof of his sense of guilt and the reproach it would bring from Isabella, holding fast to her image of the noble savage, *My subjects*, who should be converted to Christianity and treated *like the freemen they are.*

Two years later, In April 1497, Columbus proposed a new colonial policy based on his experience in Hispaniola. Circumstances were difficult: half of his men were in open revolt in Xaragua province, seizing food from the Indians and concealing much of the gold they collected. Added to this were the Indian rebellions. He proposed to bring order to all this chaos: two thousand settlers would found three or four villages to be governed by a mayor and town clerk, *as is the custom in Castile*; abbots and friars would administer the sacrament and convert the Indians; gold sifting and mining would be strictly controlled, via a system of assay marks and accounting, and limited in season, *so that way more farming will be done.*

As he faced revolts and anarchy, the natural condition among the conquistadores, self-sufficiency, settled villages, organized collection of gold and conversion of the Indians to Christianity were so many dreams to Columbus. His proposals depended on colonizers to farm the land and mine the gold. Implicitly, he had accepted that the sort of work and economic responsibilities expected of the Queen's subjects were unsuited to the Indians' temperament and culture. If the Spanish Crown and its adminis-trators had accepted this unpalatable, but undeniable, fact, they could have avoided centuries of indescribable suffering.

Six years later, on the Veragua coast of Panama, Columbus discovered more gold and wrote to Isabella and Ferdinand:

6th February 1503, raining, I sent seventy men inland and at a distance of five leagues they found many mines. The Indians who accompanied them brought them to a high hill and, from there, as far as their eyes could see, they were told there were gold mines; and twenty days travel to the west they named towns and places where there were more. Later I learned that this Cacique Quivian, who had loaned us these Indians, ordered them to show us the mines of another Quibian, his adversary, far away, when one of his own people can collect a cupped handful of gold in ten days. I am bringing these Indians with me as witnesses.

In Hispaniola and Veragua, one finds the greatest amount of gold in the mountains, where the trees are as thick as barrels and dense, born where God created the first man and where the sun does not reach the ground for foliage. In Hispaniola one finds nuggets of sev-enty marks, as your Royal Highnesses well know. In the territory of Veragua we have seen more signs of gold in two days than in four years in Hispaniola.

Unfortunately, the Veraguan Indians were fierce, attacked the Christians, killed several and forced Columbus to abandon his attempt to establish a settlement at the mouth of the River Belén. In the same *Account of the Fourth Voyage* he returned to the problem of extracting gold from the Indians. The Gold Tax and indentured labour were unhappy experiences he did not want repeated. *It is not right nor does it serve your Royal Highnesses to take by theft the gold of Quivian of Veragua and the other regions, though it be a great quantity according to my information. Good order avoids scandal and ill-fame and will enable all of it to be deposited in the Treasury, without the loss of a nugget.*

Sure of the immense wealth in Veragua, Columbus's descen-dants assumed the title of the Duke of Veragua which they carry to this day. But, as heavy rainfall and flooding prohibited gold extraction in commercial quantities, the gold in Veragua was almost worthless and it remained a chimera. Towards the end of his life, Hispaniola began to produce larger quantities of gold, but this was insignificant compared to what he had dreamed. By 1501 the gold mined and shipped reached 5.25 million maravedis, but in 1502 it was lost, in 1503 2.6 million reached Castile and by 1504 the figure was 17.4 million, still short of the twenty million he had promised. To console himself and Isabella and Ferdinand he wrote, in the recently discovered *Libro Copiador*:

The Genoese Gerónimo de Santestevan sailed from Calicut [first Portuguese trading post in India] in 1498 for fifty-eight days to the east. He arrived at the Kingdom of Pego [Lower Burma] and wanted to carry on to the source of rubies. But the death of his companion and the theft of his property by the King, who said he was the servant of the dead man, was the reason why he could not continue the voyage. From the letter he sent me, he said your Royal Highnesses' ships are in the best part of the Indies and one should not give importance to Calicut, and he told me that everywhere he went gold was held in as much esteem as in Italy.

By then Columbus also held that *The wealth of the Indies is the Indians*. But in the vigour and ambition of his prime on Hispaniola, he saw things differently. Disappointed by the amount of gold he could ship to Castile, worried that Isabella and Ferdinand would abandon the whole venture, insecure from the never-ending rebellions beginning with Martín Alonso Pinzón a few weeks after making the landfall at Guanahani, sensible of his position as an outsider and afraid of reverting to the poverty of his childhood in Genoa, Columbus looked for other sources of wealth. Mastic, spices, slavery, lignaloes and brasil wood offered, he believed, further riches. Slavery was the ultimate break with the people he described as, *The best in the world, they love their neighbours as themselves, speak sweetly, are gentle and are always laughing. They have fine customs… they want to see everything and are always asking 'what is this and what is it for,' and they memorize everything… I see them so robust and well disposed it is a wonder. They are the cleverest people with their hands and their workmanship is a witness to it.*

Under the devil's breath gold is transformed into dung.

9

ON SLAVERY

Columbus's advocacy of slavery is often ignored, but if it isn't Columbus receives a black mark – or plain abuse – which does little to illuminate Columbus's thinking on the subject. Madariaga, writing in a period when Colonialism and Empire seemed to be an eternal condition of the world order, takes what might best be termed an unjudgemental view of the occasional enslavement of the Tainos, with whom he has few sympathies. Morison despatches the issue with a sharp rebuke for Columbus, while Fernández-Armesto concentrates on the historically important issue of the *encomienda* (concession), whereby Indians throughout Spanish America were allocated to their conquerors as serfs in a throwback to medieval Europe. But as Columbus was opposed to the *encomienda*, for, among other reasons, it meant a limitation on his own and the Crown's authority, it is his advocacy of slavery which interests us.

As the Crown authorized the conquest of new territories for material gain, Columbus had to be a practical merchant explorer. After gold – his leitmotif – he was eager to report other riches to the sovereigns. By mid-December 1492, now on Hispaniola and disenchanted by his failure to discover the source of gold, he reported on the benefits of a large, docile population.

Believe me that this, and all the other islands, are as much yours as Castile and all that is missing is a settlement. You can order these people to do what you wish, for I, with the people I've brought, who aren't many, could traverse all these islands without opposition. I have already seen just three of our seamen go ashore and a multitude of these Indians flee, without us intending to do them any harm at all. They have no armaments, they go naked, have no skill in the use of arms and are very cowardly, so that a thousand will not oppose three. They are easily ordered to work and plant and do everything else that is necessary, and build towns and be taught to go dressed and use our customs.

At sea on the return voyage, Columbus drafted his famous letter announcing the discovery of the Indies. He summarized all the economic benefits for the King and Queen.

This island [Hispaniola] will yield for your Royal Highnesses as much gold as required, as many boatloads as you send for spices, peppers and mastic... as much lignaloes and cotton as you want to ship, innumerable slaves and they will be idolaters and I believe I have found [Chinese medicinal] rhubarb and cinnamon. Then he made the great promise he would never forget: *Seven years from now I will be able to pay your Royal Highnesses 5,000 cavalry and 50,000 infantry for the war and conquest of Jerusalem, the reason this venture was undertaken. And in another five years, another 5,000 cavalry and 50,000 infantry, making 10,000 cavalry and 100,000 infantry, all this for the little that your Royal Highnesses have spent on this venture, that you may have all the Indies.* The Reconquest of Jerusalem, which began with the Crusades, was still one of the main objectives of the Christian kingdoms and particularly of Ferdinand, to whom the letter was addressed.

The merchant in Columbus slips slaves between cotton and medicinal rhubarb. As Oswald Spengler points out, a slave in the Classical period had become a thing, not a person. Men waged war for the sake of booty in slaves and private enterprise hunted slaves along the shores of the Mediterranean. Little had changed by the 15th Century when Moors raided the Andalusian coast and the Andalusians the Moorish coast for slaves; when Malaga fell to the Christians in 1487, the victors seized all its inhabitants and enslaved eleven thousand Moors who failed to pay a ransom of thirty gold doublets a head.[18] Isabella sent a hundred as a gift to the Pope, and the auction of the remainder yielded fifty-six million maravedis. In Columbus's home city of Genoa, wealthy citizens bought slaves for domestic help and he had seen slaves landed and sold at Porto Vecchio. Slavery was also an acceptable means of financing discovery and conquests. Portuguese mariners helped to finance the annual discovery fleets by landing on the African coast, or islands off the coast of Africa, seizing as many people as they could to sell in the slave markets of Lagos (on the Algarve) and Lisbon. Later, they established the Cape Verde Islands as a central slave market from where slaves were often bought by the Genoese and transported to Southern Europe. Similarly, the Spanish conquerors of the Canary Islands enslaved many Guanches who were sold in the slave markets of Cadiz and Seville.

Reasonably, Columbus couldn't fail to mention the potential for slaves in his business report to Isabella and Ferdinand. Yet Isabella had established certain rules. She would not tolerate the enslavement of Christians nor of people who had not defied by arms the Spanish army; this explains why the Castilians enslaved the inhabitants of Malaga, who fought for their city, but not those of other cities which surrendered.

Columbus had traded with Guinea and the Cape Verde Islands – there was no other explanation for his presence – and the most valuable goods were gold, which takes up little space in a ship, and slaves; and the Genoese were great gold and slave traders, African chiefs prizing Arab horses brought from Iberia. Historians have either shied away from this part of Columbus's life, pretending that he sailed only once to Guinea (but he wrote, *Often, sailing south from Lisbon to Guinea...*) or cast him as a voracious slaver. He was neither. Slavery was an acceptable business; and a business once undertaken, proved profitable and repeated, ceases to be viewed in ethical terms by those engaged in it. This was one of the reasons why Columbus had difficulty coming to terms with Isabella's opposition to slavery in the Indies. She outlined her Indian policy to Columbus in the short gap between the First and Second voyages:

Their Highnesses, desirous that our Holy Catholic Faith be augmented and increased, order and charge the Admiral, Viceroy and Governor that, in every way possible, he is to work to bring the inhabitants of said islands and mainland to be converted to our Holy Catholic Faith. To help in this, their Highnesses send there the devoted Father Fray Buil with other clergymen the Admiral has managed to ship... The Admiral will procure and ensure that all those who accompany him treat the Indians well and with love, without upsetting them at all, procuring that the one and the other become familiar and converse with one another, as best they can... If person or persons mistreat the Indians in whatever way, the Admiral, as Viceroy and Governor of their Highnesses, will punish them severely...

Columbus respected the rules by qualifying the Indian slaves as idolaters, but these instructions discouraged him and his next proposal hung on the beastly man-eating habits of the Caribs. In his memorandum to the Sovereigns sent from Hispaniola 30th January 1494, he made a modest proposal:

It is reported to your Royal Highnesses that, profiting from the souls of the said cannibals, and of those who are here, raises the thought that the more we deliver [slaves] there [Spain] the better and, in this way, your Royal Highnesses may be served as follows: given that there is a great need here of cattle and beasts of burden to sustain the people who are here and in the other islands, your Royal Highnesses could license and allow a sufficient number of caravels each year to bring the said cattle and other supplies to populate the country and exploit the land; and these could be brought to these coasts at a reasonable price to be paid in exchange for the fierce cannibal slaves, who are so clever and well proportioned and quick to learn that, once this inhuman practice is removed, which will surely happen once they are away from their country, we believe they will make the best of slaves.

Unlike his other proposals in the same memorandum, which the Royal Council universally approved, they turned down his slavery proposal.

At first, Columbus took Isabella's policy as his own. His instructions, dated April 1494 to Margarit in charge of St. Thomas's Fort, on the treatment of the Indians were emphatic: *The main thing you are to do is to look after the Indians, do them no wrong, nor harm nor take anything against their will... Their Royal Highnesses more greatly value the salvation of this people by becoming Christian than all the riches which can be obtained from them.*

By the end of 1494 events had turned from a brilliant success to near disaster. The Gold and Cotton taxes fuelled the Indian rebellions raised by the undisciplined march of Mosén Pedro Margarit and his men, stealing, killing and raping their way across the island. Columbus's youngest brother, Diego, trying to stop Margarit, turned the focus of this undisciplined force into a rebellion. Margarit marched on Isabela, seized three caravels recently brought by Bartolomé Colón from Castile, and sailed for Spain. Fray Buil, responsible for converting the Indians – which he hadn't – joined Margarit and the rebel party to sail back to Castile. Illness, hunger and death (from malaria, amoebic dysentery and syphilis) hung over the Christian community in Isabela, and Columbus suffered a third recorded attack of arthritis (or malaria), leaving him bedridden for five months; and his reports of great wealth went unrealized. The Gold and Cotton taxes yielded almost nothing; the resin he thought was mastic wasn't; the spices were not appreciated, and the rhubarb was not of the medicinal variety. Arriving ships brought provisions and men, but what could he send back to pay for them and make a good profit for the Crown and himself? From Juanoto Berardi, his agent in Seville, he learned that, on orders of the Crown, *for the expenses are great*, Fonseca had refused to distribute Columbus's share of the income from Hispaniola.

It is a sign of how quickly events had deteriorated in Columbus's mind that he returned to the slave trade. This time he captured 'rebel' Indians who remained pagans due to the inactivity of Fray Buil and his men. Therefore they qualified as *enemies* and *idolaters*.

Columbus had five hundred of the best men and women boarded on four caravels, which sailed from Isabela on 24th February 1495. Michele de Cuneo, Columbus's Genoese friend, witnessed the slave drive and the ocean voyage. After they had loaded the men and women aboard the caravels and supplied the local Christians, four hundred Indians remained. *They, to better escape us, since they were afraid we would turn and catch them again, left their infants anywhere on the ground and fled like desperate people. Some fled so far they were removed from the settlement of Isabela seven or eight days beyond mountains and across huge rivers.* On board the caravels, *About two hundred of these Indians died, I believe, because of the unaccustomed air, colder than theirs. We cast them into the sea. The first land we saw was Cape Spartel and very soon we reached Cadiz, where we disembarked all the slaves, half of whom were sick. For your information, they are not working people and they very much fear the cold, nor have they long life.* Strangely, De Cuneo makes no mention of the fear, claustrophobia and insanitary conditions the Tainos suffered, locked in the black hold, its bilge-water mixed with excrement and vomit slopping around in the rolling ship.

Juan Fonseca, future Director of the Office of the Indies saw them *naked as the day they were born with no more embarrassment than wild beasts. They are not very profitable since almost all died, for the country did not agree with them.*

Isabella, horrified at the enslavement of her Indians, had twenty-one survivors released and returned to Hispaniola. Columbus could not have received a greater rebuke.

Four years later, under pressure to justify the colony, he again proposed a slave trade to the Sovereigns. Columbus wrote to Isabella and Ferdinand in October 1498 from Hispaniola, and six hundred enslaved Indians on board five caravels accompanied the letter:

From here one can, in the name of the Holy Trinity, send all the slaves one can sell and brasil wood. If the information I have is certain, I am told one can sell 24,000 slaves of little value and it will be worth twenty cuentos [twenty million maravedis], and four thousand quintals of brasil wood which should be worth as much again. The expense here may be six million and there should be forty million to the good, if it is as I expect. There are good grounds for this, because they use many slaves in Castile, Portugal, Aragón, Italy, Sicily, and the islands of Portugal, Aragón [Baleares, Sardinia] and the Canaries. I believe fewer are now coming from Guinea and, of those who come, one of ours is worth three of theirs. At the time I was in the Cape Verde Islands, where there is great traffic in slaves and they continually send ships to capture them, I saw in the port that they were asking 8,000 maravedis for the weakest.

They say there is a great demand for brasil wood [for dyeing cloth] in Castile, Aragón, Genoa, Venice, France, England and Flanders. So it does seem that from these two things one can obtain forty million if there was no shortage of ships to collect them... and there is still the gold, if it pleases Him that gives it... I believe that soon there will be seamen aplenty to do it, for all the officers and seamen of the five ships I am sending are already said to be rich, and intend to return later to transport the slaves at one thousand five-hundred maravedis the piece, and they pay for their food... If they die now, this will not always be the case, just as it happened to the Negroes and Canary Islanders at first.

Isabella, with the occasional relapse (she permitted three hundred Taino 'rebels', accused by Columbus of killing Christians, to be transported in 1497), was resolutely against the enslavement of the Indians. The Pope justified dividing the non-Christian world between Spain and Portugal on the grounds that the conquering Catholic monarchies would see to the conversion of the conquered peoples to Christianity. Isabella had a high sense of religious calling; she believed she was acting on behalf of God and she was eager for converts, be they Moors, Jews or

Tainos, and the Tainos, apparently innocent of religion, were both more susceptible and deserving of baptism. Also Columbus's praise of their virtues, her favourable impression of the first Tainos she had met in Barcelona, and their innocence and passivity, making them vulnerable to her more predatory subjects, appealed to her heart. Both politically and emotionally she was committed to the defence of her Indians.

Columbus, with the merchant's mentality, never understood this commitment and differences over the slave trade would bring her to withdraw him as Governor of Hispaniola in 1500. When Ovando went to replace Bobadilla as Governor, he had strict instructions to treat the Indians, her subjects, well. Again, in December 1503, Isabella wrote to Ovando, authorizing him to employ Indians under certain conditions: they must receive instruction in the Holy Catholic Faith, they must be paid for their work, no damage must be done to them or their property and *all this must be fulfilled and done as with free men, as they are, and not serfs*. And she remembered them in her will (1504): *I plead most affectionately to the King, my Lord, and order the Princess [Juana], my daughter, and the Prince [Philip the Handsome], her husband, that they do not consent nor enable the Indian inhabitants of the said Indies and mainland, won and to be won, to receive any ill-treatment in their person or property. Moreover, I order that they be well and justly treated, and if they are ill-treated that this be made good.*[19]

Why did Columbus insist on the slave trade when so many had died on the voyage to Castile and it went against Isabella's policy? Of course he needed to make the Indies pay, so he would try anything. This was his motivation but it is not a sufficient explanation. When he was convinced he was right, Columbus persevered despite the facts and despite the opposition. I thought of the seven years importuning at the Spanish Court, when commissions in Lisbon and Salamanca had declared his venture impossible; his insistence that the Indies were Asia, that Cuba was the mainland, that enough gold would be mined to enable a huge army to conquer Jerusalem. The slave trade was both profitable (by quoting the value of Cape Verde slaves and the relatively low cost of transport from the Indies to Spain) and right. Right because the Indians belonged as much to him as the

Crown, right because he would enslave only the rebels and idolaters among them, right because of the demand for slaves in Southern Europe. Slavery was a business and the mind-set of his age was not that distant from Aristotle, who summarized his argument in favour of slavery as 'It is clear, then, that some men are by nature free and others slaves, and that for these latter, slavery is both expedient and right.' Or the slave-owning American Constitutionalists, whose highflown statements on the Rights of Man included a valuation of a slave as three-fifths the value of a freed man, to establish each State's representation in the United States Congress.

Columbus had worked out his own ethic of slavery, similar to that which Isabella had applied to the conquest of Granada and the Canaries: there were good and bad Indians, as there were good and bad Moors and Guanches. The good Indians were the pilot-interpreters he had taken on board in the Bahamas, his loyal allies on Hispaniola, the friendly, helpful Indians he met on the Taino-occupied Islands and the Paria coast of Venezuela. The bad Indians, the Carib cannibals, the rebels on Hispaniola, the aggressive warriors at Veragua (Panama) were the people to enslave, inseparable from the stout defenders of Malaga or the fierce Guanches in the Canaries. And why not enslave cannibals and Indian rebels when you enslaved Malagueños and Guanches? According to this rationale, he was logically right, knew it and persevered. Of course, as he could only sell one hundred and fifty healthy Indians of a shipment of five hundred – and most died shortly afterwards – the first trial had not been a success. But if he were to evaluate all the initial sources of wealth in the same terms, he might as well abandon the whole venture of the Indies. *Gold is best,* yet he persevered for over a year before discovering any source and another seven years before, with the help of Christian mining experts and organized labour battalions of Indians, they began to extract gold in significant quantities. Columbus saw no reason to halt the slave traffic just because at first it was not a success, *and if they die now, this will not always be the case, just as it happened to the Negroes and Canary Islanders at first.* He may have been right: better ways might have been found to transport and look after them, beginning by avoiding winter voyages (the five hundred were sent in February), providing them with warm clothing and their own food for the voyage and allowing them daily exercise on deck in the fresh air.

There was another influence working on Columbus which has gone unnoticed: Juanoto Berardi, his agent and financier in Seville. Four documents attest to Berardi's slave trading activity, and Berardi financed Alonso de Lugo's conquest of La Palma, where the immediate financial return could only be realized by the sale of its Guanche inhabitants in the slave markets of Cadiz and Seville. Berardi, it will be remembered, syndicated the loan to finance Columbus's share of the expenses of the First Voyage. It is reasonable to assume that he expected a good and quick return on his investment. When Columbus's discovery of the Indies proved financially unrewarding, it is not hard to imagine Berardi demanding slave shipments and Columbus, with the memory of his unpleasant experience in Portugal where he feared arrest for failing to repay debts, was all too willing to comply.

Later, when no longer Governor of Hispaniola, he took a more enlightened view of the Indians. I sense repentance when he wrote (another insight from the *Libro Copiador*), *The wealth of the Indies lies in the Indians,* and, *Lose the Indians and the land is lost.*

Bartolomé de Las Casas, colonial, priest and historian, was the greatest defender of the Indians' rights in the Sixteenth Century. Both his father and uncle, who shipped with Columbus on the Second Voyage, were friends of the Colóns. Las Casas, a university man of twenty-six, followed them to Hispaniola in 1501 soon after Isabella and Ferdinand had virtually banned Columbus from the island. In 1510, Las Casas was the first priest to be ordained in America, and he settled in Cuba as a missionary where he became a passionate advocate of Indian rights. Later, as Governor of the Pearl Coast (Venezuela, where he established a model community of farmers, soon routed by the local Indians) and Bishop of Chiapas (a Maya area in Mexico), he continued his defence of the Indians. He began to write the *History of the Indies* in 1527, while still in Hispaniola, and returned to the College of San Gregorio in Valladolid in 1550 to finish his great work in 1563 – not published in full until 1857. He befriended the Colóns and used many of Columbus's papers which Fernando Colón kept in his library in Seville. Las Casas is the greatest single source of historical information on Columbus and he frequently takes Columbus to task for the ill treatment of the Indians. It is very significant that this holy man and historian, who had dedicated his life to defend the indigenous population against the injustices committed by the conquistadors, should have held Columbus in high esteem:

Columbus was extraordinarily zealous to serve Our Lord; he desired and was eager for the conversion of the Indians and that in every region the faith of Jesus Christ be planted and extended. He was especially devoted to the idea that God should deem him worthy of aiding somewhat in recovering the Holy Sepulchre...

He was a gentleman of great force of spirit, of lofty thoughts, naturally inclined (from what one may gather from his life, deeds, writings and conversation) to undertake worthy deeds and signal enterprises; patient and longsuffering, a forgiver of injuries, he wished nothing more than that those who offended against him should recognize their errors and be reconciled with him; constant and endowed with forbearance in hardship and adversity, which were always occurring and were incredible and never-ending, he always held great confidence in Divine Providence. Truly, from what I have heard from him and my father, who was with him when he returned to colonize Hispaniola in 1493, and from others who accompanied and served him, he was always loyal and devoted to the Sovereigns.

Trying to understand Columbus's insistence on slavery, Las Casas wrote: *I often believe the Admiral's blindness and corruption [towards the slave trade] was learned and infected by the Portuguese in this business or, in truth one might say, the execrable tyranny of Guinea.* Las Casas could both admire Columbus and deplore the slave trade because, in the discoverer's life, slave-trading was a minor, almost insignificant diversion. In general, Columbus's Indian policy was remarkably enlightened. This was the Columbus Las Casas admired.

10

FIRST GOVERNOR

Chance, in the form of the grounding and breakup of the *Santa María*, caused Columbus to found the first European settlement in America since Karlsefani abandoned Leif Eriksson's hamlet at Ainse les Meadows, Newfoundland, five centuries earlier.[20] This was after the 1492 Christmas Eve celebrations which had left the officers and men of the *Santa María* in a stuporous sleep and the helm in the hands of a cabin boy. The ship grounded on a sandbank inside a reef off the northwestern shore of Hispaniola. Columbus took the men off in the ship's boat and, with the aid of the *Niña* and the Indians and their canoes, ferried the ship's stores ashore. The *Santa María* began to break up. Columbus turned this setback to advantage, writing on the following day:

This, as we had so many things at hand, was truly not a disaster but good fortune. If I had not run aground, I would never have anchored here, for there are two or three reefs in the middle of this large bay; nor, on this voyage, would I have left our men here and, even if I had wanted to leave them, I could not have given them so many supplies, so much equipment nor such support or preparation for a fort. It is true that many men here have requested permission to stay. I have now given them the order to build a good tower and fort and a large ditch, not that it is needed for these people, because I take it as a fact that the men I have brought could subject the entire island, which is bigger than Portugal [it is somewhat smaller] and with twice the population [it had two-thirds or less]. These people go naked and unarmed and are irredeemable cowards.

Ten days later, Columbus set sail from this improvised settlement he had named *Navidad*. His report to Isabella and Ferdinand, on the precautions he had taken to secure the safety of his men, suggests a preoccupation with their security that was absent ten days earlier.

I went ashore this morning to take leave of the Cacique Guacanagarí and, in the name of Our Lord, I gave him a shirt of mine. Then I showed him the force and effect of a lombard. I had one loaded and shot at the side of the ship, which was on land, because we

had been talking about their enemies, the Caribs, and he saw the lom-
bard shot pass through the side of the ship and a long way further over
the sea. I also organized a skirmish with armed men from the ships,
telling the Cacique that he should not be frightened if the Caribs came.
And I did all this so that he would be friends with the Christians I left
behind, and to frighten him sufficiently to respect them.

I left thirty-nine men in the fort on Hispaniola, which the Indians
call Bohio, and I told them they had many friends of that Cacique
Guacanagarí. I left them all the ship's trading truck, a huge quantity,
to trade for gold. I also left them a year's supply of ships' biscuit, wine,
artillery, and the ship's boat from the Santa María so that they, as the
seamen they are, could, when they saw a good moment, discover the
gold mine.

I also left in this town of Navidad seed to sow, their officers, secre-
tary and Marshal, a ship's carpenter, a caulker, a good lombardsman
who knows these devices well, a cooper, a physician and a tailor, and
all are men of the sea. When Columbus returned to Navidad ten-
and-a-half months later, on his Second Voyage, he took a more
southerly route, making landfall at Dominica, and island-hopped
northward to the southeast point of Hispaniola. Looking for a
better port than Navidad, they anchored in a harbour Columbus
had named Monte Cristo, 45 miles from the settlement. They
went ashore and found four dead men, one of whom *had been
heavily bearded. Some of us suspected more evil than good, and with
good reason, since the Indians are all beardless,* reported Dr.
Chanca, Surgeon-General of the fleet.

Arriving in the dark off Navidad, they fired lombard shots, but
*They never replied and no fires were to be seen or sign of houses in that
place. From this the men were very depressed, and they formed the
suspicion to which such a situation naturally gave rise.*

Then one of Guacangari's men caught up with them in a
canoe. Columbus wrote (in one of the letters of the *Libro
Copiador*):

*All the fleet set sail [from Monte Cristo] and half way there [to
Navidad] I saw a canoe coming towards us at great speed, but I did
not want to wait because it was getting late if I were to arrive at the
port by day. But I could not arrive before dark, and I had to anchor
outside the harbour. Much later that evening the canoe arrived. A
favourite of the Cacique Guacanagarí came alongside, boat by boat,*

calling me by name, and he would not come aboard until he had seen me and heard my voice. He brought a gold mask from Guacanagarí for me and another for the Captain of the ship, Antonio de Torres. As he had followed us all day and had not eaten, I had him fed and clothed as well. He told me [Columbus had at least two Indian interpreters from Spain in the fleet] how the people I had left in the settlement had argued among themselves and killed one another and how Pedro, Butler of the King's Dais, had gone with many of the men to another cacique, Cahonaboa, who owned much land and gold; and a Basque, Chacho, had gone with other Basques and men, leaving Diego de Arana with only eleven men. Three of them had died of illness, and they themselves said the cause was the great intercourse with women; after we had left them, each man took four women and even they were not enough, and they took girls. He said the discord began after I left, when no one wanted to obey nor take gold that was not for himself, except Pedro, the King's Butler, and Escobedo, left in charge of these matters. The rest did nothing more than live with the women, and Pedro and Escobedo killed one called Jacome [a Genoese seaman] and afterwards they went with their women to Cahonaboa; and one night this Cahonaboa came to put fire to the settlement... and eight were drowned and three killed in their sleep, as we later saw from their wounds...

Although I know and it is true that they were to blame, this was very painful, and I grieve more than any of their family, because I had so wanted them to come out of this with great honour. If they had followed my instructions, they would have been in little danger; especially to leave the women alone and all that belonged to the Indians, never to leave the fort unless it was a group of six and to wait until they returned before the next group left... but they gave themselves up to food and the pleasures of women and, that way, they were lost. It gave me and gives me much sorrow. The following day I went ashore. I found the whole site destroyed without sign of a house except the fort which, damaged and burnt as it was, would still be defensible against many men for many days in the middle of Castile. I found eight men buried on the shore and three in a field, and these had received a blow on the forehead from a stone, and it seems they were killed while asleep; and it must be this way, because the fort was full of artillery. It is my judgement this happened less than a month ago.

The destruction of his settlement and the murder of his men marked a turning point in Columbus's relations with the Taino Indians, who had proven themselves capable of killing well-armed Christians. The Cacique Cahonaboa had to be punished if Hispaniola was to be a safe place for Christian settlements but Columbus, cautious at sea, was equally cautious to take revenge on a people and in a country still unknown to him. He first exculpated from any blame his friend the Cacique Guacanagarí, with whom he exchanged gifts, much admired by Guacanagarí's twenty wives.[21] He then set about founding a new town, calling it Isabela, on a better site than Navidad; and he sent expeditions to explore inland to find the source of their gold and control the countryside from a series of small forts. It was only on 9th April 1494, five months after discovering the bodies of the murdered Spaniards near Navidad, that Columbus sent Alonso de Hojeda with a message to Mosén Pedro Margarit, in the newly built fort of St. Thomas, with the order to seize Cahonaboa. He described his capture to Isabella and Ferdinand:

I sent the said Alonso de Hojeda with ten men to Cibao because if more men went, they would all, especially the guilty, flee. I wrote to him that he should see if he could find out who had been the evildoers, and take and punish them... and Hojeda went in person with ten men to their square where, as is their custom, three hundred men were gathered with the Cacique and at least as many women and children again. There, one of the three men who had lost his clothing recognized the Indian who had stolen it and another who had taken a sword. They knew the Cacique had known of it all, because it is their custom to give everything to the Cacique, since they do not have private property, as far as I know. Hojeda seized the Cacique [he duped Cahonaboa into donning an elegant pair of brass handcuffs, 'which are worn by the King of Castile'] and had the two wrongdoers and the brother of the Cacique seized. They manacled them in the presence of all, over six hundred souls. He sent the Cacique and his brother to me tied up...

Columbus had Cahonaboa confined in Isabela for over a year waiting for a ship to take him to Spain. Columbus got to know him – rather well since he confined the Cacique to one of the rooms of his modest house: *I am sending Cahonaboa and his brother to your Royal Highnesses. He is the greatest, strongest and most intelligent of the caciques of this island. If he decides to speak, he will tell us better than anyone the things of this land, for there is nothing he does not know.* Cahonaboa never 'spoke'. In March 1496, he died at sea when the ship carrying him to Spain foundered.

After contemplating what to do about the murder of the men of Navidad, Columbus acted with remarkable astuteness. By letting several months pass before moving against the perpetrators, he gained important advantages: he was as sure as he could be that Cahonaboa was the only cacique responsible for their deaths; by establishing a strong presence on the island, at Isabela and St. Thomas, he could resist a full-scale Indian attack; he fooled Cahonaboa into believing he had nothing to fear from the Spaniards, thereby simplifying his capture; and, by allowing the recent memory of their victory over the Spaniards to fade and the Spaniards lust for revenge to cool, he avoided a general war with the Indians. His decision to seize the men responsible, Cahanoboa and his brother, showed the right mix of authority – if the Spaniards could seize the greatest, most belligerent cacique, what hope was there for the rest? – and justice; the cacique, and not his people, was held responsible.

This incident on Hispaniola, the first test of Columbus's skills as Viceroy and Governor, augured well. So what went wrong? Columbus would never forget his promise to send enough gold to raise an army to conquer Jerusalem. To fulfil it required far more wealth than the island could possibly produce. According to Las Casas, he was under pressure from men at Court to bring home the riches quickly, and he had to repay Berardi and his backers. So Columbus chose to tax the two main cash products of the island, gold and cotton, taxes not based on any estimate of what was reasonable – itself an impossible task in the early years – but what he required to fulfil his promise. Failure to pay the taxes led, inevitably, to punishment, punishment to Indian rebellion, rebellion to repression, repression and rebellion to ever less income and security for the Crown and settlers, and poverty and insecurity to rebellion within the ranks of the Spanish settlers. Add in the anarchic, buccaneering temperament of the conquistador, Columbus's inexperience at managing an unexplored island as big as Scotland with an alien population of perhaps 300,000, and the inevitable cultural clash between the Christians and the Tainos, and it is a wonder he survived with his life.

In Castile, remote from the practical difficulties of managing a new, populous domain with so few loyal men, Columbus's administration seemed to be in chaos. The Crown sent Juan Aguado, as their public auditor, to report on the situation. Columbus, rarely the diplomat, treated Aguado with the disdain a duke might treat his steward, only adding to his enemies at Court.

After a year and a half's 'misrule', Ferdinand and Isabella suggested Columbus return to Spain to give a personal account of events on Hispaniola. This was to give him an opportunity to counter the accusations of disgruntled, returning settlers and their representatives, including Fray Buil, whom Columbus had also unwisely antagonized. But he waited a further year. After two-and-a-half years in the Indies, where he added Jamaica, the circumnavigation of Hispaniola and the long southern coast of Cuba to his earlier discoveries of the Windward Islands and Puerto Rico, Columbus returned from the Second Voyage, arriving at Cadiz the 11th June 1496. He was not in favour with the Crown.

11

FROM EDEN TO SHACKLES

Columbus returned from the Second Voyage intent on mounting a Third. Isabella had received reports from the rebel Mosén Pedro Margarit, their spiritual envoy, Fray Buil, and their Auditor, Juan Aguado, confirming the complaints of returning settlers: there was no wealth in the Indies, Columbus and his brothers ran it as a personal fiefdom, the Indians were oppressed, the Spanish colonizers were ill, starving or dead, overworked and subject to summary punishment. A Seville goldsmith, Formicedo, even claimed that the little gold shipped in from the Indies was impure.

Columbus had to wait two months to receive a Royal Audience, another eight months before Isabella and Ferdinand gave the orders for the preparation of a fleet, and thirteen months more before he could assemble and provision it. In Seville, Bishop Fonseca, responsible for the provisioning of the Indies vessels, seemed to take delight in thwarting Columbus, who wrote to the Sovereigns: *I beg your Royal Highnesses to order those responsible for the business in Seville that they be not against it and impede it not. For it would be much appreciated if there was someone in charge of this business who had some love for it or, at least, that was not against it, and did not set about destroying and defaming it.* His letter had no effect and Fonseca continued in his post long after Columbus was dead. Dressed in the coarse grey-brown habit of a Franciscan friar, living simply with clergymen, Columbus struggled to finance and organize the fleet, and he worried about the situation in Hispaniola. He wrote to his brother, Bartolomé, who ruled the island in Columbus's stead:

I would make the most of this if, by suffering this misery, it redounded to the service of Our Lord, for whom we must labour with a happy spirit; nor would I forget to remember that nothing great can be achieved without hardship and, in the same manner, one is consoled by the belief that everything that is laboriously obtained one possesses with the greatest sweetness.

In these two years he read, or reread, Marco Polo, D'Ailly's

Imago Mundi, and Pope Pius II's *Description of Asia*. The original volumes are dense with notes, underlinings and markings, confirming his concept of the world. For the hated scholars had begun to contest his claim that the Indies were proximate to the lands of the Great Khan, and Columbus was obliged to relive the early years of futile discussion. Even in his moment of triumph in Barcelona in 1493 there were doubters. Bernardino de Carvajal told the Pope that Columbus had discovered *Unknown islands towards India* and Peter Martyr, the Prince's Tutor, speculated that *Columbus has discovered Antilla*. Doubts about the position of the Indies were so great that, by December 1494, Guillermo Coma, a medical doctor and shipmate on the Second Voyage, could write that *I am inclined to think that these are the islands of the Arabs* off the east coast of Africa, but thought to be further east than they really are, confusing them, perhaps, with the East Indies.

Columbus, hankering back to the seven years importuning, would write at the beginning of the *Account of the Third Voyage*: *Those persons who understood such matters were sure it was impossible... I had to speak of the secular authorities, who related that in these regions there were many riches, and, in the same way, I had to bring their opinions of where this was placed in the world. At last your Royal Highnesses decided to go ahead with this task. Here you showed the great heart you always do in great matters, because all those who understood it and heard the discussions treated it as a joke, except two friars [Peréz and Marchena] who were always loyal.*

After recounting his discovery of Cuba, mistaken for the mainland, and *seven hundred islands*, he attacked his detractors: *Evil rumours began to circulate in Spain scorning the new venture because I had not sent shipfuls of gold, giving no allowance to the little time that had elapsed, nor the many difficulties I had encountered. Because of this venture, for my sins or my salvation, I was hated and impeded from doing anything I said or asked. Therefore I decided to come to your Royal Highnesses, astonished by it all, showing you I was right in everything. I told you of the people I had seen and by which we could save so many souls, I brought you the submission of the people of Hispaniola, who would pay tribute, I brought you sufficient samples of gold... of copper, many types of spices, and I told you of the great quantity of brasil wood and of other infinite things. But this was not enough for some people, who had wanted and had begun to spread evil rumours of this enterprise; nor even speak of the service of Our Lord with whom we saved so many souls… nor to point out that the things great princes customarily did in this world to increase their renown.* After citing Solomon's voyage to Ophir, Alexander's expedition to *Taprobana* (Ceylon/India), the Emperor Nero's search for the source of the Nile, and the Portuguese kings' conquests in Africa and their exploratory voyages, he reminded Isabella and Ferdinand, *Nor was it worth saying I had never read that princes of Castile had ever won lands outside Spain… The more I said, the more they insulted the venture, showing a hatred for it…* Diplomacy was not Columbus's forte. *Your Royal Highnesses answered me smiling, saying I should not take notice of anything, because you gave no credence to those who spoke badly of this venture.*

Though Isabella must have had her doubts about his administrative ability, she still trusted him with the venture of the Indies, for his arguments were substantial: the development of the new territories required time; her priests could save souls; they had established a settlement; and it did redound to the fame of the two Sovereigns. Also, he was an outstanding captain, still *my Admiral.* Linking the seven years of *great hardship* with the two years it had taken to assemble, man and provision the six ships for the Third Voyage, was not casual; the same class of men who had obstructed the First Voyage obstructed the Third. They were wrong, small-minded and unworthy subjects of such illustrious princes. That Columbus raised the whole matter again, five months after he had left Spain, shows how strongly he felt he had been mistreated and how worried he was that, in his absence, his detractors would gain ground with Isabella and Ferdinand. His worries, augmented by news of the Roldán rebellion, were well founded.

After nearly two and a half years away from the sea, he finally set sail on 30th May 1498 from the port of Sanlucar,[22] at the mouth of the Guadalquivir, and, in a little-appreciated text, Columbus explained his objective: *I sailed to the South with the purpose of arriving at the Equator and from there continue westward until the island of Hispaniola fetched due north… and I wanted to see what was the intention of the King Dom João of Portugal who said there was mainland to the south; for this reason, it is said that he had*

148

differences with the Sovereigns of Castile and, finally, it was agreed the King of Portugal would have all the lands up to 370 leagues west of the Azores and the Cape Verde Islands, from north to south, from Pole to Pole. It is also said that the King Dom João was certain he would find famous lands and things within these limits.

No mention of India, Asia, China or the Great Khan, none of which was this far south on contemporary world maps. Already, Columbus realized that if he were to discover King John's mainland at a southern latitude, it would be something new. It could only be a new, Southern continent.

For once, Columbus didn't have to worry about Portuguese opposition. With John's death and the marriage of his successor, Manuel, to the Infanta Isabel, relations between the two countries were superficially excellent, if flawed by conflicting interests in India-Indies. Columbus sailed to the Portuguese Cape Verde Islands, sixteen degrees north of the Equator, where he took on water, cheese and goats, and departed on a southwesterly course with the intention of making landfall in what is now Brazil. Nine degrees north of the Equator his ships were becalmed in the doldrums and they drifted for ten days, in great discomfort from the heat, before an easterly wind came up. He sailed due west, making landfall, on 31st July 1498, at a large island with three peaks he named Trinidad. From there he discovered the mainland of South America, as he recounted in the *Account of the Third Voyage*:

On the afternoon of 4th August 1498, I arrived at the mainland I thought was an island...

I asked the Indians [with whom he had extensive dealings and who offered him and his men a banquet] where they found and fished pearls, and they showed me mother of pearl and replied clearly they were born and collected to the west, beyond the island that was Cape Lapo, the point of Paria [Venezuela] of the mainland, which I believed was an island.

The topography from the sea – mountains appear like islands between plains submerged below the horizon – initially fooled him into thinking he had discovered new islands, but: *All the sea was freshwater and I did not know where it came from, and I say that because there did not seem to be great rivers and, if there were, it would still be a wonder...*

Columbus speculated that he had arrived close to Earthly Paradise, generally placed on the Equator by scholars of his time. Also the immense area of fresh water – about 9,000 square miles, the effluent of the Orinoco – much more than he had ever experienced, fitted the theory that *the Earthly Paradise is at the end of the Orient, in a very high mountain rising beyond the turbulent winds, where the waters of the Flood never reached and where Elias and Enoch used to be. From there sprouts a great spring, falling to the sea, where it makes a great lake from which come the four great rivers [Nile, Euphrates, Tigris and Ganges].* After further speculation that the Earth is more pear-shaped than round, with a point, like a nipple, which is Earthly Paradise, he returned to practical exploration:

I sent a small caravel to see if there was an exit to the north because, bordering on the mainland and the land I called Isabeta to the west, there appeared to be a high, beautiful island. The caravel returned and they told me they had found a large gulf and, within it, four large openings that seemed to be small gulfs, at the end of each was a river. I gave it the name of the Gulf of Pearls. It seemed to be a corner of the great gulf where we sailed close to the mainland and the island of Trinidad. I believed the four openings were four islands, and there did not seem to be a trace of the river that made all the water of the gulf, which is forty leagues long and twenty-six wide, sweet; but the seamen asserted that these openings were river mouths...

I believe this is a very great continent that has been unknown until today. And I am greatly helped in this belief by this great river [the Orinoco] and this sea, which is sweet, and by Ezra 4.vi saying six parts of the world is land and one part water... and I am also supported by many of the Cannibal Indians I captured who said that to the south was the mainland.

After this well-reasoned discovery, Columbus, full of a sense of history, wrote: *Your Royal Highnesses will never leave anything that will be remembered more greatly... and you won the lands that are so great it is another world.*

Madariaga accepts that Columbus divined the existence of South America, as does Morison, which makes it all the stranger that Fernández-Armesto should not. He cites a later letter (October 1498, *Textos* XXXVI) to 'prove' Columbus retracted his first impression that he had discovered a new world. But

Fernández-Armesto has confused Columbus's two mainlands – Cuba-China, which Columbus believed to have been known to the Ancients, and later in the same letter, *and now this [the Other World] that is so wonderful I believe it is going to be spoken of by all the Christians as a marvel.* Further evidence supports Columbus's unwavering conviction he had discovered a new world: the primitive Juan de la Cosa map, now known to have been painted under Columbus's direction, shows a great, unnamed southern landmass; and the objective of his last voyage was to sail through straits separating the known northern landmass of Asia from the southern, by definition not Asia and therefore new. There still lingered a suspicion that *I feel in my soul that the Earthly Paradise is over there;* and in a sense it was.

Even when Columbus was full of his discovery of the *Other World*, he anticipated his destitution as Governor of Hispaniola. Only two weeks after making the landfall at Trinidad, he abandoned his voyage of discovery and set a course for Hispaniola. He gave several reasons to Isabella and Ferdinand for this surprising change of plan: after over two years away from Hispaniola and with no news from his brothers in several months, he was anxious to see them and his island; he would hand over the three ships to Bartolomé for further discovery of the mainland; the stores he carried for the island were beginning to spoil; the crew were tired and he didn't have the money to pay them any longer; and his eyes were badly afflicted, so much so he was almost blind. However, neither ill-health nor the wishes of the crew, and certainly not rotting stores could stop Columbus from exploration, his obsession for the last fourteen years, especially after it had cost him such *great hardship* to raise a fleet; and the pearl beds were literally just over the horizon. Only the strongest premonition that his title to Hispaniola was at risk can explain his decision to leave the newly discovered continent and the pearl beds for Hispaniola. But he could hardly say so to his Sovereigns.

Events had turned nasty on Hispaniola: Francisco Roldán, the man he'd made District Commissioner (*Alcalde Mayor)* of the island, led a rebellion against the Colón's regime. Columbus reported his version to Isabella and Ferdinand (October 1499):

After I arrived with so many people and the powers of your Highnesses, Roldán moved to his primary purpose, saying he wanted to leave, and I found it was true that most people here were on his side. As they were workmen and for their work I would have paid them, this Roldán, and those with him, had a way to secure that they pass to his side. They would not have to work, would have plenty of food and women and, above all, the freedom to do what they liked. So I had to dissemble and finally they came and would have me give them two of the three caravels the Adelantado [Bartolomé Colón] had prepared to leave on a voyage of discovery, and letters commending their good service to your Highnesses, their salary and many other dishonest things. So I sent them over there to the western cape of the island, where they are now settled. In fact, they had free run of the island.

Rather than confront Roldán, Columbus agreed to his new demands: reinstatement as Alcalde Mayor with the right to distribute land, as well as the Indians who lived on it, to his men – first intimations of the *encomienda*. Other rebellious acts distracted and exhausted him. He wrote to Juana de Torres at Isabella's court, knowing she would pass it on to the Queen:

When I came from Paria, I found nearly half the people of Hispaniola in revolt, and they warred against us up to now like a Moor and the Indians too on the other side. Amid all this arrived Alonso de Hojeda, who proved with the royal seal and said their Royal Highnesses had sent him with promises of gifts and payments. He added a large band of men and in all Hispaniola there are few who are not vagabonds, and no one with a wife and children. This Hojeda drove me mad. He had to leave and left, saying he would return, with more men and ships, and he had left the royal person, the Queen, Our Lady, close to death. And then arrived Vicente Yañez [Pinzón's younger brother] with four caravels. There was a brawl but no damage. Afterwards, the Indians said there was news that the brother of the Alcalde Mayor Roldán had brought six more caravels, but it was with mischief, and, at the very end, when my hope that the Royal Highnesses would ever send ships to the Indies was broken, it was commonly said Her Majesty was dead. At this time, one Adrian de Mugica tried to rebel again like before, but Our Lord did not want him to realize his evil purpose.

Everything was going wrong. By authorizing voyages of discovery without even troubling to inform Columbus, the Crown had deliberately and clearly broken the Capitulations of Santa Fé. Hojeda, with Amerigo Vespucci aboard, explored the coast of Venezuela, which he named, exploiting the pearl beds discovered, charted and reported to Spain by Columbus. Vicente Yañez Pinzón, Captain of the *Niña* on the First Voyage, sailed south to discover the Amazon, and Pedro Alonso Niño, former pilot of the *Santa Maria*, reaped a rich haul of pearls at the island of Margarita. Columbus, alarmed that this presaged his downfall on Hispaniola, wrote an apology to Isabella and Ferdinand, trying to counter the arguments of his detractors:

Over there [in Castile] they said I had founded the village [Isabela] in the worst place in the island, and it is in the best of it, and so it is said from the mouth of all the Indians of the island. They said they died of thirst, and a river passes the town nearer than Santa María of Seville to its river. They said this place was the most unhealthy, and it is the healthiest. They said there were no provisions, and there is meat, bread, fish and an abundance of other things. They said I had taken all the cattle brought here, and nothing was brought here except eight pigs, which I brought. They said the land of Isabela is very poor and did not give wheat; I harvested it and ate the bread from it, and it is the most beautiful land one could covet.

Columbus chose the site of Isabela under adverse circumstances but no other site would have significantly improved the first colonizers' lot. Malaria-carrying mosquitoes infested large areas of Hispaniola[23] and new colonizers contracted amoebic dysentery and syphilis from the Indians. Many European crops couldn't flourish in the tropical climate – the settlers had to select them by trial and error – nor were most Spaniards willing or able to cultivate them; and the Indian diet, with hardly any meat and based on cassava bread, was totally foreign. Ships came intermittently from Spain with no real appreciation, in Seville, of the need of the colonizers, Columbus excepted, who, via his Florentine agent, ordered about a ton of sweetmeats for his household as well as perfumes, 6 dozen handkerchiefs and a bed of six Brittany mattresses; the friar had removed his habit.

The colonizers had to come to terms with the Indians, and Columbus had no experience to guide him through difficult times. Identical problems were to dog the first English settlements at Roanoke Island and Jamestown (Virginia) and the French settlements at Santa Elena (S. Carolina), Isle Saint-Alexis (Brazil), and France-Roy, Sable Island and Charlesbourg-Royal (all in Canada), all of which were abandoned or destroyed by the Indians. By these standards, the Spanish colony on Hispaniola was an outstanding success, and the credit must go to the perseverance of Columbus and Isabella and Ferdinand. It is a useful reminder that a century later, in the year 1600, there was not one European settlement in North America.

Columbus's choice of site for Isabela, 'a foul and ill-watered spot' according to Fernández-Armesto, has been so universally condemned that I went to see it for myself. It has a short history. Founded in 1494, it was abandoned two years later by Bartolomé Colón who moved the 'capital' to the southern shore of the island, where he was closer to the fertile plain and gold mines of Cibao. Hawkins used Isabela's warehouse to store goods and slaves which he sold to the islanders, but it was soon forgotten until a United States naval expedition under the command of Lieutenant Colvocoresses made a brief survey of the ruins in 1891. In the interim, the buildings had been destroyed by an earthquake (1749) and part of the rocky bluff on which it had been built was eroded and washed away by the sea. Thereafter the ruins were visited once in a while by a curious historian or archaeologist, until excavations on the site were undertaken in 1986. Today the whole area has been beautified and turned over to a National Park, visited by jeep-loads of blond tourists shipped in from Puerto Plata.

In January 1495, Columbus described the site of Isabela (text from the *Libro Copiador*): *Here there is no closed port, but a great bay which would hold all the ships in the world. A storm will never enter here, and there is an ideal place on higher land, almost an island, at the foot of which a great ship can moor and discharge its cargo. Within a lombard's shot there flows a mighty river, better than the Guadalquivir, from which a canal can bring its water to the town. It flows through a wide valley, whose end I have yet to reach... Here, where I have decided to build the town, were certain houses belonging to the Indians.*

How does this recently-discovered text match the present site? Columbus built Isabela on a rocky outcrop which protrudes about twelve feet above the water into a shallow bay. Several metres of the outcrop have been washed away, and it is reasonable to assume it reached out to a point where, from swimming, I found a good six feet of water. This is barely enough for a caravel and insufficient draft for a larger ship, but hurricanes can move vast amounts of sand, and one cannot discard the possibility that lode from the River Bajabonico has silted up this part of the coast. As an anchorage, it has a good, sandy bottom, is free of coral reefs and rocks, and offers excellent protection from the prevailing easterlies (a Force 6 easterly was blowing while I was there, yet the water around Isabela barely rippled). However, though a coral reef acts as a breakwater against northerly seas, the anchorage is exposed to northwesterlies. 400 metres from the settlement flowed a sizeable river, the River Bajabonico. The 1749 earthquake changed the course of the river, moving its outlet 900 metres further from the settlement, which explains why Morison and others report that the settlers had to travel 'a mile' or 'an hour' for water. The old course is clearly visible from Isabela, a short walk along the beach, and there used to be signs of an old canal to bring water to the settlement.

After the disaster at Navidad, Columbus chose the site of Isabela for its defensive situation. On three sides the settlement was protected from attack by its elevation and on the fourth by dense undergrowth 'which a rabbit couldn't penetrate'. The first settlers raised a rectangular wall to enclose the 'city' which comprised a small stone church, a large warehouse 40 metres long, an arsenal, Columbus's fortified house, incorporating a watchtower on the edge of the bluff, wells, and two hundred smaller huts and houses built for his men (and a few women). Mangrove swamps on either side of the rocky outcrop ended in beaches where longboats could be safely beached.

Columbus's comment that some Indians occupied the bluff confirms its favourable position for the site of a settlement. Archaeologists have discovered Taino remains, dating from about 1200 A.D., and when digging the site, they found a Taino cemetery beside Isabela's. Among the Spanish dead are four women.

Anyway, the rebels didn't complain about Isabela's harbour facilities or defensive qualities: mosquitoes, dysentery, malaria, a protein-deficient diet, the hard labour required to get any colony off the ground and, above all, the lack of ready gold were the real sources of their complaints.

Columbus, desperate to disqualify the rebels, wrote: *Against justice they accused me of all this because they would have your Highnesses abandon me and my venture; and what is more, the author of all this is a Converso, because the Conversos are the enemy of the prosperity of your Royal Highnesses and of the Christians; further, by destroying my reputation, they found the way so that everything would be lost. They say some of those who are with Roldán and at war with me are Conversos.* The Converso accusation merely countered, in a sort of tit-for-tat, the rebels' accusation that Columbus was a Converso.

Fernando Colón, as a page at Court, saw the other end of the dispute: *Many rebels sent letters from Hispaniola and others, who had returned to Castile, did not stop giving false reports against the Admiral and his brothers. They said they were cruel and incapable of governing, because they love foreigners and they had never had the experience from which they could have learned to govern an honourable people. They asserted that, if their Highnesses did not remedy the situation, all those countries would be ruined, if not destroyed by such a perverse administration; the Admiral who, on the pretence that all was his, because he had discovered it with his effort and labour, would ally himself with a Prince who would help him.*

As both Columbus and the rebels agreed Hispaniola was being ruined, it is not surprising the Crown was obliged to act. Logically, they should have acted against the rebels and not their appointed representatives, the Colón brothers. The accusation that the Colóns might switch allegiance must have irritated the King and Queen, with insinuating courtiers reminding them of Antonio di Noli, the Genoese Governor of the Cape Verde Islands, who had changed allegiance from Portugal to Castile twenty years earlier. Still, given the improved relations with Portugal and the predominance of Spaniards on Hispaniola, this accusation must have seemed farfetched. However, the unpleasant behaviour of returning settlers brought the disagreeable issue of the Indies home to the King and Queen. Fernando Colón witnessed it:

More than fifty men bought a large quantity of grapes, seated themselves in the patio of the Alhambra, and shouted that their Highnesses and the Admiral made them live like this because they were unpaid, and a thousand other impudences. They were so shameless that when King Ferdinand parted, they surrounded him chanting, 'Pay us! Pay us!' If I or my brother, who were pages of the Most Serene Queen, passed them by, they would raise their voices to the sky saying, 'Look at the sons of the Admiral of the mosquitoes, of he who has discovered the lands of vanity and cheating to bury and destitute Castilian hidalgos.

In May 1499, Isabella and Ferdinand signed the order permitting the withdrawal of Columbus's authority over Hispaniola. Fernando, who was now reporting his own, courtier's knowledge, blamed Ferdinand: *The King decided to send an investigating judge to Hispaniola to inform him on all these matters and he ordered that, if he found the Admiral to blame for all these complaints, he should send him to Castile, remaining himself as Governor. The Sovereigns sent Francisco de Bobadilla, poor Knight Commander of the Order of Calatrava, as their investigator.*

As this coincides with what transpired, it is evident that Ferdinand had already decided to withdraw Columbus. He wanted to replace a difficult and, according to the Capitulations of Santa Fé, powerful plenipotentiary with a simple delegate of the Crown, but Isabella was reluctant to remove Columbus. She wouldn't put the order into effect for over a year. Then Columbus sanctioned something which inflamed her sense of justice and order in the Indies. On 21st November 1499, two caravels left Santo Domingo with some of Roldán's rebels. As part of the agreement which ended the rebellion, Columbus allowed them to take some Indians with them and, possibly in misguided generosity, he also gave Indians to the other voyagers (including Las Casas's father).[24] When Isabella heard of this new shipment of Indian slaves, she was furious and ordered all the voyagers, under pain of death, to release and return their Indians to Hispaniola, saying, *What power from me has the Admiral to give my subjects to anyone?*

Bobadilla arrived at Santo Domingo on 23rd August 1500. Bedraggled Spaniards told him the Colóns' administration had hung seven Christians that week and five more were in prison and would be hung. He met only disgruntled Christians and an uncooperative and unconvincing Diego Colón who, in the absence of his brothers, had been left in charge of the settlement. Bobadilla ordered the arrest and confinement of the Colóns and assumed the Governorship of Hispaniola. Isabella and Ferdinand had decidedly breached the Capitulations of Santa Fé. Columbus, writing to Juana de Torres at Isabella's court, opened his heart to her and, by extension, to Isabella:

*In all this [the Roldán rebellion] the Knight Commander Bobadilla arrived at Santo Domingo. I was in the plain and the Adelantado [Bartolomé] in Xaragua where this Adrian de Mugica had made his headquarters, but everything was now calm and the lands rich and everyone in peace [*evidently not so, but let's allow Columbus his self-serving preamble*]. On the second day of his arrival, Bobadilla created himself Governor and appointed officials and proclaimed the freedom from the tenth [a tax] and everything for twenty years, which is the age of a man. He came to pay everyone, even those who had not served properly. He proclaimed he would send me and my brothers in irons, just as he has done, and neither I nor anyone of my lineage would return, adding a thousand indecent and rude things. This he did on the second day of his arrival, when I was absent not even knowing he had arrived.*

He carried a quantity of letters from their Highnesses, signed in blank, and sent to Roldán and his company favours and commissions; he never sent me a letter or a messenger, not even up to today. Think what whoever had my office would think: to honour and favour him who had tried to rob their Highnesses and who had committed such wickedness and damage, and drag down him who, with so many dangers, had supported them.

Bobadilla made Don Diego prisoner, shackled him in a caravel and, when I arrived, he did the same thing to me and later the same to the Adelantado when he came. I never spoke to him nor has he consented, up to now, that anyone speaks to me. I swear I cannot think why I am a prisoner.

While Isabella and Ferdinand had their reasons to remove him from Hispaniola, they were under a contractual, not to add moral obligation to compensate him for his services. The method used – seizure, imprisonment and shackles – was not Isabella's and one must assume that either Bobadilla acted independently of his brief or that Ferdinand, wary of the Colóns' possible reaction, instructed him to deal with them ruthlessly.

Aboard the caravel, Columbus stubbornly refused to have his shackles removed, arguing that *since Bobadilla had executed, in their name, the orders of the Sovereigns and it was with their authority he had been put in irons, he would not have anyone, save the Sovereigns, do anything about it.*

They arrived at Cadiz on 20th November 1500, and for three weeks Columbus trailed the streets of the port and of Seville in chains until a letter arrived from the Sovereigns; it ordered his release, summoned him to court at the Alhambra and enclosed 2,000 Ducats (750,000 maravedis). He decided to keep the shackles in memory of his many services, recalled Fernando, *And so he did, because I always saw them in his chamber and he wanted them to be buried with his bones.*

Isabella received him warmly at Court. Now forty-nine years old, no longer in good health, removed from office by the Sovereigns with no realistic hope of reinstatement (in spite of the contractual agreement of Santa Fé), with his sons well established at Court and his beloved brothers at his side, almost any man would have happily retired to an estate – which Ferdinand is said to have offered – and live off a reduced share of the revenues from Hispaniola. But not Columbus. Herein lies his greatness and the torment of his life.

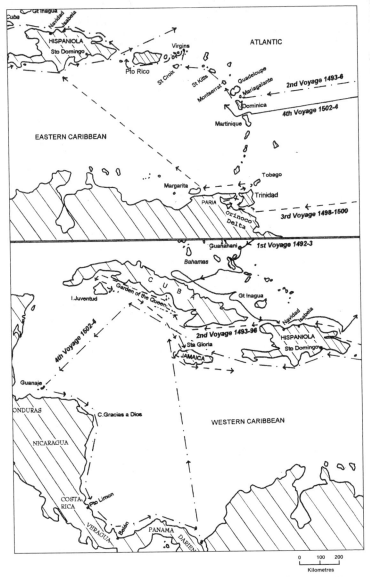

Map 4 – The Caribbean Voyages

12

To the Ultimate Victory

From Columbus's notes in his copy of Pliny's *Natural History*, which he read after returning from the Third Voyage, one gets an idea of how he treated his infirmities: loss of hair, toothache, gall stones and *How to cause disgust in Venus and the love of women. On the hatred of sexual intercourse.*[25] The mystery of why Columbus should have taken an interest in quenching the passion of women has gone unnoticed. Either it was from curiosity – doubtful since Columbus never showed signs of prurience – or he really felt threatened by the attractions of a younger woman.

Beginning with his Journal entry of 16th February 1493, Columbus described the symptoms of weakness in the legs, sore eyes and pain in the joints, a condition contemporaries diagnosed as gout – thought to be arthritis. We have the first news of his illness in 1491, when he received permission to travel by mule. These symptoms recurred in his accounts of his three later voyages, sometimes leaving him bedridden for months. A recent 'diagnosis' is Reither's syndrome, the extension of a urinary infection to arthritis, conjunctivitis and diarrhoea.

Illness, the humiliation of being brought to Castile in chains, the shattering blow of being replaced as Governor of Hispaniola by Bobadilla and, soon after his return, by Nicolás de Ovando, and the regular departure of discovery fleets sailing west from Spain and Portugal, did not deter Columbus from proposing a new voyage of discovery to Isabella and Ferdinand, while seeking redress for his destitution as Governor. His robust reaction to adversity is typical of the man; he would never give up.

While still in chains aboard the ship carrying him to Castile, Columbus worked to recover his position with his Sovereigns. On the caravel he wrote a long letter to Juana de Torres appealing to Isabella through God. This was the most passionate of his many passionate letters: *If my complaints of the world are new, her ill treatment is old. She has given me a thousand battles and I withstood them all, up to now, when I took no advantage of arms or warnings. With cruelty she has thrown me into the abyss. Only the hope of*

Him, who created everything, sustains me. His help has always come quickly. Another time, not so long ago, when I was even lower, He raised me with His right arm saying, 'Oh man of little faith, rise up, have no fear!'

I came with such love to serve these Princes, and I have served them as never heard or seen before. Our Lord told, by St. John in the Apocalypse after it was said from the mouth of Isaiah, of the new sky and land, and He made me the messenger and showed me that region. No one believed me and He gave to the Queen, my lady, the spirit and intelligence and great strength, as to a dear and much-beloved daughter. I took possession of all this in her royal name. They wanted to correct their gross ignorance by using the little knowledge they had to talk about obstacles and expenses. But, to the contrary, her Highness approved the enterprise and she sustained it, as long as she could.

I spent seven years talking and nine in executing memorable deeds; they had no idea of this. I arrived and I am in such a state there is not a villain who does not think to revile me. He who will not consent it will be among the virtuous.

Columbus then turned to the accusation of his doubtful allegiance: *If I had stolen the Indies and the land next to it, which is now fabulous, from the altar of St. Peter and given it to the Moors, Spain could not have shown me greater enmity.*

I believe you will recall, when the storm, with no sails left, threw me into Lisbon, that I was falsely accused of going there to give the Indies to the King. Later, their Highnesses knew it was not so and it was all done with wickedness. Though I know little, I know not who thinks I am so stupid I would not realize that, even if the Indies were mine, I could not maintain them without the aid of a Prince. Where could I find more support and security than with the King and Queen, Our Lords, who from nothing have elevated me to such honour and are the greatest Princes, on sea and land, in all the World? These I have served and who look after my privileges and favours, and, if someone ruins me, their Highnesses raise me with advantage. As I have said, their Highnesses have already received my service and have my sons as pages, which could never have happened with another Prince, because where there is no love everything else is worthless.

How could Isabella ignore such an appeal to her heart, her sense of justice and religious fervour? A second letter to the Royal Council reminded them of his long and loyal service, and asked them to review all his previous correspondence; and he wrote a third, shorter letter to Isabella and Ferdinand, playing on Isabella's religious fervour with a postscript that ended: *I swear I do not know, nor can even think, why your Highnesses [sent Bobadilla to send me back in irons] unless God, Our Father, wanted to do this by way of your Highnesses, me, Spain and Christianity, as He did with Abraham and Isaac, with Moses and the Israelites in Egypt when He brought them out, as with many others of which we have knowledge.*

Later in the year he would write to Isabella, offering her his body and soul:

I am your Highness's servant. The keys of my will-power I gave you in Barcelona [where he saw her in 1493 after discovering the Indies]. If you try it now, you will find its scent and savour have only improved since then. I am always thinking of your repose [she was ill]. If it pleases you to test my industry, you will discover my good intentions... I gave all of myself to your Highness in Barcelona and, as it is with my spirit, so it is with my honour and property.

Twenty-seven days after landing in Cadiz, only six days after being released from his chains, he was at Court in the Alhambra with his sons and brothers. According to a contemporary chronicler, *The Admiral went to kiss the hands of the King and Queen and with tears made his apologies, as well as he could, and, when they had heard him, with much clemency they consoled him and spoke such words that he was somewhat content.* They commanded the restitution of all his income and rights in Castile but refused to reinstate him as Governor of Hispaniola. This was not sufficient for Columbus who had insisted, in 1492, on a full, contractual agreement with the Crown precisely to avoid this situation. Whatever the interests of state, the Crown was contractually obliged to reinstate him and his descendants as Viceroy and Governor of all lands he conquered 'for all time'. He knew he was right, and he planned an offensive against the Crown that ended in the Columbian lawsuits of thirty years' duration. To support his case he prepared two lengthy documents, which he called *The Book of Privileges* and *The Book of Prophesies*.

The Book of Privileges provided the legal basis for his claim against the Crown. It included all the agreements and correspondence with the Crown beginning with the Capitulations of Santa

Fé. Adding further pressure, in 1501 and 1502, he sent several letters to Isabella and Ferdinand to remind them of their contractual obligations, without, however, receiving the satisfaction he wanted.

The purpose of *The Book of Prophesies* was the same as *The Book of Privileges* – to reinstate his former position with Isabella and Ferdinand – but its line of attack was more oblique. He prepared the ground in a 1501 letter to the Sovereigns, later incorporated as an introduction to *The Book of Prophecies*. After reminding them of his great experience at sea, where he picked up the arts required for navigation and map-making and *Our Lord, with His Palpable Hand, opened my understanding that it was feasible to sail from here to the Indies,* he wrote: *All the sciences of which I speak above were of no advantage to me nor were their authorities. Only your Highnesses kept faith and constancy. Who can doubt that this light was not from the Holy Spirit as well as from me?*

After establishing himself as a Prophet, he prophesied:

There are only 155 years left to complete the seven thousand, by which time, according to these wise men, the world will be concluded. Our Redeemer said that everything written by the Prophets would have to be fulfilled before the end of the world.

And what remained unfulfilled? *I have already said that I made no use of reason or mathematics or world maps to execute the venture of the Indies; it fully fulfilled the words of Isaiah. This is what I want to write here, to limit this statement to your Highnesses because you are going to rejoice in the other prophecy from the same authorities, that I will speak of Jerusalem and of this venture, if there is faith, I am certain to be victorious.*

One might wonder if he seriously meant that he – or they – would conquer Jerusalem, and of course he did. All the gold in the Indies would be devoted to raising an army to conquer it, his 10,000 cavalry and 100,000 infantry.

The *Book of Prophecies*, a collage of extracts from the Bible and other authorities assembled by Columbus, Father Gorricio[26] and Fernando Colón, was supposed to support this ultimate idea of St. Columbus, the instrument of the Catholic Sovereigns and Our Lord, Prophet and provider of the means to conquer Jerusalem.

It was this lonely sense of being the Chosen One that drove

Columbus onward to his next objective: to circumnavigate the world. I had arrived at this unconventional conclusion by a process resembling a game of 'Go' where my white stones, scraps of information from a variety of sources, gradually strangled the black stones, all the familiar arguments against such a theory. Now I assembled the evidence that Columbus had considered the circumnavigation a quarter of a century before, and attempted it seventeen years before Magellan.

In 1495 Columbus wrote, *If I had sufficient supplies, I would try to return to Spain by the east, coming to the Ganges, then the Persian Gulf and afterwards Ethiopia [i.e., Africa].* This was two years before Vasco da Gama had reached India, and since then everything he had learned of the world confirmed his belief that he could circumnavigate it.

The 1502 Cantino map – and the primitive 1500 de la Cosa map – describes the world as Columbus believed it to be before his Fourth Voyage.[27] To the north of the Indies is a large mainland, thought to begin at Cuba, which he called Mangi, Marco Polo's South East China. To the south of the Indies is another immense landmass whose northern shores he discovered in 1498 – his 'Other World', possibly including the Earthly Paradise. Subsequent voyages by Vicente Yañez Pinzón, Alonso Vélez de Mendoza and Pedro Alvarez Cabral had proven it to extend at least 2,000 miles southward, beyond seventeen degrees south of the Equator.

Africa was, after Vasco Da Gama's 1497 voyage, well charted and the Far East ended in a mess of islands and the northern mainland. Columbus believed in a passage between the two great landmasses, on the same latitude of the Indies, but further west, by which a ship could pass to Vasco da Gama's India and Africa, round the Cape of Good Hope, and return to Spain. His world looked like this: (see Map 5)

Fernando Colón, who shipped with his father, wrote: *On setting out on the Ocean, the Admiral's intention was to reconnoitre the land of Paria [Venezuela] and continue along the coast until he arrived at the Straits which he knew for certain was towards Veragua and Nombre de Dios [Panama].*

As Columbus had requested a letter from Isabella and Ferdinand to give to the Portuguese Captain in India, it is rea-

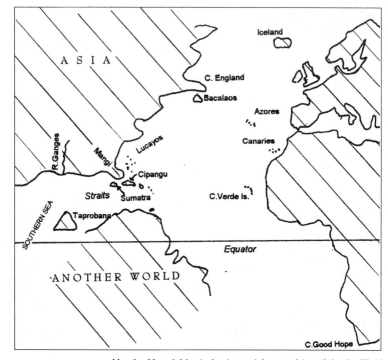

Map 5 – Map of Atlantic showing strait between Asia and Another World

sonable to assume that he intended to pass through these straits, between the two great landmasses to the north (Asia) and the south (Other World), and sail on to India. Once he had reached the legendary spice islands and India, traded his truck for gold, gems, spices and pearls and established a trading post, Columbus had to sail westward and circumnavigate the world; according to Columbus's notion of the world, there was no alternative.

He believed the distance to Taprobana (Ceylon) and Portuguese India with a favourable wind would not be great. *The World is small*, as he put it. As Vasco da Gama had already proved, it was possible to sail around the Cape of Good Hope and return to Europe – and he had seen Bartolomeus Dias's chart from the Cape to Lisbon. Not only was it possible, but it was the *only return route with favourable winds*. All Columbus's experience and knowledge of the wind systems confirmed his original belief that the easterly trades dominated the Ocean Sea from the latitude of the Canaries to the Cape Verde Islands. The latitude of his Straits coincided with this band of easterlies, making a return voyage through them virtually impossible. In fact he was right; the first Spanish sailors leaving the west coast of Mexico could easily reach the Spice Islands with a following wind, but then found it impossible to return by the same route. Also, what would be the point of returning by the way he had come when he could be the first man to circumnavigate the World? No mariner could ever outshine his ultimate victory.

Columbus had excellent reasons to keep his objective to himself. He was naturally suspicious of princes, justified by King John's use of his proposal to send a fleet into the Atlantic and by the Sovereign's approval of Hojeda's voyage to follow the route to Paria he had charted and sent back to Castile. And if the crew had learned of his real objective, he would have had a mutiny on his hands. It had to be kept secret, even from his brothers and sons.

There is other evidence to support the idea that he was about to take the extraordinary risk of circumnavigating the Globe. In the year of his departure he made his *Mayorazgo*, a will which, with special authorization of the crown, permitted him to pass on the bulk of his estate and rights to his eldest son. Almost simultaneously, he sent copies of his *Book of Privileges* to Father Gaspar Gorricio (2nd April 1502) and Ambassador Nicòlo de Oderigo for safekeeping. Further, this coincided with the first known letter to the Bank of St. George of Genoa (2nd April 1502. I had read aloud from the original, signed letter for Sr. Tarducci) in which he wrote: *Because I am mortal, I have left to D. Diego, my son, that of all the income there would be, a tenth of it all would be paid there every year for ever, to discount from the tax on wheat, wine and other edible provisions... I request as a favour that you take charge of this son of mine.*

His last letter before crossing the Ocean, sent late May from Gran Canaria to Father Gorricio, confirms his intention to leave all his affairs in good order, in case of his death: *Now I continue my voyage in the name of the Holy Trinity and I hope from Him, the victory. Remember, your reverence, to write often to D. Diego and*

167

remind Miçer Francisco de Ribarol of the Rome business, as I haven't written to him in this hurry. The Rome business was to provide Father Gorricio the license to handle his affairs.

If all this seems mere speculation, less than seven years after his return from the Fourth Voyage, Fernando, then twenty-two-years' old, wrote to Ferdinand (Isabella was then dead) proposing to sail around the world.[28] That is ten years before Magellan and Sebastian Elcano.

By February 1502 when, in a letter now lost, he proposed a Fourth Voyage of Discovery, his standing was sufficiently high to receive immediate authorization and ten thousand gold pesos (4.3 million maravedis). A warm letter from Isabella and Ferdinand recognized his rights and those of his heirs and said they wanted him to be well treated. Only the condition that he not land at Hispaniola on the outward journey was unacceptable to the legitimate Governor and discoverer of the island, and he had no intention of keeping it.

It is a tribute to his resilience and perseverance that only eighteen months after his arrival in chains at Cadiz, stripped of all his rights and properties in Hispaniola, Columbus was at the head of a discovery fleet of four vessels, financed by the Crown, and with all his rights, except the Governorship of Hispaniola, and properties restored to him. Columbus had bombarded them with letters and, undoubtedly, personal pleas, reminding Isabella and Ferdinand of his long service, their reneging on the Capitulations of Santa Fé and subsequent concessions, and their duty towards him, God and themselves. Not comfortable letters, leading some biographers to assume that Isabella and Ferdinand agreed to the new voyage to get rid of him. This wasn't the case: neither sovereign would spend 10,000 gold pesos to get rid of anyone; and their support was enthusiastic, energetically encouraging Columbus's proposal to meet hands with the Portuguese in India.

They (the wording is Isabella's) wrote to him: *With respect to what you say about Portugal, we have written appropriately to the King of Portugal, our son-in-law, and send you herewith the letter addressed to his Captain, as requested by you. We notify him of your departure eastward and if you meet on the way, you are to treat each other as friends, as is proper among the captains and subjects of mon-*

archs between whom there is so much love, friendship and blood ties, telling him we have ordered you to do the same. We shall ask our son-in-law, the King of Portugal, to write to his Captain in the same terms.

As the Portuguese brought back valuable shipments of spices, gems and pearls, Isabella and Ferdinand had every reason to be as interested in Vasco da Gama's India as their own Indies. Despite the words of friendship, both nations raced to gain position in the East, and Isabella and Ferdinand aimed, with Columbus's Fourth Voyage, to forestall Portugal's eastward advance. Ten years after discovering the 'Indies', Columbus was still driven by the desire to *learn the secrets of this world.*

13

THE HIGH VOYAGE

The Fourth and last voyage – the High Voyage he called it – was the hardest of all. An epic struggle against infinite storms, dangerous Indians and treachery, with the great, secret objective of circumnavigating the globe blocked by the Isthmus of Panama. Thanks to Fernando Colón, who shipped with his father, it was the best documented of all the voyages and gave new insights into the man.

Columbus's last voyage is universally described as a great failure: a series of missed opportunities, bad luck and even poor seamanship that almost destroyed the entire expedition and drove him to madness when he was marooned on Jamaica. This is, however, a serious misjudgement. Although Columbus was now, at fifty, a sickly old man, he was capable of great seamanship and made some worldshaking discoveries. Moreover, the expedition's perils were the result of his crew's near mutiny and the new Governor of Hispaniola's perfidy, and all would have perished if it hadn't been for Columbus's discipline and intelligence. He came through the most horrifying trials with great, but unacclaimed, honour and opened up a new land of discovery for younger sea-captains. Yet on a personal level the High Voyage was in every way a disaster, bringing him so low in spirit and body that he died within eighteen months of his return to Seville.

Fernando Colón was a thirteen-year-old boy when he left with his father and uncles on the Fourth Voyage of Discovery. Bartolomé, the *Adelantado*, was de facto Captain of the *Santiago* and Diego Auditor of the Fleet and the Crown's representative. The fleet of four ships left Cadiz on 11th May 1502.

After a quick, twenty-one day crossing from Las Palmas to Martinique, his heart drew him, in spite of the Sovereign's orders to the contrary, to Hispaniola. Columbus observed the warning signs of a hurricane and advised the Governor to order a fleet offshore to port. The new Governor, Nicólas de Ovando, refused him entry to the port of Santo Domingo and ignored his warnings; the Crown denied him the right to land at the island he had discovered and loved best in the Caribbean. If he was bitter and complained of his treatment in the *Account of the Fourth Voyage*, what man wouldn't? As he wrote to Isabella and Ferdinand, *I came to serve you when I was twenty-eight and now I have not a hair on my person which is not white and my body is ill for ever... After twenty years of serving with so much labour and dangers, I do not have a roof in Castile and, if I want to eat or sleep, I have nowhere to go but an inn or a tavern and often I cannot pay my share.* His ships successfully weathered the hurricane, but the treasure fleet bound for Castile mostly foundered, taking the lives of Bobadilla, who had put him in irons, the rebel Francisco Roldán and the Taino Cacique Guarionex, leader of the rebellion against the Gold Tax and Christianity. The only vessel to reach Castile happened to carry his share of the gold production of the island, causing superstitious seamen to speculate on Columbus's supernatural powers.

Columbus's fleet sailed due west in heavy weather, through unknown waters, over 500 miles west of Jamaica where he discovered the island of Guanaja, thirty miles off the coast of Honduras. They intercepted a trading canoe, reported by Peter Martyr as 'Mayan', off the island, the first sign of a higher civilization. Doubts as to exactly which Indian nation occupied the canoe do not consider Bartolomé Colón's letter nine years' later where he says – and this before the discovery of Mexico – that the canoe came from 'the province of Maia or Iuncatam'. Fernando's description of its contents exactly match those that a Mayan canoe would have taken on a trading mission and the older man they took aboard to pilot and interpret was called Yumbe, meaning Lord of the Ways in the Mayan language of Yucatan. Fernando described the meeting, which took place at the end of July 1502:

The Admiral ordered the most valuable and noticeable goods [which he paid for in truck] removed from the canoe. There were cotton blankets and sleeveless shirts, variously woven and coloured, shorts with which they covered their private parts and cloth that covered the Indian women from the canoe, similar to the Moorish women in Granada; long wooden swords, with grooves down both blades filled with flint and bound in with string, that cut like steel into naked flesh; their hatchets for chopping wood were similar in design to the stone hatchets the Indians used, but they were made of good copper. They brought small bells and crucibles to melt the copper [smelting was unknown on Hispaniola]. They carried the same roots and grains as those they eat on Hispaniola, a maize wine tasting like English beer, and lots of almonds [cocoa beans] they seem to hold in great value. For when some spilt on the ship's deck, they all tried to gather them up, as if there had fallen out an eye.

From Guanaje, in the Bay Islands, Columbus sailed the thirty miles to make a landfall at Cape Honduras, which lies on a coastline running east-west. From there he decided to sail east against the wind, instead of running west. Why? Columbus offered no explanation, but Fernando, who was on board with his father, wrote: *Seeing that these lands were to leeward, he could sail to them from Cuba whenever he wanted, and he continued his search to discover those straits, between the mainland and open navigation and the Southern Sea, which he needed to do to discover the spice lands.*

Historians, with a map of the Americas before them, claim that this was Columbus's great missed opportunity. If only he had sailed west and discovered Yucatan! What if he had? The Mayans gave the first Spaniards a bloody nose and their lands were so poor (no gold) that, once discovered, they were ignored for almost twenty years. Also, Columbus had neither the warrior temperament nor the resources of Cortés, without which he could never have penetrated Mexico. Columbus's sailing instincts were impeccable. He wanted to find the Straits to the Southern Sea and, according to his map of the world, they were to the south. If he sailed westward, he would find himself locked into a bay or gulf with no exit to the Southern Sea. He had to sail east to sail south to sail west.

This was consistent with Columbus's objectives and idea of the world, but it meant he sailed away from Yucatan and into the teeth of a month-long gale and torrential rain at great cost to his men and ships. Rounding a cape he appropriately named 'Gracias a Dios', the four caravels sailed due south along the Nicaraguan and Costa Rican coasts with favourable winds but foul weather, making only 330 miles in eleven days. Fernando was ill, *which tore at my soul*, he noted. It wasn't until late October – five months after leaving Cadiz – at Cateba, on the

Veraguan coast of Panama, that they noticed again the presence of a higher civilization. *Here, for the first time in the Indies, one saw an example of a building and it was a large piece of stucco that seemed to be worked in stone and lime, from which the Admiral took a piece, in memory of that antiquity.*

The coast gradually turned east, then east north east, and, now in November 1502, the fleet anchored in a harbour Columbus called Puerto Bello, about twenty-five miles beyond the present opening of the Panama Canal. Columbus wrote:

I arrived at Cariay, where I stayed to repair the ships, obtain provisions and give a rest to the men who had become very ill and I, as I said, had arrived near death many times [he'd had a doghouse built on the poop from where he could direct the fleet from his bed]. There I learned of the gold mines of Ciamba [Marco Polo's Cochinchina] I was looking for...

They tell me this [Puerto Bello] is near the province of Ciguare [Ptolemy's Catigara] which is nine days' walk to the west... they also say the sea approaches Ciguare and, from there, it is ten days to the River Ganges. It seems that this land is to Veragua as Tortosa is to Fuenterrabia [either end of the neck of the Iberian Peninsular] or Pisa is to Venice.

Columbus had correctly understood from the Indians that he was at an isthmus blocking his passage to the Southern Sea, Portuguese India and Taprobana. Bartolomé Colón marked the isthmus clearly on his sketch map of the region and, loyal to the family's sense of geography, called them the Chinese Mountains (see Map 6). A linguistic scramble enabled Columbus to fit the places he discovered in the Caribbean into his concept of the world. Hence Cibao, Hispaniola's gold-producing province, sounded like Marco Polo's Cipangu, or Japan. Cubanacan, the Taino name for Cuba, sounded like it belonged to the *Gran Can.* Jamaica, to his ear Janahica, sounded like Java Chica, or Sumatra. A place sounding like Polo's Ciamba on the coast of Panama convinced him this was South Vietnam which seemed to fit the approximate location of another Indian word for the Pacific coast of Panama which Columbus heard as Ciguara, Polo's Lesser Sunda Islands. As he was convinced Cuba was the eastern extremity of China, the big island just south, which is now the Isla de la Juventud, must be Polo's Aurea Cheronezo, or

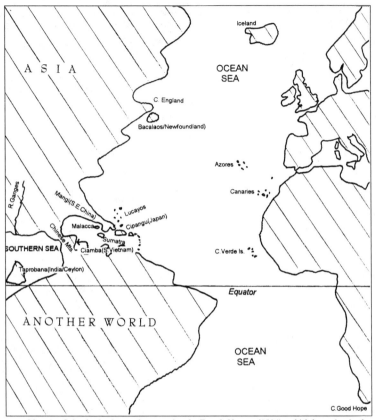

Map 6 – Columbus's view to the west after the Fourth Voyage (1504), which he maintained to his death in 1506. (Based on Bartolomé Colón's sketch-map (about 1504) and Juan de la Cosa's world map of 1500 corrected for subsequent voyages.)

Malacca. This does not detract from his identification of the South American mainland as *another world*, a new, previously unknown continent; it merely places it closer to Asia.

Sixty miles through jungle paths and over mountains, *nine days walk* and he would have discovered the Pacific, a task left to Nuñez de Balboa, eleven years later. Another missed opportunity! lament his biographers. Not at all. He had good reasons not to attempt the journey: it had no practical use; without trusted guides, the expedition would get lost – they had lost a group of

174

seamen for six days in the tropical rain forest of Guadeloupe; and the men, after living and sleeping on deck through four-and-a-half months of storms and rain, were too exhausted for a strenuous march through the mountains. He didn't need to march across the isthmus to discover the Southern Sea; he knew it was there, that his straits were blocked, and he and Bartolomé made the correct assumption that a spit of land connected the northern landmass to the southern. By proving that the Caribbean was a gigantic Gulf, he inspired other mariners to search for the Northwest passage and the Southern route to Asia.

To confirm that no strait existed, he left Puerto Bello and the ships flogged along the coast a further seven weeks in foul weather, with *violent easterlies which never ceased,* great thunderstorms *sometimes with so much thunder and lightning that the men did not dare open their eyes.* There were huge seas which *it seemed would sink the ships,* clouds so low that *the sky would hit us* and torrential rain *which did not let up in two or three days, so that it seemed like a new Flood.* A waterspout passed between the ships, *water rising to the clouds in a column thicker than a barrel, twisting like a whirlwind.* Some men believed it an evil omen when, resting on a calm day, *so many sharks came to the boats,* though they provided much-needed food. In one port *the inhabitants lived in the trees, like birds, traversing poles from one branch to another, making their huts, if you can call their homes that.*

Columbus decided to find a good port on the Veraguan – Panamanian – coast, *where there are greater signs of gold in the first two days than in four years on Hispaniola,* and found a settlement. Fernando reported their entrance into the River Belén (named Bethlehem because it was the Epiphany, 1503) *and the Indians came immediately to exchange things they had, especially fish.* The local Cacique, Quibio, exchanged gifts with Bartolomé Colón and Columbus, the Spaniards trading hawks-bells, so beloved by the Indians, for gold. For five weeks the ships were confined behind the sandbar of the river by a great storm: *if we set sail, we would soon have been broken into pieces at the river mouth.* Finally, Bartolomé sailed out in the ships' boats to explore the coast and choose the best place *to build a village.*

After finding his passage blocked to India, Columbus was desperate to find another worthy objective for a voyage that had cost the Crown 10,000 gold pesos; and Veragua, with the promise of infinite gold, was the most suitable. To ensure that Alonso de Hojeda, Vicente Yañez Pinzón or some new upstart in the Crown's favour wouldn't dispute his claim to the area, he needed a substantial physical presence, the eighty men he intended to leave behind under the command of his brother, the Adelantado. This coincided with practical considerations. Teredos had eaten deep into all the ships, all leaked badly, especially the *Gallega*, and it would be safer to return in three lightly manned vessels than with the entire expedition. And, as at Navidad, many men would have preferred to stay in their village, protected from storms and rain and trading gold with the Indians, than risk the return journey against the prevailing easterlies to Santo Domingo.

The only improvement on the settlement of Navidad was the presence of a sailable ship but, 900 miles south west of Santo Domingo, they were that much further from Castile. It was a wrong decision and fortunately the Indians attacked on 4th April 1503 before Columbus had left with the good ships. In all fifteen men were lost, but, while some defended the settlement, others transferred the village's provisions safely to the three ships standing offshore. They had to leave the *Gallega* inside the sand bar at the mouth of the river and abandon the *Vizcaina*, without any loss of men, soon afterwards.

This incident is cited as another failure and from Columbus's perspective it was. But, with hindsight, where was the failure? His fleet was provisioned and manned for discovery, not conquest, and Veragua's gold mines were an illusion, though in 1611 Domingo Colón of Córdoba fought a legal battle over its bones with a host of other claimants, including a Mendoza, a Carvajal, Pedro Colón of Portugal and Diego Colón of Larreategui. By discovering supposedly gold-rich Veragua, he encouraged the westward expansion of Spanish colonization leading to the conquest of the Mexican, Chibcha and Inca empires.

To return to Hispaniola, Columbus decided to sail along the north coast (Colombia) towards Paria until he could make the island in one reach; this was the best route against wind and current. But his men, fearing that he was really tricking them into taking them back to Castile without stopping to reprovision and refit the ships, mistrusted him. When they reached a point from where they calculated (mistakenly) they could tack across to Hispaniola (1st May 1503), they mutinied. They insisted he make the long tack north. After a terrible voyage, working the pumps day and night to keep the two ships afloat, twelve days later they made Cuba, far downwind from Hispaniola. This navigational error was not Columbus's but his rebellious men's, whose nautical skills were nowhere near his equal.

They took on fresh water and Fernando recalled:

We left Cuba for Jamaica because the easterly winds and the great current which runs to the west did not let us sail for Hispaniola, especially with the ships eaten so by teredos. Day and night we worked the three pumps and, if one should break down, we used mess pots to bail out until it was repaired. Even so, on the eve of St. John's Day [24th June 1503], the water rose so high in our ship, almost to the deck, that we could not overcome it; with great weariness we reached Jamaica – nine weeks after leaving Belén.

After entering the port of Santa Gloria – St. Anne's Bay – discovered by Columbus in 1495, *unable to keep the ships afloat any longer, we ran them ashore as best we could, one alongside the other, side by side, and we fixed them with many struts so they could not move. Water filled them almost to the deck, and we built cabins on the forecastle and sterncastle, where the men could take shelter and we could secure ourselves against a possible attack from the Indians; for, at that time, the island was neither populated nor subdued by the Christians.*

Marooned and out of provisions, Columbus was at the mercy of the large Indian population – perhaps 100,000 – whose contacts with the Tainos on Hispaniola had warned them of the dangers of allowing a Spanish presence on the island. Against the greatest odds and despite his illness, Columbus managed to survive this trial thanks to discipline, imagination and perseverance. First he organized another settlement, managing it with a discipline unknown in the Indies.

To control the market in such a way as to avoid disputes between Christians and Indians and to make sure no one went short, the Admiral appointed two men to account for sales and purchases, and every day they were decided by lottery among the men on the ships. By then we had nothing on the boats to sustain us, because we had eaten most of the provisions and the rest was rotten...

By nature we are disrespectful, and no order or punishment would have prevented us from going to the places and houses of the Indians to take what they had, and to offend their wives and children, causing many squabbles and turmoil, making them our enemies... This did not happen because our people lived in the ships, and no one could leave without permission and leaving his name registered. Columbus traded sewing thread for hutias, beads for cassava bread and hawks-bells, mirrors and coloured caps for provisions *of greater value.*

Then, to seek help from Hispaniola, Columbus chose two trusted men, Diego Méndez, who had performed the most daring deeds in Veragua, and Bartolomé Fieschi, a fellow Genoese, to lead a small expedition. Méndez and Fieschi each had six Spaniards to accompany them and ten Indians to paddle their canoes the one hundred and twenty miles separating Jamaica from the western end of Hispaniola. With Méndez and Fieschi, who left within a month of their arrival in Jamaica, he sent a letter to Governor Ovando, requesting help, a note to Father Gorricio and a long letter (7th July 1503) to Isabella and Ferdinand. He wrote with great candour, giving us insight into his state of mind. After reminding them of his years of service *and now each and every one claims its authorship... and even tailors ask permission and it is authorized,* he summarized the situation in the Indies:

All the coast of Paria and the islands of the region have been pillaged [by the successive voyages of Hojeda, Rodrigo Bastidas, Cristóbal Guerra and the 'discoverer or destroyer' (Las Casas) Diego de Lepe] and many people killed. Those who survived will not be our friends. They are rich and not to be held in low esteem. Much gold, pearls, spices and brasil wood is there for Christians, Moors and everyone.

The lands, which here obey your Highnesses, are greater than all the others belonging to Christians and richer. After I, by Divine Will, placed them in your royal and supreme domain... against your command I was made prisoner with my brothers, thrown into a ship, weighed down with chains, naked in body, and treated atrociously without having disobeyed you or called before or vanquished by justice. Neither privileges, letters, promises nor position were worth anything...

Columbus denied earlier accusations of disloyalty and pleaded the *restitution of my honour and injuries,* ending, *If I die here, you have my son there.* He moves on to exonerate the Indians:

I always said and put it in writing to your Highnesses that the Indians were the gold and riches there, because the Christians who arrived, as humble as they might be, say they come from King Priam and should be treated as such. Lose the Indians and the land is lost; only good order can save all this.

After reminding them of his poverty – *nor have I squandered my rewards* – he describes the terrible reality of being marooned on Jamaica:

In spiritual matters, in the normal sense of the word, I have come to a stop in the Indies, isolated on this rock, ill, waiting every day for death, and surrounded by a million savages, full of cruelty and without pity and our enemy, more mobile than the leaf of a poplar. I am so separated from the sacrament of the Holy Church that it will forget this soul, if it be separated from this body. Weep for me whoever has charity, chastity, truth and justice. I did not come on this voyage to win honour or riches. This is certain: I came to serve your Highnesses with all good intentions and conscientiousness, and I do not lie.

I beg your Highnesses that, if I have said anything against your royal wish, forgive me. I am in such anguish and despair it is a wonder I am alive and have not turned mad or broken down. One could not write about my suffering in a thousand pages. All my blood has turned into a tumour.

On the basis of this letter biographers have speculated about Columbus's mental health. Was he delirious? Did he suffer a nervous breakdown? Was he just plain mad? He was certainly ill with 'gout' or malaria and he was under great strain: his hoped-for 'victory' wasn't to be; he had lost his ships and the ten thousand gold pesos Isabella and Ferdinand had invested in the venture; it was possible they would all perish on Jamaica, including his young son Fernando and his brothers; and there were no guarantees that the Sovereigns would respect their promises or their agreement to transfer his privileges to his other son, Diego, in Castile. However, the letter included nothing new that Columbus hadn't written, directly or indirectly – via Juana de Torres or the Royal Council – to Isabella and Ferdinand before. And what madman has the self-awareness to write that he fears for his sanity? The key is the phrase, *if I die here, you have my son there*. It was a plea to look after his son if he died on Jamaica, reminding the Sovereigns of his years of service, his suffering, his gift of the Indies and his penury.

The letter was also a *cri de coeur*, an outlet for the worries and anguish he couldn't share with his men on the two beached caravels. In his baking cabin, lying prone and in pain in his cot, pestered by mosquitoes, exhausted by his extraordinary efforts, first to save his ships at sea, and then to establish order on land, Columbus contemplated death. Never had death so many faces. The agony of intensifying pain in his joints until his heart would no longer bear it, or accompanied by the desperation of slow starvation. Eventually one of these furious storms, called *huricanes* by the Indians, would strike the helpless vessels, propped up in water to their gunwales, tearing them – and him – to pieces; most likely death would be a knife or lance, thrust into his defenceless body by one of the mutineers who had plagued his life in the Spanish possessions; or the kindest of all, a sudden blow to his brow by a heavy stone wielded by an Indian, like the men at Navidad. This last letter smells of death.

Columbus was to be marooned for a year on Jamaica. Fernando reported on the deteriorating situation.

Soon after the canoes [carrying Méndez and Fieschi] left for Hispaniola, our people began to fall ill from the great hardships they had suffered at sea and from the change of food.... and the healthy men, fed up with this harsh life, so long confined, grumbled about the Admiral.

These *healthy men*, seeing the Admiral bedridden in his cabin, believed he was too ill to undertake the *arduous and dangerous voyage* in canoes to Hispaniola, where he might be arrested anyway. After half a year confined to the makeshift fort on the shore, on New Year's Day 1504, many men rebelled under the leadership of Captain Porras. Though both Columbus and Bartolomé tried to resist, they were held back by their own men, and the rebels seized the canoes Columbus had bought from the Indians *so that they could not use them against the Christians*.

Though the mounting tension in the reduced space of two sixty-foot caravels had exploded harmlessly, Columbus, himself bedridden, was left with only a few faithful retainers and men too ill to contemplate a voyage to Santo Domingo. They were suddenly vulnerable to an Indian attack, which the predatory violence of Porras and his men, freed from the Admiral's discipline, might provoke. Fernando continued:

Captain Francisco Porras and the rebels followed the route Diego Méndez and Fieschi had taken in their canoes to the eastern point, from where they had left for Hispaniola. Everywhere they went they committed a thousand outrages against the Indians, seizing their supplies and anything else they liked by force, saying they should go to the Admiral who would pay them and, if he did not, they had permission to kill him or do whatever seemed fitting...

They set out for Hispaniola... but not four leagues from land a headwind blew up, which frightened them so they decided to return to Jamaica.

To lighten the canoes, the rebels first threw everything, except their weapons, overboard and then some Indians, chopping off their hands if they tried to reboard. After failing a second time to cross to Hispaniola by canoe, they wandered about the island, living off the Indians. It is a tribute to Columbus's resourcefulness and the Indians' peaceful ways that he managed to supply his men for a whole year on the island, half the time with a rebel band of his men stirring up the Indians against him. *However, as the Indians work too little to cultivate large fields and as we consume in a day more than they eat in twenty and they did not have the desire to barter our goods, which they now valued lowly, and, as they saw so many Christians were against us, they took little care to bring us the victuals we needed.*

Columbus's self-made rules did not allow him to seize food from the Indians and his men seemed unable to catch enough fish to sustain them, so he relied on a stratagem described by Fernando: *The Admiral recalled that in three days there would be an eclipse of the Moon. He sent an Indian from Hispaniola, who was with us, to call on the principal Indians of the province to tell them he wanted to talk to them at a fiesta he had decided to give them. The caciques arrived a day before the eclipse and he told them, through an interpreter, that we were Christians and we believed in God who lives in Heaven and has us as his subjects; He looks after the good and punishes the bad... and touching on the Indians, God, seeing the little care they took to bring supplies in exchange for our goods, was angry with them and was resolved to send them a great famine and plague. As they might not believe it, He would show them a clear sign in the sky, so they might know more clearly the punishment that would come from His hand. They were to pay great attention to the rising moon that night.*

The eclipse duly arrived, persuading the Indians to bring food to Columbus. This was Leap Year Day 1504. Méndez and Fieschi had been gone for over seven months. What had happened? They had reached Santo Domingo and *Governor Nicólas de Ovando,* wrote Méndez, *detained me there for seven months until he had burned and hung eighty-four caciques.* If Ovando had sent a ship directly to Jamaica, there would have been no rebellion and none of the terrible anxiety which must have shortened Columbus's life. The perfidious Ovando, not Columbus or bad luck, was to blame for the trials his men suffered on Jamaica.

While Méndez waited at Santo Domingo for ships from Castile he could hire, man and sail to Columbus's relief, Ovando sent a small caravel to salute him, give him *one* cask of wine and *half* a salted pork, and inform him he couldn't send a large enough ship to rescue them all, *for the time being.* This was March 1504, eight months after Méndez had left for Hispaniola. Fernando accurately speculated that Ovando sent the caravel to spy on Columbus and see *how he could assure that everything would be lost.* This was not to be Columbus's last trial.

After sending off Méndez and Fieschi for help, Columbus did nothing to contact Hispaniola; there were no more voyages in canoes and no attempt to build a small boat from the materials at hand. Though Columbus often spoke of God's divine intervention, he never depended upon Him to get him out of a difficult situation. The best explanation is that his illness sapped his strength to such a degree that he no longer had the initiative to start the design and construction of a boat, without such key materials as pitch, nails and tools, nor the confidence to attempt another crossing to Hispaniola in canoes. Under these circumstances, it was easier on mind and body to await a visit from a passing ship or to reason that Méndez or Fieschi must have got through, and it was only a matter of time before they would bring a ship to rescue him. Nevertheless, this inaction, as Fernando reported, was the main cause of the Porras rebellion, for which Columbus must take part of the blame.

At the end of May 1504, a month before Méndez came to his rescue with two ships, Porras and his men marched on Santa Gloria to *rob them of what they had.* They refused Columbus's offer of peace, believing that, as they were mainly *men of the sea* and Columbus's were mainly *men of the palace,* they would easily overcome them. The rebels attacked Columbus's loyal men under the command of his brother, Bartolomé. Bartolomé's strength and leadership once again won the day and he personally captured Francisco Porras; they killed *many* of the rebels (five) and the battle was over. Columbus had Porras shackled and, to secure the submission of the remaining rebels, he offered them a full pardon.

A six-week long voyage, against wind and current in the chartered ships, brought the hundred odd survivors, of a hundred and forty who had left Cadiz, to Santo Domingo, where Ovando released Porras and made snide remarks to Columbus. Columbus chartered another ship and with Fernando, his brothers and twenty-one of the original crew, sailed for Spain, arriving at Sanlucar 7th November 1504, two and a half years after leaving Castile with high hopes of 'victory'. He returned poorer in spirit, in health and in wealth than when he'd left, with only the memory of the goldfields of Veragua to warm the corner of his soul where 'Gold is best'. Yet this last voyage was actually a triumph, opening the gates to the westward expansion of the Spanish Empire and redirecting other, younger explorers to the northern and southern perimeters of the great landmasses.

14

LAST MONTHS AND THAT IMPOSTOR VESPUCCI

On 26th November 1504, three weeks after Columbus returned to Castile from Jamaica, Isabella died. Her health had deteriorated after the death of her only son, Don Juan, in 1497, which the Royal Family blamed, incredible as it might seem, on an overactive honeymoon. Peter Martyr had warned the Sovereigns of Juan's *paleness*, advising them that his doctors wanted to separate the couple, *alleging that such frequent copulation constituted a danger to the Prince.* Further blows were the death, in childbirth, of her daughter Isabel, Queen of Portugal in 1498 and two years later the only fruit of that marriage, Miguel. To this must be added the dispiriting reports from Flanders on the mental health of the future Queen, her daughter Juana, so reminiscent of Isabella's mother, another Juana. Juana was married to Philip the Handsome, a Hapsburg prince and had lived from the age of sixteen in Flanders. Beautiful, intelligent and sensitive, and lonely in the foreign climate of Brussels, Juana was prone to fits of depression aggravated by her husband's infidelities. She disfigured one of Philip's lovers with a pair of scissors and, as a result of being locked away by Philip, became claustrophobic, on one occasion, now in Castile, refusing to enter a village fearing she would be locked away. She spent the night in the open.

After his death – Philip had lived a mere 18 days as king – Juana's depressions intensified enabling Ferdinand to become Regent. She became known as Juana *La Loca*, and Ferdinand had her locked away in the isolated, inhospitable castle of Tordesillas, where she suffered a long, tormenting confinement until her death.

Contrary to Columbus's expectations, Isabella did not mention him in her will, and he did not see her before she died. He now entered the last phase of his tumultuous life. Almost universally, it is agreed that this period is marked by self-pity and whining, hardly flattering his character. Though bedridden his energy was still there in reserve, like a mothballed battleship waiting to be recommissioned for its ultimate battle. In this last year and a half he wanted to assure Diego's succession to his rank and privileges, recuperate his position of favour with the Crown and receive the moneys owed to him. New evidence reveals the extent of Ferdinand's deceit, and if Columbus seemed to whine, he had every reason to do so.

Before learning of Isabella's death and despite being confined to bed in his house in Seville – shared at this time with Amerigo Vespucci – he was still full of optimism, energy and fight. Between 21st November and 4th December 1504 he wrote four letters to his son, Don Diego, now a knight at court. This is a sample:

1st December 1504.

My Dear Son,

...It seems to me that you should write, in a clear hand, the clause of that letter their Highnesses wrote me, where they say they will fulfil their promises with me and will place you in possession of everything; and give it to them with another note explaining I am ill and it is impossible for me to go and kiss their royal hands and feet; tell them we are losing the Indies, and there is fire in a thousand places and, as I have not received any of the income due me nor has anyone required them to send me anything, I live on loans. Some moneys, which I had over there, I spent to bring home the people who had shipped with me, for it was a great burden on my conscience to leave them abandoned.

If my letters are not enough, I will also work so that your brother and uncle leave to kiss their Highnesses' hands and tell them of the voyage. Have plenty of respect for your brother: he has a good mind and is no longer a boy. Ten brothers would not be too many; I never found a greater friend anywhere than my brothers.

One must look to obtain the Governorship of the Indies and, after that, the delivery of the revenue. What they have delivered to Carvajal [his factor on Hispaniola] is nothing... I am tired of saying, in the past, that the contribution of an eighth has come to nothing; the eighth and the rest belong to me for the favour which their Highnesses made me, as I made clear in my Book of Privileges, also the duties and tenths. I have not received the tenth of all income, only the tenth of what their Highnesses receive [i.e. 2%], and it should be from the gold and other goods found in any way within the office of the Admiralty; and a tenth of all traded goods that come and go to there, once their costs are deducted...

My illness only allows me to write at night, because the day deprives me of the strength of my hands...

The caravel that was dismasted on embarking from Santo Domingo has arrived at the Algarve. In it comes the investigation of the Porras brothers. Such ugly, brutish cruelty was never seen. If their Highnesses do not punish them, I do not know who will choose to go in their service [Porras was never punished].

Today is Monday. I will get your uncle and brother to leave tomorrow [they left the day after]. Remember to write to me very often and Diego Méndez too. There are messengers every day from here to there.

May Our Lord look after you,

your father who loves you like himself.

After hearing of Isabella's death, he wrote to Diego revealing his real feelings for Isabella and Ferdinand: *The main thing is to affectionately commend to God, with much devotion, the spirit of the Queen, our Lady. Her life was always Catholic and saintly and close to everything of His Holy Service. For this, one must believe that she is in her holy glory, away from the demands of this harsh and tiresome world. After that, in everything and for everything, one must be watchful and vigorous in the service of the King, our Lord, and work to remove his anger.*

Though his financial affairs are not well documented, there is no reason to disbelieve Columbus's tenuous financial situation as he described it to his son. We know he received a substantial quantity of gold which escaped the 1502 hurricane that sank Bobadilla and Roldán's ships off Santo Domingo, and Giovanni Colombo sold twenty-two marks worth of gold (484,000 maravedis) for him in 1504 and 1505. This may have come from a chest of gold he received from Ovando on his departure from Hispaniola in 1503. Against that must be set his expenses of the Fourth Voyage, including the 1.2 million maravedis spent repatriating his family and crew. To put this into perspective, Grandees had yearly incomes of eight million maravedis or more.

Without Columbus's knowledge, Ferdinand instructed Ovando to impound his assets in Hispaniola until he had paid all Columbus's debts, both confirming that Columbus owed money and that he no longer received any income from there. It is reasonable to suppose he lived comfortably, but that his income fell far short of what it should have been.

He was right to blame the King. The Sovereigns had breached every one of the Capitulations of Santa Fé, except for his titles of Don and Admiral, without compensation. This smells of Ferdinand's doing. Ferdinand, *who was always in need, cannot be said to be generous*, reported the Chronicler of the period.

Not until May 1505 was Columbus well enough to make the journey from Seville to the Court at Segovia, a distance of more than 500 kilometres. Columbus received special permission to travel by mule. The audience with miserly Ferdinand yielded nothing but pleasantries. After writing at least three letters to Ferdinand to remind him of his unfulfilled promises, Columbus confided in Fray Diego Deza, now Archbishop of Seville, *It seems his Highness is unwilling to comply with what he has promised with his word and in writing with the Queen, God rest her soul. I believe that for a mite like me to fight such an opponent would be like flailing in the wind. It will be for the best for I have done what I can, and now let it be left to the Lord, Our God, to do it, whom I have always found very favourable and prompt when I needed Him.*

But he wouldn't leave Him to do it alone. Although he was in the grip of chronic disabling arthritis and his great patron had died, the relics of his character – perseverance, a powerful sense of justice and pugnacity – clanked on under its own steam. He added to the *Book of Prophecies*, took warrants out against a former mutineer, Gonzalo Camacho, for spreading falsehoods about him in Seville, tried to intervene in the appointment of three bishops to Hispaniola and continued to use Diego and his friends at Court.

By December 1505, Columbus was in Salamanca where he had followed the Court. The next news we have of him is in Valladolid shortly before his death, in May 1506. He had passed the winter in Castile, where it can drag on through April or even May. What was Columbus doing in Valladolid?

When Philip and Juana, now King and Queen under the terms of Isabella's will, arrived in Castile, he sent them a letter offering his service and apologizing for the illness that prevented him from presenting himself. The letter is not dated, but Columbus must have composed it in the Spring of 1506 when Ferdinand had agreed to retire to Aragon with his new French wife, Germaine de Foix, whose sexual appetite would eventually

187

be responsible for his death (ten years later, Ferdinand died from an aphrodisiac prepared by their French cook and reputed to include bull's testicles – still today a popular dish in Spain).

Philip and Juana would make their triumphal entry into the Royal city of Valladolid in July. Evidently, Columbus was in Valladolid to receive them, plead for his son's rights to assume his titles and privileges and recover his share of the income from the Indies. His life had turned a full circle. Once more, he had to importune Monarchs he had never met but, on 25th May 1506, his importuning was interrupted by his death. Surrounded by loyal retainers, including Méndes and Fieschi, and his sons and brothers, Fernando heard him murmur, *in manus tuas, Domine, comendo spiritum meum.* He had lived fifty-four or fifty-five years, and was buried in the presence of his family, friends and servants, probably in the cemetery of the Monastery of San Francisco.

In his last will and testament, confirmed on the eve of his death, Columbus left the bulk of his estate and titles to his son Diego. He left large annual incomes to Fernando and his brothers Bartolomé and Diego, *But I cannot say this definitely, because up to now there has not been nor is there a known income, just as I say.* He left bequests to *members of the family who seem to have most need,* and Beatriz Enriquez. He discharged debts due to Genoese merchants and left half a silver mark for *A Jew who lived at the gate of the Judería in Lisbon.* He ordered Diego to found a chapel *which should have three chaplains to say three masses a day, one to honour the Holy Trinity, another Our Lady of the Conception and the other for the soul of all the faithful deceased, for my soul and those of my father, my mother and my wife,* preferably on the island of Hispaniola.

I took the road from Madrid for Valladolid mid-May to coincide with the 500th anniversary of his death. It was raining heavily, the mountains shrouded in cloud so low that as I reached the tunnel which burrows through the Sierra de Navacerrada, the car was engulfed in fog. The external temperature dropped to 8°C. Emerging at the other side, the sky cleared and snow lay on the shoulder of the dark mountains behind me, strangely out of place in a countryside greened by the recent rains. Ahead lay the big country of the *meseta,* boulders like great cow-pats to the left, stretching towards Avila, on land good only for sheep grazing, and green wheat fields to the right through which an occasional farmhand, waist-deep, waded as through a lake. As I approached the Duero, cultivation intensified, copses of chestnuts and poplars appeared and rivers began to flow in sight of the road.

A phalanx of orange-brick apartment blocks, their windows meanly small, signifies the beginning of Valladolid and, as in so many of Spain's cities, one has to find a way through suburbs of flat-topped apartments, industrial estates and ever-narrowing streets to the old, historic centre, marked by the lofty ambitions of men from a more noble age. Valladolid has celebrated its Columbian connection by erecting a replica Isabeline mansion on a site of a house it chose to identify as the likely deathbed of the Admiral of the Ocean Sea. In the main exhibition room an aged, white-haired Columbus peers above his sheets from an oil painting facing on to a collection of Amerindian objects, including a case of Taino pottery and three, three-sided stone zemis resembling snails on the march. The museum has collected fourteen different portraits purporting to be Columbus, offering a choice of colouring and features from a haughty dark knight, which might be Don Quixote, to a youthful, blond George Washington, a dull-witted Roman burgher or an intellectual Jew. We have no portrait of Columbus painted by a man who had set eyes on him.

A world map I had not formerly heard of, by Contarini and Roselli and dated 1506, is on display. Significantly, it shows the world almost as I had imagined Columbus thought it to be before he embarked on his last voyage: there is a broad strait between two continents, Asia to the north and a southern continent to the south, with the Canaries, West Indies, Cipangu-Japan and Mangi-China in a line on about the same latitude. Cuba is closer to Cipangu than the Canaries and Cipangu is equidistant between Cuba and Mangi. It is Toscanelli's map updated for the discovery of the West Indies and the Southern continent of South America.

Also of interest are legal documents concerning Columbus's descendants, including one signed by Don Jacobo Francisco FitzJames Stuardo Colón de Portugal, *Gran Almirante de las Indias* and *Adelantado Mayor* of them, Marques of Jamaica and

Duke of Veragua. This distinguished Stuart proudly bore the title of Admiral in 1736.

Downstairs I talked to the guardian, who confirmed that this was the site of Columbus's death though there is no record of where Columbus died in Valladolid. But the city is economical with the truth when it comes to its historical sites: the house which Cervantes lived in for three years does not, contrary to its claims (forcibly upheld by its guardian), contain a single piece of furniture used by the creator of Don Quixote, and there is no evidence Columbus's funeral service was held in the once fine church (with a Romanesque campanile reminiscent of northern Italy) of Santa María la Antigua.

Most likely, as Jesús Urrea suggests, Columbus died in the Monastery of San Francisco's hospice, and not a stone remains of the Monastery. It used to lie on the west side of the Plaza Mayor between Santiago and Tornero streets, and its entrance was where a theatre turned cinema, Teatro de Zorilla, now stands.

Columbus achieved his desire to found a family of Grandees in Spain. Though the family never recouped what was owed to them by the Crown, Diego married María de Toledo, niece of the Duke of Alba, and Ferdinand appointed him, with reduced powers, Governor of Hispaniola. But, with the persistence of his father, Diego obtained a second governorship of the Indies with the superior title of Viceroy. Bartolomé, Diego and Fernando Colón were a formidable trio, determined to recover the titles and privileges contracted with Isabella and Ferdinand. They launched the Columbian lawsuits against the Crown which only ended in 1536, when the Colón family renounced all their claims and titles in exchange for an annuity of 10,000 ducats (3.75 million maravedis), the Duchy of Veragua and Marquisate of Jamaica. Fernando received enough income from his father's estate to allow him to travel widely and purchase books to build the largest private library in Europe. From his mother, Beatriz Enriquez, he received a house with a shop, a winepress, two market gardens and three small vineyards near Santa María de Trassierra (a village up in the hills behind Cordóba), proving that she did not die in poverty, as is sometimes suggested.

It could have been worse. It was the fate of the early discoverers of America to die violently or in poverty:

Giovanni Caboto (John Cabot) of Genoa and Venice, discovered Newfoundland and three hundred leagues of the East Coast for the English Crown in 1497. Henry VII paid him ten pounds and Cabot disappeared at sea on his second voyage.

Vicente Yañez Pinzón, Captain of the *Niña* on Columbus's First Voyage and, with Cabral, discoverer of Brasil, faced debtors' prison on his return to Castile in 1500. He only escaped it by royal pardon.

Juan de la Cosa, Captain of the *Santa María* on the First Voyage, first map-maker of the New World and indefatigable explorer, was killed by the poisoned tip of an Indian's arrow on the coast of Colombia and eaten by the Indians.

Alonso de Hojeda, who accompanied Columbus on the Second Voyage and explored a thousand miles of the Venezuelan coast, died in extreme poverty in Santo Domingo, possibly from a wound incurred in a skirmish with Indians.

Pedro Alvares Cabral, joint discoverer of Brazil for the Portuguese crown in 1500, was denied a second voyage by King Manuel and retired to a small estate, marrying into the nobility.

Vasco Nuñez de Balboa, discoverer of the Pearl Islands and the Pacific Ocean in 1513, unjustly tried by Pedrarias de Avila for treason and murder, was beheaded in a public square in Darien and his body left to the vultures.

Juan de Solís, explorer of the River Plate in 1515, a few months later went ashore in Uruguay, where unfriendly Indians killed, dismembered, roasted and ate him.

Giovanni da Verrazzano of Florence and in the service of France, discoverer of the coastline from Maine to the Carolinas in 1526-8, was killed by Carib Indians on Guadeloupe and consumed in full view of his men, lying offshore in the ship's boat.

Jacques Cartier, discoverer of the St. Lawrence River in 1534, explored the river 1,000 miles inland in search of the Northwest Passage. François Premier granted him two ships and he lived in comfort until his death at the age of sixty-six.

Death did not end Columbus's voyages. Three years after his burial in Valladolid, his family disinterred him and deposited his remains in the family mausoleum Diego had built in Seville. When Diego became Governor of Hispaniola, he had his father's remains removed and buried beneath the High Altar of the first cathedral of the Indies, in Santo Domingo. He lay there for the next three centuries until the island was ceded to the French and, in 1796, what were believed to be his remains were reburied in Havana's cathedral. In 1898 the United States went to war with Spain, capturing Cuba, and the Spaniards brought Columbus back to Seville where he rests, or so it is believed, in a grand sarcophagus borne by four crowned princes in the nave of the cathedral. However, in 1877, when restoring the cathedral of Santo Domingo, Padre Billini discovered two lead caskets marked as belonging to Cristóbal and Luis (his grandson) Colón. The Dominicans have been generous with his ashes, distributing them to eight places, including Genoa, New York and Boston, though how Columbus came to ashes – he was never cremated – isn't explained. As I remarked earlier, the 'ashes' in Genoa are the colour of sawdust. His last 'move' was organized by the Dominican Government in 1986 to a monument worthy of a Pharoah, set in a park by the sea in Santo Domingo.

Death saved Columbus from the final indignity of seeing the land he discovered named after a perfidious friend. For America, that land of hope and disappointment, tripped up at its first step, its baptism. But, of course, continents can't trip up. We leave that to man and, in the case of America, to two men: a young German scholar eager to win his academic spurs and an Italian merchant who, in his declining years, suddenly discovered an overweening sense of history.

The year is 1507. Amerigo, Americus, America rolls off the tongue like a Latin declension. I can see a youthful Martin Waldseemüller seated on a hard oak bench in a stone-cold chamber, his back warmed by an elm-wood fire now low and long unattended in the grate. He ponders over two flimsy, recently-translated epistles authored by one Amerigo Vespucci. In the tiny college of Saint-Dié, lost, scholastically speaking, in a corner of Lorraine, Waldseemüller is adding a fourth part of the world for a new edition of Ptolemy which will make his reputation. The cosmographer dips his goose quill into a pot of a dark, muddy-looking liquid made from iron salt, gum and the tannin extract of nutgalls. Easing a large drop off the quill's point into the well, he scratches on a sheet of vellum: *Since Americus Vesputius has discovered a fourth part of the world, I do not see why anyone should object to it being called after Americus the discoverer, a man of natural wisdom; Land of Americus or America, since both Europe and Asia have derived their name from women.* To support his suggestion, he included one of Vespucci's epistles, known as the *Soderini Letter*, as an appendix to the great work. In this letter, Amerigo wrote to the *Gonfaloniere* of the Florentine Republic describing his four voyages to the South American mainland. It was the first, the 1497 voyage to Paria at the mouth of the Orinoco, that staked his claim to have discovered the mainland because it preceded Columbus's voyage there by a year. He called his discovery *Mundus Novus*, the title of the second epistle on Waldseemüller's desk. Waldseemüller painted a new continent (South America), separated from the Eurasian landmass, and wrote *AMERICA* in large letters across her Brazilian bulge. He had a woodcut made from his painted map and ran off a thousand copies. America was born.

If Waldseemüller had tried to corroborate Amerigo's 1497 voyage, he would have found out what all Seville knew. Amerigo Vespucci had spent 1497 on his chandler's business in the city and only signed up for his first ocean voyage in 1499.[29] This was a year after Columbus had discovered the South American continent at Paria (on 4th August 1498 by the Julian calendar), identifying it as a mainland *which was another world.*

Vespucci didn't just lie about the 1497 'voyage'. He exaggerated his protagonism of the three voyages in which he participated to such a degree that the expeditionary leaders go unnamed, and his discovery claims, in terms of latitude and longitude, were impossible. Only recently have historians realized that his wonderful navigational feats, winning him great renown in Castile, were so much hogwash.[30] Las Casas, who had a good eye for a faker, takes Vespucci to task and proposes calling the new continent *Columba*. What do we make of Vespucci's lies?

No one seems to have explored Vespucci's friendship with Columbus. They were so intimate that Amerigo lived with Columbus for several months in 1505. Columbus, at that time bedridden with an attack of arthritis and out of favour at Court, wrote to his elder son: *I spoke with Amerigo Vespucci, bearer of this letter, who is going there [to Court], called on matters of navigation. He always wanted to please me and is a man of good deeds; as with so*

193

many others, fortune has been against him. His work has not been rewarded as reason demanded. He is going on my behalf and, if it is within his power, he very much wants to do something which brings me favour. He is going determined to do for me whatever he can. Of course, Amerigo did nothing.

Columbus, discoverer of the route to the Indies, discoverer of the mainland (the *Other World*), discoverer of the Caribbean islands from the Bahamas to Trinidad and the coast of the mainland from Honduras right down and around to Darien, was everything Amerigo Vespucci, the discoverer manqué, was not but yearned to be. The poisonous drip of ambition and envy worked at Amerigo, *whose fortune has been against him,* and, *whose work has not been rewarded.* In 1504, he decided to write *a small work... which will acquire some fame for me after my death.* The language of his 'discovery' letters, as Formisano has recently noted, is strikingly similar to Columbus's. Were they also invented?

Vespucci's claim to have discovered the New World was dated 4th September 1504. Aha! By then, nothing had been heard of Columbus since July of the preceding year when he wrote from Jamaica, where he was marooned, that he was *isolated on this rock, ill, waiting every day for death.* Amerigo, now fifty-three years old, concluded that his rival was dead. I am happy for Columbus that he never knew of his 'friend's' duplicity and that he died before Martin Waldseemüller published his new edition of Ptolemy and the *mappa mundi.*

15

THE GREAT SEAFARER

In Columbus's era exploration of the unknown world was almost entirely by sea. The great explorers – Columbus, Vasco da Gama, Magellan and Cook – were great mariners. The contrary biographers who have undermined his reputation as a sailor are all, I believe, landlubbers. Morison reckoned Columbus's seafaring skills were only matched by Captain Cook. New material from the Tarragonan *Libro Copiador* helps to flesh out his mastery of the sea.

Columbus's home was the sea. He wanted wealth, titles and estates, but women, family and the exquisite life of a Grandee meant little to him compared to the adventure of discovery on board a well-equipped caravel. He shared with his contemporary, Giovanni Caboto, the Genoese tradition of mariner-discoverers in the Ocean Sea. The Vivaldi brothers sailed into the Atlantic in 1291 *To make a new and unusual voyage* but they never returned; Lucas di Cazzana promoted voyages under the Portuguese flag after the discovery of Tercera in the Azores; di Noli explored and settled the Cape Verde Islands, also under the Portuguese flag; and Lancotti (or, according to Taviani, Lanzarotto Marocello) rediscovered the Canary Islands – hence Lanzarote. Before 1492, Columbus had spent eight years in Portugal, home of the greatest maritime explorers ever, and there he learned the latest techniques in navigation and ocean sailing. As he wrote, *I have sailed for twenty-three years on the high seas, without leaving it for any length of time, and I have seen all to the East and West and I have sailed northwards to England and I have sailed south to Guinea.*

Many elements make up a great mariner-explorer: selection of ships, crew and provisions; map-making and navigational skills and knowledge of winds, tides and currents; management of the crew, handling of the ships at sea, inshore and in extremes of weather; maintaining communication between them at night and during storms and the leadership to encourage men to go where no ship has ever gone. Columbus possessed all these qualities to a high degree. Perhaps his greatest achievement, unparalleled among the discoverers, was to have never lost a man at sea. This extraordinary record was the result of careful preparation, good seamanship and his spectacular ability to learn the conditions of new waters and coastlines. It was much appreciated by his men. The crew of his Fourth Voyage included many men from the Niebla region, which had supplied most of the men for his First Voyage.

Caution dictated that he always sailed out with at least three vessels in case one, or even two, foundered. Sailing in modern boats with aluminium masts, spliced-steel cables, nylon ropes and lines, I have frequently suffered breakages, often at the most awkward moments. Fifteenth-century vessels' sails, tackle, even hulls – the dreaded teredo could only be combatted by frequent careening and tarring and wasn't finally vanquished until shipbuilders covered the timber bottom in copper – were far more suspect on long voyages, only adding to the usual risks of being dismasted, pooped or breaking up on a rock in uncharted waters. His three-ship policy saved him and his men on both the First and Fourth Voyages.

Next, Columbus took great care over the provisioning of his ships, especially to ensure there was a good margin of fresh water: seamen could survive for many days without food – there was always the possibility of catching fish – provided their thirst was slaked. By the frequency he mentions landings to take on fresh water, his ships were well watered. Although it was only common sense to prefer the nimble, shallow-draft caravel of the Portuguese, Columbus had clear ideas on how to improve their design for the inshore waters of the Indies: *I believe your Highnesses will remember that I wanted ships to be made in a new way; this shortness of time has not made it possible...* we have no more details about his ship designs.

Knowing the superstitious nature of seamen, their fear of the unknown and of distance from land, Columbus used ingenuity, which is sometimes confused with deception. Three days out of Gomera, on the First Voyage, he wrote: *We sailed fifteen leagues today but I decided to count less than we had sailed because, if it was going to be a long voyage, it would not frighten the men so.* Some days later, on 17th September 1492, he noted: *The Pilots took a reading of the North and found the compass needle northwested a quarter point and this frightened the seamen, not understanding why. I know it [he'd discovered this for himself four days earlier] and, at dawn, I again took a star reading of the North and it seemed it was the star that moved, and not the compass needle.* He had reassured his men that the compass, their principal navigational tool, was still reliable. When the fleet of the Fourth Voyage encountered their first waterspout, Columbus had the men sing from St. John's Gospel, *which if we had not stopped it would have sunk whatever it met beneath it,* wrote his son Fernando.

It is easy to overlook his skill at keeping the ships together at night and in the foulest weather. This was important on voyages of discovery where it was impossible to agree a rendezvous in advance. To keep the seventeen-vessel fleet of the Second Voyage together on the Ocean crossing was quite a feat, given the difference between the fastest and slowest ships and the confusion of lights at night. He seems to have used a system of lights and lombard shots to keep the four vessels together in the torrential rain-blackened skies and heavy seas off the coast of Central America, where night visibility was sometimes reduced to a few yards.

The best pilot in the fleet was invariably Columbus. On returning from the First Voyage, he wrote in his *Journal* 15th February 1492: *After sunrise we sighted land; it seemed to be ENE from our bow, some said it was Madeira, others that it was the Rock of Sintra of Portugal, near Lisbon. The wind rose ENE on our bow and the sea high, coming from the west; there were five leagues from the caravel to land. By my navigation I found us to be in the islands of the Azores and I believed it was one of them. The pilots and seamen found us to be in the waters of Castile.* Columbus was right, it was Santa María of the Azores. On the Fourth Voyage, the pilots' errors so frustrated him that he confiscated their charts.

His sense of direction was impeccable, based on the position of the stars, Sun and Moon, cloud formations, winds, flights of birds, seaweed and flotsam, colour of the water, and the scent of the sea air. He used native pilots wherever he could find them. Dr. Chanca, on the Second Voyage, marvelled at his navigation: *The Admiral, by the indications the Indians of the islands of the first voyage gave him, directed his course to the new islands because they were the nearest to Spain; also the route from there to Hispaniola, where he had left people, was direct. We came to those islands, thanks to God and the good judgement of the Admiral, as if we had been following a known route.* On the Third Voyage, after discovering the mainland at Paria, he decided to sail directly for Hispaniola. After a 700-mile voyage NW he landed twenty-five leagues further west than he anticipated. He correctly explained it was due to the greater strength of the west-flowing currents *which one does not notice at sea.* His extraordinary sense of direction showed itself again on the Fourth Voyage. Returning from Veragua, he decided to tack along the northern coast of South America, where the contrary currents were weaker, until he could make Hispaniola on one tack. His crew, convinced that he wanted to take them directly to Castile, mutinied and insisted they tack north prematurely. Due to adverse currents and winds, they reached a point in Cuba impossibly far west from Hispaniola – just as he had predicted.

This sensitivity to phenomena at sea provided Columbus with the most useful insights. Michele de Cuneo, shipmate on the Second Voyage, noted, *At only seeing a cloud or a star at night he said what was to come and if there would be bad weather.* He was the first sailor to understand the Atlantic wind system, enabling him to sail to the Indies and back with favourable winds. He was the first pilot to note the magnetic variation of the compass on 13th September 1492. On 18th November, he reported from Cuba, *The tide is the reverse of ours, because there the Moon is in the SW by South; it is low tide here.* A correct observation. In the Account of the Third Voyage, *I have plenty of experience that the sea-water moves from east to west with the sky [the N. Atlantic Equatorial current] and that here in this region, when it passes, it passes more quickly.* Another correct observation. On 29th June 1502, off Santo Domingo, he noticed the warning signs of a hurricane – 'Oily swell rolling in from the southeast, abnormal tide, an oppressive feeling in the air, low pressure twinges in his rheumatic joints, veiled cirrus clouds tearing along in the upper air while light, gusty winds blow on the surface of the water, gorgeous crimson sunset lighting up the whole sky.' (S.E. Morison). All of Columbus's ships survived while nineteen vessels of a treasure fleet went to the bottom.

As impressive to the seamen was his deft, almost faultless, handling of the ships inshore in the Caribbean Islands where reefs, rocks, sandbanks, currents and the sheer number of islets are frequent hazards. These islands are difficult enough to negotiate with beacons, a good chart and a pilot's guide at hand. His method was simple but required immense patience and self-discipline: never run an unnecessary risk. Even when the harbour was immense and sounded by a ship's boat, he preferred to jog to and fro all night rather than risk entering in the dark.[31]

Some of Columbus's *Journal* entries are as precise as a Pilot's Guide. 1st December 1492, Cuba: *I placed a large cross on a rock at the entrance to this harbour I called Porto Santo. The point is on the SE side of the entrance to the port, but whoever wishes to enter must approach nearer the NW point. Although at the foot of both points there are twelve fathoms of water, off the SE point there is a rock jutting above the water... At the entrance one should turn the bow SW.*

Columbus's 'feel' for latitude was remarkable. On arriving at Guanahani after a month in uncharted waters he reported that *it is at the same level as Hierro.* Hierro, the most southerly of the Canaries is at 27.45°N, San Salvador, Bahamas, at 24.35°N. Hierro was the closest Old World approximation to Guanahani he knew. Columbus used the astrolabe and quadrant, both recent innovations in maritime navigation, during the First Voyage, as is clear from his entry on 3rd February 1493: *The North Star seemed to be very high, as at Cape St. Vincent [an accurate observation]. I could not take a reading with the astrolabe or the quadrant because the sea was too high.* At sea, the sea would almost always be *too high.* On land, his readings of latitude were for a long time consistently too far north, something he recognized. This has given rise to speculation that he abandoned his instruments and depended on measuring the length of daylight and then read it off a table he had copied from D'Ailly's *Imago Mundi* to find his latitude. The table contained errors which match his errors. At some point he corrected these errors because, in the *Book of Prophecies* he wrote, *In the port of Santa Gloria in Janahica [Jamaica] the Pole Star rises at 18 degrees*, just half a degree too far to the south. His navigation at sea was based on dead reckoning – taking the compass course for the day and calculating the distance travelled by estimating the speed of the vessel (easily calculated by throwing something over the bow and counting the seconds until it passed the stern), adjusting for leeway and any known current. He confirmed his latitude, as well as he could, by observing the position of the Pole Star; his years of piloting had given him an excellent 'feel' for its height. In one of the recently discovered Tarragona documents, Columbus explained his map to Isabella and Ferdinand. It is part of the *Account of the Second Voyage*.

I am sending you a chart of all the islands that have now been discovered together with those of last year, which I have composed with much effort; for I am very busy with the construction of the town [Isabela] here and the return voyage of the fleet. With it well finished, your Highnesses will see the lands of Spain and Africa and, opposite them, all the islands found and discovered on this and the previous voyage. The vertical lines show the distance from east to west; the horizontal ones show the distance from north to south. The space of each line signifies one degree which, counting fifty-six and two-thirds miles, is the equivalent of fourteen-and-a-sixth sea leagues. This way one can measure from west to east or north to south the number of leagues. Using Ptolemy's measure, comparing the degrees of longitude with those of the Equator, saying that every four degrees on the Equator is equivalent to five at the latitude of Rhodes which is thirty-six degrees north. So every degree shown on the chart corresponds to fourteen leagues and a sixth from north to south and east to west. From this one can measure the distance of the route from Spain to the beginning and end of the Indies, and so the distance from one territory to the other. On this chart it will be seen that there is a red line passing from above Isabela to the end of Spain. Above this are the territories discovered on the First Voyage and below this are the territories discovered on this voyage. I hope, with Our Lord, that each year we will paint more on the chart because they will be continually discovered. From this description, Columbus's map was superior to Juan de la Cosa's, whose famous map was based, as H. O'Donnell Y Duque de Estrada has recently shown, on Columbus's.

In every sphere, Columbus's mastery of the sea was outstanding. What was it like to be on a discovery ship in the Caribbean? The closest description we have we owe to Columbus in the miraculously discovered Tarragonan *Libro Copiador*. Most of the details were faithfully reported by Bernaldéz and Las Casas, but there is a freshness and directness in Columbus's own words, writing to Isabella and Ferdinand about his exploration of the southern coast of Cuba. They had requested him to undertake such a voyage and he reported it in detail.

The year is 1495, Hispaniola is in the secure hands of his brothers Bartolomé and Diego, and he sails to Cuba from Jamaica which he has just discovered. *From the crow's nest I saw the sea clotted with islands on all sides, all green and full of trees, the most beautiful sight that eyes can see.* The narrow channels twisted, making it difficult to navigate, but he landed at the 'mainland' of Cuba and *On the seashore sprung two eyes of water, more than a foot high...* He painted an idyllic scene: they rested in the grass beside the springs enveloped with the scent of flowers, *in the shade of these great and beautiful palms;* further on scarlet flamingos dazzled his vision, and he called this mass of lovely islands The Garden of the Queen.

From his prow, still in the Garden of the Queen, he saw Indians using sucker fish to hunt turtles. *They were like a conger eel, and they bring them tied by the tail with a very long cord. And these fish have a long head full of cavities, like an octopus, and it is very bold and will take on any other fish, regardless of size. It sticks its head into the most vulnerable spot and will not let go until it dies. The hunters catch the fish they want, and it is very fast and sticks where I said, and then they pull the cord and pull out the one and the other, to the surface of the water, where they kill it and take it with a heavier rope.* The Indians, *speaking like lambs,* asked his men to keep away from the canoe until they had finished fishing. Then they gave Columbus four large turtles.

After leaving the Garden of the Queen, he found a large island with a big settlement. The inhabitants fled at the sight of his sails. He reported seeing their dogs (*guaminiquinajes*), *not large and very ugly, as if suckled on fish, nor did they bark and I knew the Indians ate them and even our Christians have tried them. They say they taste better than kid.* The villagers also kept tame blue herons and smaller birds. To reassure Isabella that he had behaved properly, he wrote *I left them without touching anything.*

Along the southern coast of Cuba he found villagers who, believing they came from the heavens, offered them gifts of *fruit,*

bread, water, spun cotton, rabbits, pigeons and a thousand other birds.
He had his interpreter, 'Diego Colón', tell them that they had
come from Castile, *but they still believed and believe that this is the
sky and your Highnesses are there.*

The small fleet entered a sea *as white as milk and thick, like the
water leather curers tan hides in.* The ships keels touched the soft,
muddy bottom and they sailed thirty miles ploughing along it.
They passed rockier islands, the ships grounded and the men
had to kedge them for several days, backbreaking work.
Columbus, always on the lookout for new plants, reported sea
grapes and he collected samples of their vines and *a barrel of soil
from the bottom of the white sea.*

The men were now exhausted from kedging the ships, but
Columbus carried on. He discovered an island *as great as Corsica*
he immediately assumed was *Cheroneso*, the Malacca Peninsular.
This was the Isla de la Juventud, formerly the Isle of Pines,
about half the area of Corsica, to contain a prison which would
include such illustrious inmates as José Martí and Fidel Castro.
He wanted to land but found the mangrove swamps impenetrable, *so thick a cat could not get through.* But he consoled the
Monarchs with reports of huge mother of pearls, an indication
that pearl beds lay nearby. His men fished out boatloads, but
found not a single pearl though they enjoyed the huge oysters
they cooked and ate on the shore. By now, his men were near
mutiny:

*The ships were badly damaged by the many times they had
grounded; rope and tackle were very worn and most of the supplies
lost, especially the ship's biscuit because of the water we had shipped;
and everyone was exhausted and fearful, although I had much hope
that God would bring us to safety. Since I had travelled one thousand
two hundred and eight-eight miles, which are three hundred and
twenty-two leagues, from Cape Alpha and Omega, and had seen infinite islands, I agreed to return. Not by the way I had come, but turning to Jamaica to sail around the southern part... which I had not
seen.*

As he was blocked in from the open sea by a mass of islands,
he was forced to retrace his steps. Nature provided more wonders. *I saw more than a hundred cormorants, together, coming from
the sea towards land. I count it as a marvel because I have never seen*

anything like it while I have been at sea. The following day so many butterflies came to the ships that they darkened the sky, and they stayed until nightfall, when a sudden squall came and released a great amount of water. Also, I saw that in all those seas there were innumerable turtles, and these twenty leagues were thick with them, huge ones, so many it seemed the ships would run aground on them. The Indians value them highly for their taste and nourishment, just as we do...

Returning to the eastern end of Cuba, a province he called Homofay, the Cacique and a man *over eighty-years old,* greeted him. After Mass held in a church Columbus had convinced the village to build, *the old man reasoned well and boldly. As he knew I had travelled to all the islands and mainland, which is where we are, his intention was that I should not be arrogant, because every man is afraid and I was a mortal like everyone else.* The old man and Columbus, in the shade of a palm, talked about the miracle of birth, the fragility of the body, death, the soul and what was right and wrong. The interpreter 'Diego Colón', *who understands and pronounces our language very well and is an excellent person* then described everything about Castile. *He spoke of the cities, churches, large houses, nobility of the people, of the fiestas, bullfights and matters of war he had seen. This pleased the old man very much, and he decided to come to see your Highnesses, but his wife and children wept, and, in pity for them, he would not come. I did not want to take him by force, as if he were a young man, of whom I took many without outraging the land. I am sending your Highnesses a Cacique I took in Sava and, although they go naked and, when they run away, appear to be savages and beasts, I can vouch that they are very clever and are delighted to discover new things, like us.*

Within half a century of his discovery of America Spain, thanks in part to America's riches, had become the greatest power in Europe.[32] In Columbus's wake, Europe colonized America and one thinks of his American legacy in terms of the conquest of the Aztec and Inca Empires, the Europeanization of a continent several times the size of the original, and the rise of the United States. However, as Columbus never knew of their existence, it is the development of his favourite island, Hispaniola, which best reflects the Columbian legacy. This was my next destination.

16

TO THE DOMINICAN REPUBLIC: FATE OF THE TAINOS

From the air, my first views of Hispaniola were the beaches which run in a continuous line along the northern coast, wiggling lightly between dark borders of land and sea. A series of inlets and rivers run down from black-green clad mountains, standing like great bastions before the water. Pico Duarte, at 3,175 metres, the highest point in the Caribbean, was over to my right, impossible to pick out from other peaks, in a sierra striking for its forest cover and strange mounds which rise from the surface like bubbles in a thick soup. Mountain ridges run inland, giving way to a broad valley in which a river meandered, at one point leaving isolated an oxbow lake. Where roads connect almost invisible settlements, red scratches cut through the green. On the bottom of the broad valley, sugar cane, maize, cacao, tobacco and yucca are cultivated, and I searched in vain for the small dark green coffee trees which must merge into the forest on the neighbouring mountainside. We flew over another sierra, dappled with these strange mounds, before dropping lower over Cibao, a land of small settlements and farms, a broad river with its tributaries wandering over the plain and up the mountains like a Virginia creeper. Here, the fields are lush and green like a thick-pile carpet you can imagine running your hands through. Approaching Santo Domingo, the fields shrink to allotments containing corrugated iron-roofed shacks, bright and silver in the sun, each with a shaggy banana palm at its side, as if it were the nation's flagpole. Taller palm trees – Royals and Palmettos – came in to view just before we touched down.

In the short walk to the terminal the sun heated my head and shoulders, accustomed still to a Madrid winter, with the force of an electric heater. A small brown man with a tray-full of glasses offered me a Cuba libre, and I sipped it gratefully as I was politely whisked past immigration and customs, with not the slightest hint of the hustling and administrative hassle I had been warned to expect from my guidebook. This was a welcome worthy of the Tainos.

Suddenly I was surrounded by men each telling me to take his taxi. I asked a white-haired mulatto with a gentle smile what he would charge me to take me the 20 miles to my hotel. '$20 is the fare,' which coincided with my guidebook. '*Rácano!*' Chiseller! shouted the others as I followed him to his unmarked taxi, a twenty-year old Chrysler. I asked him to stop at the Taino museum-cemetery at La Caleta on our way to the city. We arrived at a brick structure roofed with bleached palm leaves reaching almost to the ground on three sides. It is set in a grove of coconut palms within thirty yards of the sea and a small beach, used by fisherman, from where a group of boys emerged to ask me for money. I sniffed the air, expecting to detect something of the sweet fragrance Columbus and subsequent mariners reported scenting still days away from the islands. But the still air was vaguely sour and the scent which seemed sweet at sea was merely its contrast with the salt of the sea air.

An elderly black man in a grubby T-shirt and shorts waved back the boys and, with the green and gold insignia of the National Park Service (evidently modelled on the U.S.) on his cap, ushered me into the museum. The palm roof protects a small graveyard, not more than twenty skeletons, of which two, my guide assured me, have been identified as Caribs, one of whom, from his fractured skull, was evidently clubbed to death. In the largest grave sits a shaman with several objects around him to take to the afterlife, including the remains of one of their mute dogs which, judging by its skeleton, was about the size of a Corgi. 'Using Carbon 14 dating, they know this is about 750 years old.' The old man, his eyes glistening with enthusiasm, told me about the Taino's Cohoba ritual, and pointed out the spatula beside the shaman which was used to force vomiting as part of the ritual. Finished with the skeletons, he led me to a showcase with a few pottery shards, all that the Archaeological museum has left on the site. They are scattered in a glass case, difficult to make out in the gloom. 'They are making repairs,' explained my guide, though there was no sign of activity. We moved to photos of the dig. In one of the photos two archaeologists look down at a shallow pit where the glistening back and shoulders of a muscular, ebony-coloured man is at work. He pointed to the man in the pit. 'That's me and the man on the left is now Director of the Archaeological Museum.' He has worked here since the site was discovered in 1972 and rolled off a list of archaeologists – from the United States, Germany and Spain as well as the Dominican Republic – with whom he has worked. Was he proud of the Tainos?

'Very. They were a good people.'

'And the Caribs?'

'Evil people. They were *antropófagos*.'

'Cannibals?'

'Exactly.'

The old man pointed towards the car park. 'Fenutino is a good man, he's my friend.'

My white-haired mulatto waited patiently for me by his car and we set off for Santo Domingo. Frank's Car Wash, a medical clinic, a hardware shop called Hacha, Pica Pollo – the Dominicans' answer to KFC, Lechonera Kelvin line the highway into town, a coalition of shacks with their paint peeling in the sun, reminding me of a dilapidated Floridian shopping centre from the 1960s. The row of shacks abruptly ends and a brilliant white long, low building behind a white adobe wall came into view. A big sign advertised *Jesucristo es mi patrón*. Fenutino explained: 'They are Americans. They have shaven heads and wear white tunics. What do you call them?' Religious nuts. I don't know. How has Santo Domingo changed?

'When I was young, only 50,000 people lived here and I knew everyone. Now there are more than two million.'

'And has life improved?'

'Of course it has! when I was young I had no fridge or television, now I have everything.' Including this old, air-conditioned Chrysler with its everlasting engine. And why hadn't the Dominican Republic gone the way of Haiti? He smiled, there is no love lost between the neighbours, 'It's the people, they aren't like us. They are black. All black.'

Election hoardings and banners lined the Malecón, a boulevard which runs along the coast, tall Royal palms, grass and the deep blue of the Caribbean on one side, chic cafés turning to expensive hotels and houses hidden behind a screen of trees on the other. When prompted, Fenutino told me about the forthcoming election. Balaguer, the 89-year-old President, is retiring,

'His only problem is that he's blind.' Whom would he like to win? He waved the question aside. 'They are all good men.'

The Good men, the Tainos, welcomed Columbus and his men as visitors from the heavens. Their ships' huge sails – no one in the Americas had harnessed wind power on this scale to move their vessels – were, to eyes innocent of science, immediately associated with winds and clouds, properties of the sky. The aspect of the men – bearded, some blond and blue-eyed, fully-clothed, sometimes wearing a shell which made them invincible to the best-aimed arrow – was so far removed from anything the Tainos had experienced that they assumed they must be Gods. And Gods with the most wonderful powers. Their high, paddleless vessels, blown along with the wind, effortlessly outstripped canoes and could brave the greatest waves the sea gods could throw against them. By lighting tiny flames at the end of white sticks, they burnt the night away creating a pool of sunlight wherever they wandered, protected from the fearsome *opias* of the dead. They would point a magical *guanin*-like tube at a distant tree and, with one frightening thunderclap, it disintegrated into splinters. From a leather sheath they would withdraw a long blade which shone like white gold, and with one swipe they could wish away a human arm or head, slice in half a coconut or lob off the branch of a tree. And they had telepathic powers: one God-like man could paint squiggles on a special thin white cotton-like material and another God-like man, a day's march away, could look at it and understand what the first God-like man was thinking.

At first Columbus and Isabella recognized their responsibility as guardians of this innocent people. Isabella, distant from the daily frustrations of implanting a colony and of organizing the Indians into a European-style workforce, remained true to her sense of guardianship until her death. Columbus did not. Neither did Isabella's governors and representatives, who took advantage of their distance from Castile to impose a 'pragmatic' Indian policy opposed to hers. Why? It is easy to underrate the fears of a numerically inferior people. The Spanish population of Hispaniola in 1500 was about 300, much lower than in 1493 when Columbus arrived with his fleet of 1,500 men (and a few women). Some of the 1,500 returned to Spain with their vessels, but the majority – perhaps a thousand – stayed. Though fresh immigrants arrived from Spain, the death rate on Hispaniola was so high and so many left that the Spanish population fell to a third in seven years.

Whether the Indian population was 100,000 or half a million, the few hundred Spaniards were so greatly outnumbered that any killing of their number was viewed with horror. Each Governor was obliged to wage war against the Indians at the first sign of insubmission. Once blood had been shed, and any new colonizer would be reminded of the massacre of the men at Navidad and subsequent murders, the tiny minority could only feel secure by keeping the Indians in a state of terror. To mine gold and grow crops suitable for a European table required a large labour force which, at first, could only be satisfied by the Indians. Thus began the *encomienda* feudal system whereby Indians had to work a certain period of the year for their masters and, as the Spanish population multiplied and the Taino's declined, every Indian became subservient to a Spaniard, breaking for ever his traditional way of life.

Historians, anthropologists and statisticians have variously estimated the Indian population of Hispaniola in 1492 at 100,000 to eight million. Generally, the lower figures are estimates of Spanish scholars wishing to limit the alarming nature of the depopulation of the island under Spanish rule. The higher estimates, which as we will see are grossly inflated, come from American scholars who seem to revel in exaggerating the scale of the tragedy. Yet this figure is picked up by editors such as those of the *1996 Caribbean Islands Handbook* who wrote, 'It is estimated that up to 8 million [Indians] may have lived on the island of Hispaniola alone, but there was always plenty of food for all'. Such bliss in such number! Contemporary sources on pre-Columbian populations are scarce, contradictory and unreliable, creating an ideal battleground for the sedentary scholar, where interpolation and conjecture can rove unhindered by the obstacle of unassailable facts. Still, enough information is available to set limits on the Indian population in 1492.

Las Casas reported a conversation with Diego Deza in which Deza recalls Columbus telling him there were 1.1 million inhabitants, yet on another occasion Las Casas wrote of *about three mil-*

lion souls – but Las Casas is hopeless when it comes to population estimates and neither he nor Columbus undertook anything approaching an Island-wide census. These global numbers, thrown out to impress the Court on the size and importance of the island, are not a good starting point to estimate the native population.

In 1495 Columbus wrote that in the province of Cibao, the name given to one of the five 'kingdoms' on the island, there were 50,000 people, evidently a very approximate estimate, but at least he had visited it. Early records of village populations are in the hundreds, rising to 3,000 for an unnamed village visited on the First Voyage. When Columbus arrived near Guacanagarí's village, everyone came to the shore to see the ships, *over a thousand,* reported Columbus. When Mayobanex, Cacique of the Ciguayos, wanted to impress Columbus with the possibility of cultivating yucca, he assembled *four or five thousand men* bearing wooden spades. Already, the impression is of an island occupied by tens or hundreds of thousands. The first real census was not taken until 1508 (it counted 60,000 Indians) and thereafter there are reasonable estimates of the Indian population, for which certain adjustments must be made. All estimates begin with these figures and work backwards, assuming a greater or lesser mortality rate, to reach a theoretical aboriginal population at the moment Columbus landed on the island.

I shall start the other way around with a figure of 300,000, which is the mean estimate of two Dominican scholars who have no axe to grind and are, in all senses of the word, closer to the ground than their foreign rivals, and work forward to the first censuses. This apparently illogical method has the advantage of allocating responsibility to each Governor of the period and makes some allowance for the principal causes of the Indians' decline – the imposition of the *encomienda*, the number of Spaniards on the Island, known military campaigns and epidemics.

1492 – 1494: Population: 300,000 Indians, 0 – 1,000 Spaniards. 'Governor', Christopher Columbus. In the early years, relations between the two peoples were sporadic and, except for the murder of the Spaniards at Navidad, friendly.

1495 – 1500. Governor, Christopher Columbus. In these years he shipped about 1,500 Indians to Spain as slaves, undertook the first Indian war (1495), followed up by Bartolomé's campaign. In all, say, 1,000 Indian casualties. There is no record of epidemics among the Indians in these years, and assumptions that there must have been seem coloured by the alarming death rate of the Spanish colonizers and the later epidemics which struck Mexico. The tiny Spanish colony was too preoccupied with its civil war, the Roldán rebellion, to do more than negotiate a tribute from the Indians. Though the Gold and Cotton taxes were tiresome demands – soon commuted to cassava bread in lieu of gold by Bartolomé – they caused the Indians no casualties except those indirectly produced by confrontation with the Spaniards. Luis Arranz provides (1991) a good estimate for the population of the gold-producing areas of the island (Cibao and Vega Real) for 1496 based on the per capita Gold Tribute agreed with two grand caciques, from a new document found in the Casa de Alba. His estimate of 60 to 90 thousand would, if applied equally to the remainder of the island, suggest a population of between 200 and 300,000. Population in 1500: 297,000 Indians, 300 Spaniards.

1500-2. Governor, Francisco de Bobadilla, who established de facto *encomiendas* which, in the early years, were relatively benevolent but entailed the use of forced labour. Spanish control was concentrated in Cibao and La Vega from the new settlement of Santo Domingo, leaving the rest of the island to run itself on traditional lines. Perhaps 5,000 Indians (probably less) died directly or indirectly from working in the gold mines and in skirmishes with the colonizers. Population in 1502: 292,000 Indians, 360 Spaniards.

1502-9. Governor, Nicolás de Ovando, who arrived with 2,500 Spaniards. Under Ovando were created all the conditions for a serious depopulation of the island. Gold and the promise of *encomiendas* brought in so many Spaniards that up to 14,000 at one time lived on the island, creating a drain on its food sources, largely dependent on the Indian plantations, and a huge demand for Indians to serve and labour on behalf of the conquistadores. So many immigrants arrived that Ovando begged King Ferdinand to send no more, but Ferdinand kept up the pressure, asking Ovando why more Indians could not be put to work in the mines to bring out more gold. The Spaniards spread out across the island, creating thirteen new settlements to control all its low lying areas. It was this colonization, accompanied by outrageous demands on Indian labour and food, which caused the Indians to rise against their conquerors. Ovando put down the Indian revolts ruthlessly, in one campaign alone (the second Higuey campaign) killing 14,000 Tainos, while in Xaragua some 10,000 Tainos including 86 caciques lost their lives. It is only from Ovando's governorship that reliable censuses are available. The first census, undertaken in 1508, counted 60,000 Indians which Roberto Cassa believes understated the Indian population by 20%. Population in 1509: 70,000 Indians, 12,000 Spaniards.

1509-1515. Governor, Diego Colón. The *encomienda* system continued to take toll of the Indians and, to compensate for the consequent labour shortage, at least 15,000 Tainos were shipped in from the Bahamas which, by 1546, had a grand total of eleven inhabitants. Thus began the raiding parties which would bring in Indians from South America, Trinidad and the neighbouring islands. A 1511 census counted 33,000 Indians which, by 1514, had fallen to 25,000.

Further censuses counted 11,000 in 1518, reduced by smallpox to 8,000 in 1519 and only 2,340 were counted in 1529. But by then a large number were outside Spanish control, the Spanish population itself reduced to a few thousand as men moved on to Mexico and Central America, so that a 1534 estimate of 5,000 Indians is not inconsistent with the earlier census. In this period gold production had fallen to a tenth (1523) while the first sugar exports were recorded in 1521. By 1547 only 150 Indians remained alive. In these later years some Indians were murdered or, in the case of women, abducted by *cimarrones* (peak-people), black fugitive slaves.

If we begin with 300,000 Indians on Hispaniola in 1492 and include the very broad, and undoubtedly inaccurate estimates for the pre-census years, the population decline and annual rate are as follows:

	Indian Population	Population Decline	Rate p.a.%
1492-1494	300,000	0	0

1495-1500	297,000	3,000	1%<
1500-1502	292,000	5,000	1%<
1502-1509	70,000	222,000	16%
1509-1515	25,000	45,000	15%
1514-1518	11,000	14,000	17%
1518-1519	8,000	3,000	27%
1519-1529	2,340	5,660	12%
1519-1534	5,000	3,000	2%

I present this gruesome table only to show that the mean estimates of Roberto Cassa (between 200,000 and 300,000) and Frank Moya Pons (400,000), two contemporary Dominican historians who have studied the records, are within the realms of possibility; the high estimate of eight million Indians would require more than a halving of the population every year between 1502 and 1508. The idea of four million deaths in any one year is inconceivable, even a tenth of that number impossible without the technology of a 20th-century Germany. It even stretches the imagination to think how a small number of Spaniards could have done away with a hundredth of that number in a single year, when the vast majority were pursuing the pacific occupations of farming, construction, gold-sifting, trading, artisanry and administering the new colony. There is, of course, the powerful argument that, once the *encomienda* system had taken a hold on the island, most of the Indians' deaths were self-inflicted.

Like Las Casas and other 16th-century observers, I assume that the principal cause of the decline of the native population of Hispaniola was due to the *encomienda* and not to diseases brought over from the Old World. (Whether or not malaria was endemic to the Indies before the Conquest is one of the keys to this assumption. If the first Spaniards brought malaria with them, one would have expected a deadly epidemic among the Tainos. None is recorded.) So, exactly what was so deleterious about the *encomienda*? In theory it was a step up from slavery. At first all adult Indians, from whom were excluded women once the Spanish authorities realized that forced labour caused their decline in numbers, had to work for their Spanish *encomendero* ten months of the year, separated by two 40-day breaks when the Indians were expected to return to their villages to cultivate their land. They were paid a small salary for their work. In practice, because they cost the *encomendero* nothing to acquire, the Indians were treated worse than slaves, many – there is no exact record – dying of overwork. Their death-rate at the mines was appalling, yet this alone, once the women were freed from the obligation to work, would not have caused their extinction, even if all the men had worked there, but only about a third were so employed.

The Spaniards, by destroying the Taino's traditional way of life, quite unintentionally broke the spirit, the will to live, of their Indian charges. The Indians were prohibited from playing the ball game, from participating in the Cohoba ritual, polygamy was banned, the zemis destroyed and even the right to bathe (considered unhealthy as well as unseemly by Europeans) and dance and sing were taken away from them. The 40-day periods to cultivate their crops were not always respected and anyway were insufficient. Meanwhile, in the villages occupied only by women and children, there were no men to provide fish and game, nor give comfort to the women or a central political role or purpose to the community. Unlike slaves brought from Africa, the Tainos and neighbouring peoples were unable to successfully adapt to or resist their masters. They seem to have chosen the extinction of their race, reminding me of Quibian's Indians in Veragua who preferred death to imprisonment on Columbus's ship the *Bermuda*, hanging themselves in its hold. Many Tainos, faced with being worked to death by their oppressors, chose the same route – some committed suicide (by drinking prussic acid, the poisonous juice leached from cassava), others died resisting the conquistador, many women stopped procreating (or aborted or killed their children at birth) and deliberately left their mounds of yucca uncultivated, believing they could starve the Spaniards out. Of course they only starved themselves. In the 1514 census, of 26,334 Indians only 1,463 were classified as children, whereas there should have been around 9,000 merely to maintain the population (assuming a life expectancy of 35 years). Las Casas reports one group of Tainos escaping to Cuba, but as the Spaniards closed in, they all leapt to their death in a fast-flowing river.

The Church – led by the Dominican Order – mounted a powerful campaign against the *encomienda* and in defense of native Americans, but that is another story and came too late to save the Tainos.

Though extinct, the Tainos, via Spanish, live on in our language: from common words like barbecue, hammock, hurricane, savannah, canoe, cay and tobacco; wildlife (iguana, cayman, hutia, manatee); food-producing plants (maize, cassava, yucca, potato); fruits (guava, papaya or pawpaw, tuna); place-names (notably Cuba, Haiti and Jamaica); and the more esoteric cacique, guiro and guaiacum. And they are very much present, as I discovered, in the memory of the people who now live on their island.

17

THE DOMINICAN REPUBLIC: IN COLUMBUS'S FOOTSTEPS

In the run-up to the Presidential election, the incumbent, Joaquin Balaguer, former assistant to Trujillo and President for twenty-three of the last thirty-five years, prepared for retirement with a live TV programme dedicated to himself. He was in Azua, west of Santo Domingo, a small, ailing, pale gentleman resting on the arm of an aid, seeing nothing, saying nothing and, perhaps, thinking nothing. His face was passive, his head low in the silver-backed throne in which he sat, with ministers on either side of him and army officers, in their creased uniforms, standing behind him. Before him was a wide table of no apparent use. A besuited dignitary, the Governor of Azua, eulogized the great man, comparing him to General-cum-President Santana who liberated the country from the Haitian yoke. El Presidente Balaguer was *un patriota insigne* and he rolled off the public works undertaken – irrigation, a road tunnel, a new school, and now he would hand over the deeds of 309 smallholdings and thirty homes to Azuan peasants.

Grinning peasants crossed the stage to receive the deeds from the very hand of El Presidente, supported on his feet by two aids. At first he seemed to mumble something, but soon his face reverted to its blank look. His arm swung back and forth, as if it were on a hinge, receiving and passing on deeds to the lucky 339 peasants, and I wondered who would stop it when, like Chaplin in *Modern Times*, the production line came to a halt. But the camera moved away while he was helped back to his throne. A bishop in a purple biretta and soutane rose to give his most profuse thanks to El Presidente Joaquin Balaguer for building a new church in the province. Again, a younger man supported Balaguer while he handed over the keys of a parochial church to its parish priest, and the speeches and gifts hadn't stopped. There were bikes for boys and dolls for girls...

President Balaguer does not suffer critics lightly. A few days after the 1994 elections, reportedly fixed by his party, he had Dr. Narciso González arrested. According to Amnesty International, González, a 54-year-old academic and journalist who had criticized Balaguer, was picked up outside a cinema by police, tortured and, most probably, murdered.

The 16th century city of Santo Domingo is alive and healthy. It has survived hurricanes and earthquakes, being sacked by Drake and the Haitians and centuries of neglect by Colonial and Dominican administrations. Here Spain took a stand in the New World and created the best it had to offer. As a result, Santo Domingo is the site of the second church, the first cathedral, the first university and the first library, the first hospital and leprasorium, the first monastery and convent, the first Governor's mansion and law courts, and the first cistern and piped water of any European settlement in the Americas. All, it should be added, built with indentured Indian labour.

All these buildings are standing, most in such impeccable condition – the Dominicans restored some for the Quincentennial and others, in a burst of dictatorial enthusiasm, in 1955 – that one can imagine the glorious little city which Spain created in twenty years in a land which, until then, had not known a permanent building. Streets, lined with trees to provide some shade, are laid out in a grid with squares every few blocks, their size depending on the importance of the adjacent buildings so that the largest plazas are reserved for the *Casas Reales*, the administrative centre, and the Cathedral. The east side of the colonial city is bordered by the Rio Ozama, where ships still moor at its smooth, broad entrance. To the south the Caribbean, sparkling under the tropical sun, extends to the horizon. Both shores are protected by a series of stone forts and walls, their heavy, rusting cannon still looking formidable from a distance.

The Cathedral, whose first stone was laid by Columbus's son Diego in 1512, is a symbol of the city's past. In its almost shockingly dark and cool interior, where the scent of incense still lingered in the air, plaques commemorate Columbus's tomb, Gonzalo Fernández de Oviedo, 'First Chronicler of the Indies', and the year 1794 when, as Primate of America, its Archiepiscopal Diocese included 'Lima, Mexico and New Orleans'. The Cathedral's north side shows a hesitant attempt at

Italian renaissance, the arches too small and asymmetrical and the accompanying worked stone too modest, as if the architect worried about being too modern. Emerge at the Plaza Colón and, for a brief moment, with its brick floor, laurel hedges, wrought-iron gas lamps and white-habited nuns strolling in pairs, one is thrown back to an Andalusian Plaza Mayor on a summer's day. I sat out of the sun on a bench beside an elderly man, with a green wooden box stuffed with contraband cigarette cartons at his side, and waved away a shoeshine boy who wanted to polish my beat-up casuals. Before me a bronze Columbus stood on a stone podium with one hand on a map resting on a wharf's bollard, the other pointing, appropriately for times when the country depended on emigrant remittances, due north to Miami and New York.

I strolled on, declining the services of guides, taxis, and sellers of postcards, to a solid stone Hidalgo's house which could have been transplanted from the old quarter of Caceres. It sported the French tricolour. Behind its forbidding exterior, high-ceilinged rooms big enough to hold a ball in led to a patio given over to French propaganda. Cortés lived here before setting out for Mexico and, once known as the *Casa de Cortés*, it is now the *Casa de Francia*. A ventriloquist, against a backdrop of the Eiffel Tower, kept a group of Dominican school-children amused with a naughty female puppet who occasionally popped in a French phrase. So, pointing at the house, she saw, *un ladrón sobre el techo, UN VOLEUR SUR LE TOIT*, the odd French sounds causing hilarious squeaks from the second graders. Beside posters advertising Loire chateaus, a pair of Dominican girls served croissants and coffee and ice-cream cones for the children. I asked one of them what she thought of the puppet show. 'They want us to learn three languages, Spanish, English and French.'

Did she speak French? She gave me a lovely smile. 'Not now, I've forgotten it all.'

Penetrating further into Cortés's splendid house, its raw stone, wood-beam ceilings and pillars and smooth stone floor are, thanks to its height and galleries, surprisingly elegant. According to tradition, it was here that the first gold was smelted in the city, though by then Columbus was on his deathbed and

Ferdinand had renegged on the contract of Santa Fé. More school-children, herded into an anteroom by a pair of teachers, little ones not more than five-years old were getting out of hand, their ice-creams liberally spread over their faces and the 500-year-old floor.

Nearly opposite is Ovando's House, another formidable stone building on two floors, which Nicolás de Ovando, third Governor of Hispaniola, built for himself in 1508. It is now a Government-run hotel. I walked through to a patio, flanked by the two wings of the house, skirted the recently-built swimming pool and stood by the city walls facing on to the River Ozama. Opposite, on the east bank, is the oldest standing church in America, built by Bartolomé Colón in 1496, where Columbus worshipped. As one would expect, it is a plain prayer-house without a bell tower (they had no bell) or steeple or even a cross to blemish the smooth lines of its roof, and, with the Colóns' passion for the sea, it perches on the bank of the river. Surrounded by bushes and trees, a footpath leads down to a tiny beach where ships' boats could be pulled up – someone had left a dinghy there – well protected from the sea, just the place one would choose to anchor a ship during a storm. It was here, towards the end of the rainy season in 1500, that Columbus was led in chains, his back to the little town he and his men had carved out of the jungle, to the waiting caravel, wondering what tortuous series of events had brought Isabella's envoy to seize and imprison him without any formal charges or even explanation.

When he founded Santo Domingo on Columbus's orders, Columbus's brother brought the settlers from Isabela and suffered a repetition of everything which had gone wrong in Isabela – the hidalgos wouldn't work, his men came down with tropical illnesses and suffered from the heat and foreign, protein-poor Taino diet. In 1502 the hurricane, which sank 19 vessels but left Columbus and his fleet almost intact, blew it all, except the chapel of the Virgen del Rosario, away. Ovando rebuilt Santo Domingo on the west bank for no other reason, I suspect, than that it was not the bank the Colóns had chosen for the city. The river runs deep and broad inland, a wonderful refuge for ships from hurricane winds and foaming seas, the best in all the island,

and to deny its shelter, as Ovando did to Columbus in 1502, can only have been motivated by a hatred difficult to fathom.

In the street the sun was high now, so that everyone, vendors, tourists, passers-by, used the shaded side of the street. A few yards further on is the National Pantheon, actually an 18th-century Jesuit church which, after the Jesuits' expulsion, was used as a theatre, a tobacco warehouse and for public offices. It was deemed grand enough by Trujillo to be the site of his tomb, but the dictator went down in a hail of bullets and his tomb lies empty. The great stone nave is parted by a crimson carpet sectioned off by scarlet velvet ropes which match the red trimmings on the blue uniform of a sentry guarding an empty tomb, waiting for someone with sufficient national prestige to be interred, dies. I suspect the 89-year-old President Balaguer has himself in mind.

At the end of Las Damas Street, where colonial ladies used to stroll at sunset, fanning away mosquitoes and throwing off perfumed scents which lingered in the heavy, motionless air, is a square worthy of a great city in Spain. An immense stone building of imposing simplicity erected in the early 1500s, perhaps a hundred yards long, lines the west side, facing the River Ozama and the old port. Known simply as *Las Casas Reales*, here resided all the main organs of colonial government: the palace of the Captain General, the law courts, and the offices of the Royal Council and Treasury. All of it has been turned over to a museum, many of the rooms fitted out in furnishings of the period.

At the entrance are samples of several gold medals, the *Condecoración de Colón*, and I asked the black woman who vigilated the room what she thought of Columbus. 'He wasn't good. He took all the gold from our country.' Poor Columbus, how he wished he had! I turned to the next case and was surprised by samples of Taino objects – a tiny stone ceremonial seat, a forked hollow cane with balls of resin at each end which they would force up their nostrils to sniff a narcotic powder to enter the trance required for the Cohoba ritual, and a stone yoke not identified as a mould for the leather hip belts they used in the ball game. The yoke and Oviedo's description of the ball game, which they called *batey* (and *bate* is the Mayan name for the yoke), are so similar to the game played by Mexicans and Maya that one would assume they were in contact; and yet there's no indication that the Taino's knew of the great civilizations to the west nor that the Aztecs or Maya knew of the existence of the Greater Antilles. A collection of stone axe-heads, mortars and a seated figure are displayed beside relics from the site of Isabela. The brass hawks-bells Columbus used to trade gold (and used as a measure for gold tribute) are tiny, no larger than a gooseberry, while the Taino's beads are as large as hen's eggs and worked in a simple dogtooth design, using red, white and black stone. A copper ring, given to each Indian when he was baptized, and a curved terracotta tile made in 'La Isabela' finish off the small collection. Wall plaques explain the loss of life of the Tainos, numbered between 200 and 300,000, the importation of 12,000 African slaves in the 16th century and the consequent mix of African with Taino and Spaniard. This was my first inkling of the Dominicans sense of identity with the Tainos.

I moved on to rooms filled with colonial objects – swords, muskets, armour, lombard balls – but then military equipment outlasts most trappings of civil life. A young guardian, a small, light-coloured mulatto wearing gold-rimmed glasses like my own, asked me where I was from. He was a student. Was he proud of the Tainos?

'Of course I'm proud. They were our forefathers and we have their blood. But they have gone. It's not like Mexico or Peru where Indians survive and speak their own language.'

And the Spaniards?

'Well, they killed all the Tainos. 600,000 of them, but I don't blame them. Those were different times. They were ambitious, wanted gold and used the indigenous people to work for them. And they forced them to work if they didn't want to. Those who wouldn't they hung.'

What of the fine buildings, the university, the hospital, all the trappings of what we call civilization?

'Everyone develops with time. What would the Tainos have developed in these five hundred years? That's a long time in the period of their civilization.'

What did he think of Columbus?

'He was a most ambitious and intelligent man, but he organized the first *encomiendas*.'

By 1503 Columbus wrote that he regretted the ill-treatment of the Indians and recognized that they were the real wealth of the Indies.

'Did he really write that? It must have been on the Fourth Voyage. By then it was too late.' He made a kicking movement. 'First he put in the boot and then he withdrew it with his mouth.'

Outside the Casas Reales, in the centre of the Plaza de España, is a statue of Governor Nicolás de Ovando, he who let Columbus and his men rot for the best part of a year on Jamaica. It is dedicated to 'The Founder of Santo Domingo'. Poor Bartolomé Colón, the city's real founder, only gets a street named after him. On the far side of the square, by the old walls and port, is the most elegant building in the colonial city, a beautifully proportioned renaissance palace built by Columbus's son Diego in 1510. Two stone arcades, the smaller one surmounting the bigger one, fill most of the frontage and on either side stand a Royal Palm, two soaring sentries with their green plumes fluttering in the air. Inside there's a ground-floor room where Bartolomé, Diego's uncle, slept. Small blue ceramic tiles of a rampant lion and a tower are set in the stone floor, so that every morning Bartolomé got out of bed he was reminded of Ferdinand's kingdoms of Castile and Leon. The noble rooms have marble floors, in cream black and rose, the ceiling is painted mahogany and the entrance to the upper balconies are separated by exquisite wrought-iron gates. Here Diego, named Viceroy of the Indies, one of his father's favourite title, and his family lived, waited on by lithe Taino servants, their once tanned bodies suitably covered. Sliced papaya, pineapple, bananas and oranges from trees brought from the Canaries overflowed silver fruit bowls laid out in the shade of the upper terrace where a fresh sea breeze caressed the cheek and ruffled the women's long dresses. Here Diego, a Grandee in his own right, married to the niece of the Duke of Alba and ruling over the embryo of a new Empire, had achieved everything Columbus would have desired for him.

Turning his back to the river, the Viceroy overlooked the town where Indian labourers, under the direction of Spanish masons and carpenters, unloaded stone blocks and lengths of hardwood beside half-built mansions, houses and churches, replacing the pole and thatch huts which still littered the view. But it was the view down the river to the sea which stirred his interest. Barely a month passed without the arrival of a ship bearing news, provisions and fresh men and women from Spain or returning with news of the neighbouring islands, Venezuela, Castillo de Oro, Guatemala, Higueras, Honduras, La Florida, Mexico or Yucatan. Death came suddenly and unexpectedly in the Indies, friends – and enemies – were no more, but news came of new peoples discovered, wearing rich robes, bearing staffs of gold and living in palaces worthy of Seville with great pyramids for temples, or of rivers where gold nuggets the size of a fist lay scattered, waiting to be gathered. Land, the Indies, stretched interminably to the north, south and west and occasionally the remnants of a once powerful expedition would return with stories of great rivers and plains full of bison, of warring native tribes, each speaking a different language, of deserts and jungle, lands almost empty of man and filled with trees and game. From Diego Colón's palace the Viceroy, yet to be menaced by English, French and Dutch corsairs, looked out on lands so great and so rich that he didn't even have to dream of the empire in the making.

The oldest standing fort in the Americas, built in 1503, is a Norman tower with an adobe stairwell on one side, a strangely deformed, damp and claustrophobic place, now stinking of urine, which served as Ovando's first residence. He added walls and rooms, the whole an ugly but effective military structure to which would be added two gun platforms, more walls, subsidiary forts and barracks making Santo Domingo secure until Drake sacked it seventy years later. Trees and grass, on which hens run free, have replaced the barracks and transformed the old military complex into something approaching a village common. A lone man with a rake gathered leaves, sweeping them under the carriage of a cannon. For six weeks Columbus walked, as well as he could, these walls, waiting for a vessel he could charter to take himself, his son, brothers and twenty-three shipmates from the vessels wrecked on Jamaica back to Castile. Columbus could imagine the fine city that would emerge now that Ovando had the men and money which had been denied him, but now nothing on the island he had discovered and conquered and loved was his. He wasn't even supposed to visit it. And what awaited him in Spain? He knew Isabella was ill, possibly dead and that Ferdinand would be cursing the 10,000 gold pesos he had spent on the High Voyage. Wracked with pain, he must have known that he would never recover from the privations he had suffered on the coast of Central America and marooned on Jamaica and that he would never return alive to this island with its happy, innocent people, its lush, evergreen vegetation, and inlets and bays, fringed with white sand shelving gently into clear water.

Adjoining the Fortaleza de Ozama is what is known as Rodrigo de Bastidas' mansion, a low brick building forming a large U around a pleasant, shaded park filled with the pungent smell of boxwood, a place of repose. I reposed and thought of Bastidas's turbulent life, which had seemed ordered (he was a merchant in the village of Triana) until the story of riches coming from the Indies enticed him to lead a voyage to the west. He took Juan de la Cosa as pilot and discovered the north coast of Colombia, trading pearls and gold with the Indians. Then, as so often happens in the Indies, his luck changed. His ships were wrecked on the southwestern extremity of Hispaniola and from there he and his crew walked, bearing their treasure, to Santo Domingo. Bobadilla, who had had Columbus chained and repatriated to Castile, confiscated the treasure and had Bastidas jailed. Then Ovando arrived, released Bastidas and returned him to Spain without his treasure. Eventually, the Crown returned his gold and pearls and with this experience of the Indies behind him one would think he'd have had enough. But, 49-years old, he bought this land and set out on another voyage with a Royal Permit to found a colony at Santa Marta, Colombia. Santa Marta is a lovely site, with long beaches, close to the effluent of the Magdalena River and in the shadow of the highest mountain in Colombia, a dormant volcano which rises from the sea to its Pico Cristóbal Colón at 5,800 metres. Bastidas established amicable relations with the Indians, which meant his men, many of them hidalgos, were expected to farm and do manual labour. They rebelled, Bastidas suffered a knife wound, and he died aboard his ship bound for Santo Domingo, and his remains lie under the floor of the Cathedral. This house was built by his family and enjoyed by his son who took on the safer calling of the cloth, rising to be Bishop of Venezuela and of Puerto Rico.

A short walk along the narrow streets of the old town, is the *Casa de Tostado*, facing on to a small square with a bronze statue of Padre Bellini. Francisco de Bellini's life touched the heart of a nation. From an early age he founded and promoted public institutions which today we take for granted. After founding a school, he went on to found the first poor house on the island (1867), the first orphanage (1869) and the first madhouse (1885), financing them with a lottery, also a first for the Dominican Republic. Padre Billini was the man who discovered Columbus's remains inside a lead casket in the city's cathedral on 10th September 1877, while it was undergoing restoration. Inside the casket Bellini found a lead pellet, which caused a minor flurry in academic circles: was Columbus wounded by a musket-shot? Only once does he refer to his 'wounds', in a context which is generally assumed to refer to an illness, but it would not be a surprise if the only battle wound he received came from a Spanish musket.

Like so many Andalusian houses, the *Casa de Tostado* is of more interest inside than out, a vestige of Moorish times when houses presented an austere, blank face to the street, behind which wives and daughters were protected from the prying eyes of outsiders. This was the residence of Francisco de Tostado, the first creole Professor at the University, mortally wounded by a cannonball fired from one of Drake's ships. It is now a Museum to the 19th-century Dominican Family.

A woman in her early thirties, with a pleasant smile disclosing long white teeth which contrasted with her scarlet lips, asked me if I spoke Spanish. 'Oh, thank God for that. I'm not the cashier but if you give me the ten pesos, I'll leave them for him. He's gone for a coffee.' If she was not the cashier she had to be a guide, and she led me away – reluctantly I have to admit. She was so chatty and, as there was no one else in the museum, I let her take me on a tour of Marie-Theresa chairs, French clocks, oak commodes, brass bed-frames, Limoges china, English silver. Nothing, she confirmed brightly, was made in the Dominican Republic, only a porous stone font near the well once used to purify water. She admitted that this was a museum created by 'well-heeled families of the upper-middle class.' She, with her smart dress, good speech and interest in antiques was evidently from the middle-class herself though not, I assume, well-heeled.

'We are poor. A worker earns $240 a month, a nurse might earn $500, and with this they have to buy food and pay for a small, a tiny house, and if they have a large family...' She shrugged her shoulders.

Would she like to live in a house filled with antique furniture like this? 'Why not? I like old things.'

What did she think about the Tainos? She seemed reluctant to answer my question, which admittedly seemed out of place in this Spanish-style mansion stuffed with European antiques, but by a gilt French mirror she made a decision. 'Yes, I would like to see a Taino with my own eyes, I would like to touch him. I know the Spaniards had a higher culture when they arrived, but this was the Taino's land. Look at me. I have African lips, a European nose, oriental eyes and my hair? Well, where would you say it comes from? We have Taino in our blood and yet we've never seen a pure Taino. If one suddenly popped up, he'd be overwhelmed by scientists who would want to test his blood group, his genes... I would like to see their skin. It was a lovely, smooth brown, not like mine.' (Hers was acceptably brown and smooth, but I was not going to argue.) 'I envy the Mexicans. They still have pure Mexican Indians. And the Amazonians in Brazil, and the Redskins in North America.'

There are communities of Indians living along the north coast of South America who are cousins of the Tainos and speak Arawak. Though she'd heard of the Arawaks, she was surprised some had survived. Standing in the shade of a covered balcony overlooking the small garden (once it went all the way to the sea, she'd told me) filled with the scent of her perfume, she said, 'My grandmother told me a story of when she was a little girl. A story told by her mother, my great-grandmother. They had a brother and he disappeared for ten or fifteen years and when he returned he said, "I've been living with the Tainos underground." He stayed for a short time and then he said he had to return because he had married a Taino woman and had children by her. And he left.'

'Maybe he meant that they lived in a cave.'

'Exactly, and who knows? It was a long time ago.'

Though I broached the subject of Columbus, she wasn't interested in him. 'He discovered a new world. Why do they call us third-world? Maybe we should be happy just to be included in their world.'

She had travelled, knew Spain, had a cousin who worked for ten years in a circus and now owned a discotheque in Madrid, *Puerto Plata*. And why had I asked her about the Tainos? No foreigner had ever asked. 'But you're not a scientist or anthropologist, a writer perhaps?' Suddenly interested in me, she asked if I would deliver a letter to her cousin in Madrid. Was I staying long? We could perhaps meet at another moment... She sensed my reserve and quickly changed the subject, brightly talking about Madrid and La Coruña.

I walked along Padre Billini Street, past a park dedicated to Fray Bartolomé de Las Casas. A powerful bronze statue implying a physical force which the only known engraving of Las Casas belies – his long, bald head rests on a slender hand and a thin pair of drooping shoulders – stands in a wasteland of litter and concrete benches with only a tree to justify its denomination as 'park'. It was the first park I'd seen in Santo Domingo which was railed off and whose gates were padlocked.

A block further on, the little street widens into the Plaza Duarte on whose sea side is an imposing, freshly cream-painted complex, recently roofed in powder-pink tiles. Only the thick stone wall at the west end, a buttress and a simple stone bell-tower, the bells silhouetted against the sky as one sees in westerns shot in Mexico, hint at a possibly religious origin. The Dominican Monastery was built in 1510, becoming, in 1538, the place for the first university in the Americas. The University of Alcalá de Henares provided support and professors for the first faculties of Philosophy, Theology, Jurisprudence and Medicine, completing the colonization of an island whose original inhabitants were on the point of extinction. A man in his twenties detached himself from a wall he was leaning against and weaved unsteadily towards me. 'Gi'me a dollar. I'm hungry.' He was drugged to the eyeballs and, to avoid an unpleasant scene, I crossed the street to the Plaza Duarte.

Sitting on a bench in the shade, with the thin stream of my neighbour's cigarette smoke tickling my nostrils, I looked up at the huge statue of the writer and politician who led the rebellion against the Haitians, seemingly in a stiff wing collar and a long Victorian coat. On this spot Ovando hung the cacique Anacoana after putting to the sword other caciques he had lured to a feast. She was a woman of great character and beauty, whom it was rumoured Bartolomé Colón loved in the gentler days of Columbus's governorship. To be hung, rather than be put to the sword or burnt, was a privilege reserved for her rank, though one she could hardly have appreciated. Her Tainos and those of the new city gathered before the immense stone prayer-house raised by the white men to observe the announced death of one of their great caciques, murdered with a length of rope slung over a branch of a tree. Meant as an example, this cold-blooded murder could only confirm, if it needed confirming, the essential inhumaneness of their new lords and masters, and remind them of Caicihu's prophecy that clothed men would come and seize their food and kill them. Before the deadly weapons and physical might of the Spaniard, they knew that Caicihu's prophesy would be fulfilled.

Streets peter out at a fort, still with a rusting cannon at each emplacement, before which a grassy incline leads down to the coastal road and the sea. A striking thirty-foot statue of a black man dressed in white marble, his hand cupped to his mouth as he calls out to sea, stands on a small promontory. This is in homage to the Dominican friar Antón de Montesino, whose Advent sermon in 1511 was the first significant reaction to the freebooting ways of the conquistadors and abuse of their Indian vassals.[33] Las Casas reports part of his sermon verbatim. It is of Shakespearean eloquence. Montesino warmed up his congregation with a warning that with their *consciences as sterile as a desert* and their blindness, they walked in the path of the most vilious sins. He knew he was the voice of Christ in this desert island and that they would hear the roughest, hardest and most frightening and unpleasant condemnations they could ever imagine hearing. Montesino's voice 'made their flesh shrink and it seemed to them as if they were before the Divine Judgement'. Then:

This voice tells you that you are all in mortal sin and in it you live and die for the cruelty and tyranny which you use against this innocent people. He says, With what right and with what justice do you keep these Indians in such cruel and horrible servitude? With what authority have you so detestably warred against these people who, in these meek and peaceful lands, you have consumed with death and destruction? How can you so oppress and exhaust them, without satisfying their hunger or succouring them in illness, that, from excessive labour which you give them, they die, or better said, you kill them to mine and accumulate every day more gold? What care do you take that they know the doctrine and the faith of God and the Creator, that they be baptized, say mass and observe holy days and Sundays? Are these not men? Are they not rational beings? Are you not obliged to love them as you love yourselves? Do you not understand this? Can you not feel it? How can you sleep so deeply and for so long? Be sure that in the state which you are now, you cannot ask to be saved any more than Moors or Turks who have not and desire not the faith of Jesus Christ.

Las Casas, who was there, reported that the congregation were stunned into an awful silence. Later, over lunch at the Governor's mansion, Diego Colón and his men worked themselves into a fury, claiming Montesino was undermining Royal authority on the island. He demanded to see Montesino, but all the Dominican friars had helped in the preparation of the sermon and it was the most venerable of them, Pedro de Córdoba, who appeared. He gave such a robust response to the Viceroy's complaints that Diego Colón 'softened and spoke with humility'. Nevertheless, Diego summoned Montesino and demanded he retract his accusations the following Sunday. When the day came, 'all the city thronged the church'. Montesino climbed to the pulpit and began:

I will return to the principle of learning and truth which I preached to you last Sunday. And I will demonstrate that those words which upset you so are true.

Montesino returned to his accusations of the previous sermon, without retracting a single word. When he finished he went home, and 'everyone in the church was left to growl in anger against the friars'. Thus began the Church's offensive in favour of the Indians which would take them – via a commission of

Jeronymite friars – to rule the Indies for a brief period five years later. The immediate consequence was the Laws of Burgos, taken from the city where Montesino debated the Indian question before Ferdinand, a series of measures which were designed to protect and Christianize the Indians.

Two boys followed me below Montesino's statue where a part of his famous sermon is engraved into a vast marble slab overlooking the sea. I took a photo of the two boys by the slab and they follow me out, the elder of the two, ten-year-old Diego, asking me for money. Why should I give him money?

'To get home, because it's a long way from here.'

How did he get here then?

'I walked.'

Then he can walk back. He told me the smaller boy was Luis. He was eight and Diego claimed he was his brother though this news caused Luis some surprise. Like all Dominicans, Diego wanted to know where I come from and had a vague notion of England. Luis said, 'English from America.' Diego corrected him. We passed an ice-cream stall and I bought them each one and we parted.

It was now dusk and the central pedestrian walk of the old city, El Conde Street, was full of Dominicans strolling past the rather grubby plain-fronted shops and fast-food outlets, puffing frying odours at the pedestrians, which, but for the massive presence of pedestrians, give it the air of a Main Street in any poor Southern town in America. At the eastern end, approaching the River Ozama, the street leads to the Plaza de Colón and a well-known café, the Café Restaurante El Conde, which my guide books reported as being frequented by the city's literati. But guide books are generally decades out of date in this particular and, anyway, who wants to look at a literary set even assuming you can recognize one when you see it? I ordered a large bottle of Presidente beer – 0.65 litres to be exact – which came almost frozen, a delight in this tropical heat. A bearded, earnest man in his late twenties stopped at my table to offer me a newspaper, *Vetas*. 'It's cultural, has good book reviews.' I bought it for 20 pesos.

'Are you a writer?' He asked me, spotting my notebook.

'Of a sort.'

'So am I,' he said with pride. I wished him well.

My two boys strolled by and saluted me with affection. They sat beside me and I ordered them cokes and a packet of *Dorados*. Both were at the Casa de Francia this morning. They enjoyed the ventriloquist and the ice-cream. And the French lesson? 'It was alright,' said Diego without enthusiasm, 'Do the French always shout?' asked Luis. Though one might think it makes sense to teach French to a people who share an island with Haiti, I never met a Dominican who had been over the border and if he had, French would have served him poorly with the Creole-speaking Haitians. A tall youth passed by.

'He's Hare Krishna,' Diego informed me.

What do they do? 'They sing.' Does he like it? 'Not really.'

After a day tramping the city and the beer, I was lethargic and reluctant to move. What did they offer for supper? I chose *chivo*, a goat stew served on a bed of rice, and another Presidente. The stew was delicious, meat cooked on the bone and seasoned with local herbs, quite the best food I was going to eat in the Dominican Republic. A family settled at the next table, man, woman with baby and younger sister, from the country by the fuss they made about organizing their table. The man, a good, solid farming type, flipped out a book and began to read aloud to the family. I supposed, with the vague memory of *Jesucristo es mi patrón*, Padres Bellini, Montesino and Las Casas that it might be the Bible. But he was reading from Khalil Gibran.

A corpulent taxi driver took me back to the hotel. He asked if I were Italian – a curious question since I wouldn't come across a single Italian on the island. He added, 'Do you want a girl? There are lots of good places, lots of massage parlours.' I declined. 'So you don't like that sort of thing.' I like my wife. 'Is she here?' No. In baffled silence, he dropped me off.

Reclining in bed, I read the English weekly *The Santo Domingo News*. The ruling party had chosen a woman as Vice-Presidential running mate for Peynado, a young but very fat rich boy of Spanish descent, Balaguer's candidate for President. Maribel Ganó Diez was 'a 37-year old lawyer and business executive... scion of a prominent family of Spanish descent... She speaks three languages, graduated cum laude from the Universidad Nacional and has an M.A. from New York University.' But the party's youth section rejected her as a choice – because she was new to politics and because of her 'Spanish heritage'. Strange in a country where Spanish blood runs, more or less thickly, through all but a tiny minority of Dominicans.

Churches are dotted like a rosary over the city of Santo Domingo. San Lazaro's was once the city's leprasorium, treating the early colonizers among whom was a Luis Colón, said to be a descendant of Columbus, presumably a bastard of his unlikable grandson of the same name. Another, the Mercedes Church, hosted Tirso de Molina, one of the greatest of Spanish play-wrights and creator of *Don Juan*, who was otherwise occupied as member of the Order of Mercy, going by the less ponderous name of Gabriel Telléz. He taught Divinity here between 1616 and 1618, a short stint in a city in decline, the powerful viceroys, along with men of enterprise, having moved on to New Spain, Peru and New Granada and, abandoned by a bankrupt king, the north and west of the island had been lost to foreign corsairs. A short walk up a street of wood-clad houses painted in lumines-cent blues, turquoises and pinks, the Haitian quarter, took me to what was once the finest building in all Santo Domingo, the first Franciscan Monastery in the Americas. Built in the first decade of the 1500s on a hilly site overlooking the city, the ruins – it was sacked by Drake and destroyed by earthquakes – testify to a tall, long church flanked by a cloister which connected it to living quarters extensive enough for a large school of monks. Enough of it was standing to serve as Padre Billini's lunatic asylum a cen-tury ago, and its elevation made it an ideal location for the city's first cisterns, which are still in use. Bartolomé de Las Casas used it as a base from where he travelled, sometimes for years at a time, to Spain, Cuba, Mexico and South America, carrying con-troversy and utopian schemes for peaceably occupying huge tracts of the Americas, ventures which inevitably ended in tears.

A short way down the street, one of those magnificent stone doorways – this with a stone Franciscan's braid curling over the portal – announces the *Casa del Cordón*, built by Francisco Garay in 1509. Garay came over with Columbus on the Second Voyage in 1493, and Diego Colón appointed him Governor of Jamaica. In 1519, he sent three ships north under the command of Alvarez de Pineda to search for a strait past Florida to Asia.

Pineda landed on Florida's west coast, from where he sailed along the southern coast of North America (incidently discovering the Mississippi and proving that Florida was not the island it was thought to be) as far as Texas. Here, after several skirmishes with the Indians, Pineda was killed, flayed and eaten. Some of his men reached Cortés in Mexico and the relief vessels sent by Garay. But, not content with this loss and the Governorship of Jamaica, and with the unlimited ambition of the conquistador Garay set out to conquer Pánuco on the Gulf Coast of Mexico, in conflict with Cortés. After a series of misadventures, Garay lost his men, ships and guns to Cortés and died on Christmas Day 1523 of a stomach complaint after dining in Tenochtitlan. Since he was not the only person to have died suddenly after dining with Cortés, it was rumoured Cortés had poisoned him. The size of Garay's mansion – the ceilings are fifteen feet high, and spacious rooms are set around patios which would grace Seville or Cordóba – is a testimony to the wealth he accumulated from slaving and gold-trading in the Indies. Diego Colón occupied this house while his Alcázar was being constructed, and upstairs one can see the rooms where two of Columbus's grandchildren, Felipa and María, were born.

I emerged from the cool house into the street, wondering why they didn't build such hurricane-resistant houses today, not even in Florida where people could afford them. Nearby is the first hospital in the Americas, the Hospital of San Nicolás de Bari, now a ruin, in which the most aristocratic of palms, the Royal, has been allowed to proliferate. Ovando had it built in 1503 and its sheer size, big enough to take dozens of beds, gives some idea of the frequency with which the early colonizers came down with disabling diseases. All but the wealthiest lived, at first, in Taino huts of pole and thatch and packed dirt floors, many cohabiting with young Taino women whom the Tainos believed had sealed the friendship of a family bond. From the women they contracted syphilis, from the water dysentery, from mosquitoes malaria and yellow fever and, weakened from the protein-poor Taino diet based on yucca and the relentless heat, even the healthiest seemed, to the fresh eye of a man straight off a ship from Spain, in a wretched state. Now the hospital ruins' only residents are pigeons, thousands of them, nesting in holes pecked into mortar or strutting over the grass with that particular intensity which leaves them insensitive to everything else around them.

Now midday, I walked under the blistering sun, wishing I'd brought a hat. I wanted to see the Convent of Regina Angelorum where Padre Billini was buried. A tangle of cables and wires crisscross the stone façade, behind which Sor Leonora de Ovando and Sor Elvira de Mendoza had composed the first poems in the Indies. But, as with so many poets, their work is no longer published – or at least available. As I was sorely in need of a seat and a drink, I returned to El Conde Street, where a plump, dark mulatta with henna hair approached me, and without more ado said, 'Do you want to go to the beach?'

'No, thanks.'

'Why not?'

'Because I don't want to.'

At the end of the street is the El Conde Gate, where Duarte proclaimed independence from Haiti. Over the gate is engraved, *Dulce et decorum est por patria mori*, an exhortation which, thankfully, must be lost on all but a tiny minority of Dominicans. While I lunched on melon and beer, a series of vendors hawked their wares: packets of peanuts and chewing-gum, merengue music, the ten postcards at 60 pesos, guide services and boot blacks. One is never alone in Santo Domingo.

It is about three miles via Avenida Independencia to the Plaza de Cultura and the Museum of Dominican Man, and I decided to walk. After a hundred yards I was sticky with sweat, but it's surprising how quickly one gets accustomed to the heat. Soon I was out of range of street vendors and walking along a pleasant boulevard bordered by houses and low buildings of flats with gardens open to the pavement. Such a carefree attitude to security would be quickly punished in countries like Brazil, Venezuela or Colombia.

I hadn't gone more than half a mile when a tall, stringy grey-haired mulatto, neatly dressed in a white shirt, black slacks and good leather shoes, joined me. Was I from Europe? He liked to practice English, would I mind if he accompanied me? Where was I heading? He spoke passable English but soon lapsed into Spanish and it was my turn to ask the questions. What did he think of Columbus?

'Have you seen the monument? It cost 500 million pesos, money which should have been used for the poor. And how much went into bribes?' I nudge him back to my subject. 'The Spaniards brought good things. Crops, sugar-cane, but they took our gold, or at least most of it. There are still some mines left. And the Tainos died out, though we have some of their words in our language.'

Do Dominicans have Taino blood? 'We have French, African, Spanish and Haitian blood. You know there's a village in the west where everyone has smooth, black hair and golden brown skin.'

Had he been there? 'No.' Nor had he visited Haiti. He hadn't had the time, had a wife and three children between the ages of eight and twelve. By his hair and dark mottled complexion I had thought he was in his late fifties or early sixties, but he couldn't be more than 45.

We approached the President's Residence on Maximo Gomez, a modest white mansion outshone by its pompous neighbour which belongs to the Papal Nuncio. Who will he vote for?

'Peña, because he's for the poor. I will tell you about this man,' indicating the house, 'when we've passed it.'

I knew Peña as a dark mulatto, an earnest man past middle age, who had contested and, it was generally agreed, won the 1994 election against Balaguer. He was a populist of the left.

A jeep and half a dozen soldiers loitered on the sidewalk which was being swept by a dwarf wearing a red and white PEY-NADO/BALAGUER baseball cap. 'There's a small circle around the President,' said Johnny, 'who've taken millions of dollars outside the country. He knows they're at it but he turns away his eye. He's as guilty as they are. We need a change.'

And Peynado, Balaguer's young candidate? 'He drinks from the same cow.'

Will they fix the election as they did in 1994? 'No, there are international observers, and we're past that.'

As we arrived at the museum, he said, 'Afterwards, I'll take you to Chinatown. I'll show you the supermarkets and we'll have a beer.'

I shook his hand and thanked him for accompanying me, but I would be hours in the museum and would then return to the hotel for a swim. Should I offer him some money for a beer? While the thought was settling in my mind, he helped me out. 'I am a poor man. Will you buy me a beer?'

The Museum of Dominican Man is a spacious modern building whose exhibits have some difficulty in living up to its lofty expectations. I was practically alone in this vastness except for classes of school-children dressed in the sky-blue shirts or blouses and tan trousers or skirts, the uniform for the nation's state schools. A museum guide led them through at a good pace, stopping just once in each room to announce: 'The Tainos carved petroglyphs which are rock-carvings.' To which the entire class would repeat, 'The Tainos...' Older children carried notebooks and a few would become absorbed by a case of Taino implements, lagging behind, until herded back to the group by their teacher. Evidently independent, unguided study was not encouraged.

The early rooms are a mixture of Indian, African and Spanish objects, the Indian always identified as Taino, forgetting the contribution of the aboriginal Ciboneys and the Ciguayos and Macorixes who coexisted with the Taino majority. Perhaps archaeologists have had difficulty in ascribing finds to specific groups. Parallels are drawn with Arawak tribes surviving in Darien or, in the case of their African heritage, with the Yorubas of Nigeria and Dahomey. The Cohoba ritual is presented in depth, the Tainos snorting ground seeds of *anadenthera peregrina* but, for some reason, the ball game *batey* is not mentioned. Stone zemis are abundant. There is a fine and very rare example of a rocking-horse-sized anthropomorphic zemi carved from dark *guayacan* wood, so dense that it sinks in sea water. It must have been a similar zemi which Columbus reported was connected by a hollow cane to a bush outside the 'prayer-house', from where the cacique tricked his people into thinking the zemi spoke.

The later rooms exhibit contemporary Carnival costumes, a peasant's hut and such daily items which bring tears of nostalgia to the city folk of Santo Domingo and tears of desperation to villagers, assuming they have the ten pesos to spend on the museum's admission. Outside the main entrance is a statue of Enriquillo, a legendary Taino hero (of whom more later), who could have walked out of *Dancing with Wolves*.

The Toyota Starlet had 106,000 kilometres on the clock, a loose transmission and a worn clutch and accelerated in little jerks into the flow of Avenida J. F. Kennedy. But it was air-conditioned, which compensated for its mechanical debilities. I passed a series of billboards advertising a travel agency: *Viajes Caribe – Manhatten – Queens – Bronx*, one-way tickets, I imagine, since Dominicans are now the largest immigrant group in New York. Leaving Santo Domingo at the toll booth on the main road north, I picked up two policemen, one dressed in fatigues and the other in a T-shirt and jeans. They were on furlough and the one beside me – he introduced himself as Miguel – carried a shoe-box. He showed me the beautifully finished black army boots (size 10), which cost 600 pesos, a gift to his father from his Lieutenant.

After a while I asked them about the Tainos, but drew a blank. Where did I come from – Italy? Puerto Rico? They were both interested in the martial arts and discussed the merits of jujitsu, kung fu, karate (the boy in jeans in the back seat was a brown belt), judo and tae kwon do, Miguel's preference. With their tight, muscular bodies and clipped hair, they reminded me of boys from the parachute regiment who marched through Córdoba during Holy Week soon after Franco's death.

Did they have much crime to deal with? 'No, the Dominican Republic has less crime than anywhere else in the world,' I was told from the back seat.

'Oh, come off it,' said Miguel.

'If you walk down a street in America with a thick gold chain, they'll rip it off you.'

'Try walking the streets of Santo Domingo like that.'

In England the police don't carry guns. 'Try that here and the criminals would arrest us!' said the boy in the back seat.

They discussed police methods, a new computer with which they can correct a photo for a beard, a moustache or long hair. Identifications had soared. Were the Haitian immigrants a special problem? 'No. They have their criminal element, but they're normal people, like us.'

We drove up through hills covered in a mantle of dark greens, so unbelievably lush to an eye accustomed to the browns of the Castilian meseta and the hard dry summers in Andalusia, that it is no wonder Columbus wrote: *It is the most beautiful country I have ever seen.* I let off the boy in the back seat at the junction for San Francisco de Macoris. Alone now with Miguel, I asked him why he had chosen to become a policeman.

'At first I didn't like the idea. Country people don't like the police, but I sat the exams. It was a way to meet new people. Now I like it.' His family are peasant farmers. Who did he want to win the Presidential elections?

'As a *militar* I shouldn't have an opinion, but I do have a preference. We need more education, more help for the poor.' These are code words for Peña. 'I'm afraid there might be disturbances.' Might they try to fix the ballot like they did in 1994? 'Yes. I was guarding a polling booth then, and they didn't want us to take the ballot box away.'

He asked me where I was going. To La Vega Vieja, the remains of the fort which Columbus built in 1494. 'They say the Virgin de las Mercedes raised the ruins from the ground.' They revere the Virgin in the nearby church of Santo Cerro. 'I'll show you the way if you like. I have the time because I have the whole weekend free.' I thanked him for the offer. I would have liked his company but his family were expecting him. We arrived at his turnoff, a dirt road leading into fields high with sugar cane. Could I take him home? 'I appreciate the offer, but it is out of your way and I know that every minute is precious when you're travelling.'

Off the main highway a road climbs over the adjoining hills, now cleared for cattle-grazing but decorated still with clumps of trees which afford shade for man and beast. Running down the other side, a broad valley of fields, filled to the brim with the green tones of sugar cane, maize, cocoa trees and other crops, spreads as far as the distant mountains, which rise in a bluish hue. Columbus saw it and immediately called it La Vega Real, the Royal Valley. The remains of the Fortaleza de la Concepción, which Columbus ordered to be built in 1494, was being excavated at a Dominican pace. A fat man slept on a bench in the shade of a mango tree, and I entered a wooden hut which was supposed to be a library. There were no books, but it was a good place to write up my notebook, or so I thought before I was attacked by vicious mosquitoes.

Set on a ledge between the hills and the plain, Columbus's fortress-village commands a view and, more to the point, the natural route between the Vega Real and Cibao, to the south. Though nearly everything was destroyed by an earthquake in 1564, a thick brick bastion about six-foot high survives. It would hold ten men with ease and is pierced with loops for harquebusiers and crossbowmen. The ground plan of about twenty stone and clay houses and a church have been cleared in an orchard of mandarin, orange, mango and a single, dying breadfruit tree. Banana palms, like ungainly orangutans, throng on all sides, replacing sugar-cane which is in decline. To compensate, banana exports have risen fivefold in the last ten years. Of course, all these fruit-bearing trees were imported after 1492, so the mind has to blot them out and substitute them with pines, huge, knotty *guayacums* and broad, acacia-like red-flowering *flamboyans*.

From his writings, Columbus never seems to have left his caravels, but here in this isolated stronghold Columbus and Roldán reached an agreement which put an end to the first rebellion in the Indies. Here Fray Ramon Pané baptized 'Juan Mateo', and here were planted the first sugar canes in America, the crop which would make the West Indies wealthy, inducing the French to part with Canada rather than lose their Caribbean islands. At the end of his life, Columbus remembered this broad valley with such love that in his will he requested that they *build a chapel in the place which I found, which is La Vega, called La Concepción,* an extraordinary request from a man so attached to the sea.

On the edge of the banana plantation, a stone's throw from the fortress, lies a *bohio*, built exactly as the Tainos built their houses: a bleached palm-leaf roof sits on a few thick tree-trunks or branches, filled in with upright poles thrust into the ground to take the weight of the palm-leafed overhang. Two boys wandered in to take fruit from a mandarin tree and I ambled to the wells, dropping stones to confirm that they'd dried out.

The road from La Vega deteriorates. Only two lanes wide, a constant procession of trucks, buses and cars have taken their toll on its surface. Potholes abound and in the approaches to Santiago (a city of 600,000) they multiply to the point where no good surface is left, and the traffic has to negotiate it at walking pace. There are no signposts, so navigation depends on the help of fellow drivers or the occasional policeman. My objective was the site of Columbus's first intentional settlement in America, the much-maligned Isabela.

According to my road-map, off the main road to Montecristo I could turn north for Hidalgos and Isabela (a modern town) and cross the River Bajabonico to reach El Castillo and the ruins of Columbus's Isabela. On the ground, the route wasn't so simple. As I drove towards Montecristo, a dark wall of green mountains, whose peaks were lost in the clouds, separated me from my coastal destination. The road to Hidalgos was, amazingly, sign-posted at 17 kilometres. The road surface was rutted and broken, sometimes deteriorating (improving?) to a dirt track as it climbed into the mountains. It began to rain and the little Starlet struggled with the potholed inclines. Clusters of huts, painted in the luminescent pinks and greens so popular on this island, came and went, with dark faces peering out of open doorways. Banana palms sprouted between the huts like immense weeds which no one could be bothered to hack down. The descent through the pass, which Columbus's men had called Los Hidalgos, was equally difficult for the little car, but after an hour I entered muddy streets and clapboard houses, roofed with palm-leafs, which went by the name of Hidalgos. Plastic pennants in favour of Peynado, Leonel Fernández (a clean-cut light-complexioned mulatto bearing a strong resemblance to Eddie Murphy) and Peña were draped across the main road like bunting at Carnival. I came to a fork in the road and stopped to ask a tall, heavy man the way to Isabela.

'I'm going there. If you like I'll show you the way.'

We set off and he asked me my destination. I told him. 'But you can't get through with a car, there's the river.'

We stopped to look at my map. I pointed out the thick black line which promised a 'Secondary Road' linking Isabela with El Castillo. 'They're building the bridge.'

I turned round, my heart heavy with the thought of returning by the road I had so recently crossed with such difficulty. Once out of Hidalgo, the road seemed unfamiliar, though the thick vegetation, banana palms and clusters of bohíos were unchanged. On my map this new route promised a short cut to the other access to my Isabela, and the first town en route would be Guanico, at a distance of 10 kilometres. As the potholes were no worse than the other road, I decided to try it. After an hour and a quarter I had passed two villages not on my map and had yet to see any sign of Guanico. I had my doubts but reasoned that now I was on the Atlantic side of the mountains and heading east, I had to meet the main Santiago-Puerto Plata road, my immediate objective, which cuts north-south. Guanico suddenly announced its presence and I gave a cheer, stopped to ask directions out of the town, confirming that the road I planned to take really existed.

Within an hour I had arrived at Luperón, named after a General whose men had routed the Haitians, and ended up on the pier, looking out at the protected waters which Columbus called Río de Gracia. Not favoured because he noted, *it has a sand bank at the entrance, with only two cubits of water; inside is a good port but it has a lot of woodworm.* Yachts were anchored offshore in a well-protected bay, and their blond crews walked into the muddy streets of the town bewildered at being suddenly confronted by life in the raw. The customs post is an abandoned sentry box, still painted khaki, its door flung open and reeking of urine. I turned around to look for the road to Isabela and, to avoid a head-on collision, hit a palm frond which lay in the street. The car made a new, unpleasant scraping noise. The brakes? Transmission? A boy with a long staff waved me down. The palm frond had knocked the composite-rubber engine shield down on to a front tyre. We forced it back up, but the flange wouldn't grip its socket. Would it hold? The road was now smooth asphalt and I arrived at the site of Isabela shortly before it was due to close at six o'clock. I decided to stay the night at the Rancho Gran Sol Bed & Breakfast next door.

The view from the Gran Sol's terrace is the same as from Columbus's house at Isabela, and was the finest view I had seen on the island. Most sea views are exactly that – a strip of palm-lined beach and the sea. This view is dramatically different. Ahead, the mountain at Punta Rucia tumbles down to the sea in saw-toothed ridges, enclosing a bay which rushes in a gentle curve, past a river mouth and beaches white against the foliage, towards you. The water, limpid and quiet near in, grows in volume until, in the far distance whitecaps, whipped up by the prevailing easterlies, remind one of the protective site Columbus chose for Isabela.

The Rancho Gran Sol is run by a serene, slender Dominicana and a retiring Flem (Hermann) who avoided me, though Sonia prodded him forward – 'The Señor speaks Spanish and English' – to no avail. His vacant expression, white hair and stoop belonged to an old man, and contrasted with her youthful nature and healthy looks, though it's possible only a few years separate them. Though I had arrived in the high season, I was the only guest.

Thirsty and tired – I'd had nothing to eat or drink except for coconut juice since a seven-o'clock breakfast – I sat down with a bottle of Presidente. Sonia said, 'We had lots of people here when they were digging the site and building the church.' (There's a Temple to the Discovery nearby which is financed by a corporation) 'Archaeologists, the architect and construction engineer. We became friends. You know they were here for a long time.'

The Gran Sol was not mentioned in either of my travel guides. Would she like to note the address of their English and Spanish publishers? Without answering she showed me the *Gentleman's Guide to the Caribbean*, which recommends the 'luxury hotel run by Sonia and Hermann'. As the rooms have no hot water or air-conditioning and, by American standards, are small and spartan, luxury is not the adjective I'd chose to describe the Gran Sol. 'The German Consul was here and he's written a book about the Dominican Republic and we're in it. It will be published in German and Spanish this year. I'm sure it will be, because he's an official, from the Government. You know people have come and said we'd be in their books, but,' and with a gentle shrug of her shoulders, 'later, nothing.' I had told her I was here on holiday.

She handed me the key attached to a slab of mahogany on which was carved a Taino motif, a zemi's face. Had she taken the design from a petroglyph? 'No, I saw it somewhere and it seemed appropriate. You won't take it with you, will you? Sometimes people take them as souvenirs.' She showed me a key on brass key-ring. 'This one was taken by a Canadian couple. I ran after them, but they had gone.'

At the bottom of their neatly laid out garden is the beach and the sea. A forty-foot catamaran, its Genoa rig, short mast and slender hulls reminding me of our old catamaran *Gemini*, was anchored offshore. I swam out to it, but if it was occupied, they were down below, so I swam along to Isabela, relishing the silence and the natural state of the coastline. Dugout canoes were pulled up on the far beach, exactly where Taino villagers who had lived on Isabela's site would have beached theirs, beneath the outcrop jutting into the sea.

Dinner was a curious affair. My single place was laid at one end of the large terrace beside a noisy parrot, and Sonia and Hermann's at the other end. Hermann hid behind a voluminous vase of fresh-cut flowers and leaves, and they conversed in Flemish and the parrot squawked. The cook served me dorada fried in butter, a spicy sauce and a bowl each of boiled potatoes and lettuce which could have satisfied a family of six. I ate slowly, reading about Patrick Leigh Fermor's travels through the Caribbean in the late Forties. Unfortunately, he omitted publishing his experiences in the Dominican Republic, because his lack of Spanish had prevented him from conversing with its people. His description of Haiti is so different from my view of the Dominican republic that they seemed to live in different hemispheres, inconceivable they could share an island smaller than Ireland. When I had finished eating, Sonia asked if I'd like coffee. Hermann had gone to bed. What time would I like breakfast? At nine, ten? I had got into the habit of rising early and I suggested seven o' clock. We compromised on eight.

From my room, I heard gulls and cicadas fighting for attention, drowning the gentle whirl of the roof fan. I had almost fallen asleep when the thumping rhythm of merengue blasted through the night air. At first I couldn't believe it. The nearest hamlet is two kilometres away, yet this sounded as if it came from next door, and not from the direction of Hermann and Sonia. After a few minutes, someone put a stop to it and I slept.

I was woken by rain drumming on the corrugated iron roof. How Columbus's men must have suffered in their partly-built town, soaked by these downpours and exposed, unlike me with my mosquito netting, to relentless attacks of mosquitoes. Had they spread over their exposed skin the herbal juice the Tainos used to repel insects? Once they had taken Taino women and seen its effect, I suppose they would have. After a while the rain settled into a less furious rhythm and a bird – a blue heron? – took up a deep cackle from some point nearby. It was 1.15 a.m.

At 6.30 it was light and, to make time until breakfast, I walked under a blowzy sky to the beach and back, cutting through the garden. On my return I met the gardener, a thin silent man grooming a horse he kept in an improvised paddock. We exchanged greetings and I noticed that beyond the main buildings is an outhouse, where I assumed the gardener and his young daughters, two lightly-coloured mulattas with lively brown eyes, lived. This would explain the merengue.

Breakfast was very Flemish. Only the ubiquitous guava jam, from the fruit used by the Tainos to treat diarrhoea, was native Dominican. Hermann said, 'Good morning,' before donning his glasses and staring out at the view, with pleasure I do believe. When I went to pay, Sonia informed me that she had misquoted the nightly rate and that my stay would cost 50 pesos less. She asked me for my travel guides, carefully noting their long, foreign addresses.

I was the day's first visitor at the site of Isabela. A guide is obligatory and Manuel, in his late teens, was an enthusiastic and well-informed companion. Sonia had told me that Trujillo had given orders to clean up the site of Isabela for some visiting Spanish archaeologists, and his men had taken him at his word. They brought in bulldozers and raised the ruins. This was in 1959. The *Gentleman's Guide to the Caribbean* picked up the story and added another twist. The bulldozers had 'removed 80 cm. of topsoil'. Was this true? 'Yes, some of the walls here stood 1.50 m. high and look at them now.' When Lieutenant Colvocoresses of the U.S. Navy rediscovered the site in 1891, some of the walls were four feet high and three mounds of stones, which he thought were the remains of Martello Towers, three feet high. His native guide said that, as a child, the walls had been much higher, but that stones had been removed by visiting ships. Carlos Dobal, who visited Isabela with his father in 1966 and again in 1971, wrote, 'The condition of the site filled us with sorrow. Everything [since 1966] has been raised to the ground. The vegetation is burnt. The few stones... have been completely dispersed.' This had nothing to do with Trujillo's bulldozers (he was assassinated in 1961) but with the value of building stone. For centuries, masons in Puerto Plata have been bringing in stone from Isabela; Carlos Dobal even requested the Government to halt the imminent destruction of a house built with stones from the site. Dobal and his team had the stone blocks returned to Isabela.

It takes little imagination to visualize the early months of the fortified village perched on an outcrop into the calm, clear water of the bay. The Tainos, naked but for a loin cloth, came in canoes, which they beached beside the Spaniard's longboats, to exchange yucca, fish, peppers, beans and their succulent dogs for beads, scissors, mirrors and the tiny brass hawks-bells Columbus had laid out for inspection. They clustered around the stone and mortar church and house, fascinated by the metal tools used by masons and carpenters and the curved clay tiles baked in a fire, wandered past the cluster of pole and thatch huts occupied by smelly bearded men wearing cloth to protect their white flesh from the sun, some lying ill, groaning and sweating in the shade. And beside their cemetery, the number of fresh graves, each with its crossed stick, testified to the short life of these men. Their shaman, for all their powdered remedies and assortment of magic implements, were so unsuccessful at curing their people that one wondered why their families and friends didn't gouge out their eyes or tear out their genitals. The Tainos knew that in the southwest of the island, where the rains often failed, men dug canals to irrigate their fields. But here, where the rains rarely failed, these white men expended enormous effort on a canal to bring water from the nearby river to the village. But then they drunk so much, just as they ate. Columbus, observing his half-built town and the harmless, friendly Tainos drawn to Isabela, inspecting the simplest tool and work with curiosity, the great bay *which would hold all the ships in the world*, the newly planted fields beside the nearby river, *better than the Guadalquivir,* and inhaling the fresh sea air, could imagine the wealth Hispaniola, thirty times the size of the greatest of the Canary Islands and infinitely more populous, would bring to him and the Spanish crown.

Manuel showed me Isabela's museum, a good collection of Spanish and Taino relics and the site which I described in Chapter Eleven. What did he think of Columbus and the Tainos? 'I think he was instigated by others to do what he did.' These carefully chosen words, designed to offend no one, did not hide his sympathy for the Tainos. Standing in the middle of what was once Columbus's house, so modest compared to the mansions raised a few years later in Santo Domingo, my heart went out to Columbus. He gave his life to discovery but it was the Crown, appointed Governors, including his son Diego, the slave-trader Garay, the fortune hunter Bastidas and the official Fonseca who enjoyed its fruits.

Driving to Puerto Plata I winced at every pothole the little Starlet hit, waiting for its engine shield to drop on to the offside front tyre. Economic progress is noticeable everywhere: just as mules are giving away to mopeds, so palm-thatch is giving way to corrugated iron and clapboard to breeze-blocks. Traffic overwhelms the main Santo Domingo-Puerto Plata highway, with the surface near Puerto Plata reduced to ponds and moguls which have to be negotiated at walking pace. The entrance to the city is off-putting; rubbish tips, litter, filthy stalls, half washed away by the previous night's rainstorm, sitting beside rusting wrecks provide the welcoming committee to the nations leading tourist resort. I cut down to the Malecón, a boulevard beside the sea, where palms, beaches, a magnificent 16th-century fort and a turquoise sea are the material from which Caribbean posters are made, even if, geographically speaking, the sea is the Atlantic. Columbus passed the site of Puerto Plata on his first voyage, naming the 793- metre mountain rising behind it Monte Plata. *At the foot of the mountain is a fine port, with fourteen cubits at the entrance.* Today it is the second port of the Republic, provided with tall derricks loading freighters moored alongside a vast, concrete quay.

I had a lunch of crab *yaniqueques*, pasties, and fresh pineapple juice under the shade of a magnolia, next to Dominican families lounging in their swimwear, just a few feet from the beach. Opposite, large hotels set in pleasant gardens face the sea and the Malecón while the rest of the town is a mess of rutted roads, stalls and shanty towns emitting a vaguely sweet putrid smell, smells in the tropics nearly always reminding one of decay. Once out of the city, heading east, the road improves and occasional entrances, controlled by armed guards, signify the beginning of resorts for the mainly European tourists who fly in to the nearby airport. They are told it is dangerous to venture beyond the compound, a self-interested warning since it keeps the tourists' dollars within the confines of the hotel.

I drove on to Sosúa to see the twin town of El Batey, named after a field on which it was believed the Tainos played their ball game, founded by German Jews fleeing the Nazis in 1940. Some Jewish writers, clutching at Columbus's Jewish origins, speculate that he wanted to discover lands which Spanish Jews could colonize. Although there is no evidence to support this theory, the Americas were to become as much a refuge for Europeans as an extension of European civilization, hemmed in by the Turks to the east and the Arabic-speaking peoples to the south; and it became a refuge for the Jewish people, beginning with Sephardic colonies in Brazil, exiled from Portugal on the orders of John II. When the pressure of the Inquisition became too much for them, they moved to the Dutch colonies, which made them welcome.

My road-map indicated a Synagogue on Dr. Rosen Street but, though a number of small bungalows made from breeze-blocks, clapboard and corrugated iron dated from the period, I found no Synagogue. No one I asked had heard of it. Sosúa-Batey is thick with Germans, and the former Jewish colony is surrounded with German enterprises – bed & breakfasts called Annelisa's and Koch's, a tavern called Bayerische Belgarten, Erich Breilinger Immobilien, Dr. Quax Deutsche Bar, Arquitectur Bürt Bauenternehonen. 500,000 German tourists came to the Republic last year, more than from any other country, but El Batey, with its streets filled with mud and water, raised wooden sidewalks alternating with muddy paths and hastily-erected buildings, which would be carried away in the next hurricane, was resolutely Dominican. The sixth person I asked directed me to the Synagogue.

'They came here in 1940 and founded this town. There weren't many, but they have become rich, running some of our biggest industries,' said the narrow-faced man, greying and past middle age. 'But they don't live here anymore. The museum is interesting and there's a Jewish cemetary.'

The Synagogue's clapboard walls, narrow verandah and corrugated-iron roof are typically Dominican. Only its shape, in the form of an upturned hull, and the small, stained-glass windows are unusual. They had painted it in Star-of-David blue. Set in a pleasant garden of lawns and herbaceous borders, I opened the gate and walked around the back towards the museum. The guard from the neighbouring warehouse ran in after me to tell me it was closed until the following afternoon. Through the plate-glass windows, I could see the exhibits, all family photographs and texts. The guard said they were making a film.

My hotel was full of Germans, Americans, Dutch and English. Over dinner, surrounded by sunburnt honeymoon couples and pensioners munching international cuisine, I felt as if I had been lifted out of the Dominican Republic and deposited in a purgatory for the well heeled. Yet, as in Spain thirty years earlier, it was these tourists who were the key to the Dominicans' economic future.

I left early for my room to read about the Tainos, Ciguayos and Macorixes. Both Ciguayos and Macorixes, when it came to the Spanish conquest, put up greater resistance than the Taino majority. The Ciguayos were the first Indians to confront Columbus at the Baia de Flechas (Bay of Arrows), on the Samaná peninsular. The Macorixes, like the Ciguayos, had long-bows and heavier arrows than the Tainos and the last Indian rebellion took place in their territory, to the east, in the mountains which led down into the Vega Real. Yet it is the Tainos whose memory has lodged in the subconscious of the Dominicans.

Even by the turbulent standards of the Caribbean, the Dominican Republic's history is out of the ordinary. After the first flush of gold and *encomiendas* brought thousands of Spaniards to the island in the first decades of the Sixteenth century, with all the organizational intentions attested to by the fine colonial city of Santo Domingo, the island fell into a slumber relieved only by national disasters until well into the Nineteenth century. By the 1560s the Spaniards numbered only a couple of thousand, the Indians were extinct and the tiny economy, now based on sugar cane, depended on African slaves. But the Africans were a rebellious lot. An ever-expanding group of fugi-

247

tive slaves formed guerrilla groups, the *cimarrones*, who operated in mountainous areas. To deter flight, slave-owners devised several apparatuses, among them a metal neck-lock fixed to the slave with a wire loop rising above his head from which dangled goat bells, so that he could be located in the midst of tall sugar canes or out in the forest.

The incursions of pirates combined with the reduced Spanish population (so dramatic that in 1526 the Crown tried to impose the death penalty on any Spaniard who left the island) obliged the Governor in Santo Domingo to abandon the north and west coasts of the island in 1605. In 1586 the capital itself was sacked by a British squadron under the command of Drake. By 1630 France had taken the island of Tortuga, just off the northwest coast, and corsairs had begun to establish plantations in the western part of the island. In 1697 Spain recognized the French settlement in what is now Haiti, thus dividing the island in two. The French exploited Sainte-Domingue, bringing in African slaves to work the plantations, so that by the end of the Eighteenth Century the population of the western, French third of the island, at nearly 600,000, outnumbered the Spanish two-thirds by ten to one. It needed but a small push from Revolutionary France for Spain to cede the rest of the island. Within six years Toussaint Louverture's black troops had overrun the united island, burning plantations and terrorizing the white settlers. This initiated two hundred years of enmity between Haiti and the Dominican Republic.

With the aid of a British fleet, Spain recovered its old colony only to lose it twelve years later, in 1822, to Jean Pierre Boyer's black army of Haitians. The Haitian occupation, which lasted twenty-two years, is remembered by Dominicans as an unmitigated humiliation. The Haitians broke the Church's ties with Rome, usurped all important posts and tried to obliterate Hispanic culture by closing the University. They even objected to the royal emblems worked into Dominican buildings and had them cut out. Western culture came to a full stop, though, as his apologists point out, Boyer did abolish slavery. Under the leadership of Juan Pablo Duarte, known as the Father of the Nation, the Haitians were expelled, this time for good. But Duarte was soon in exile and a series of dictators dominated Dominican political life until Trujillo was assassinated in 1961.

To seek protection from Haitian ambitions, Dominican leaders twice tried to return sovereignty to a protecting power. For four years in the 1860s, Spain returned, at the invitation of General Santana, but that fell to a public uprising. Then President Baéz tried to unite the country with the United States. Though President Grant favoured its annexation, the Senate, disgusted by a land scandal on the island, voted it down. The Republic suffered ninety more years of dictatorship, interspersed with the occasional popularly-elected President whose liberal intentions soon saw him murdered, exiled or merely evicted by a coup d'etat. In a harking back to the days when a committee of Jeronymite priests ruled the Spanish possessions, an archbishop, Adolfo Nouel, held the presidency for a brief four months in 1912. Civil wars spluttered into life, fed by political iniquity and prolonged by the inefficiency and disunity of the country's armed forces.

American meddling, which began when the U.S. took over the Customs in 1905 to control its revenues, has caused remarkably little anti-Americanism among the cheerful, decorous Dominicans. The first occupation, lasting from 1916 to 1924, brought a modernized infrastructure and a unified, organized Gendarmerie whose successors include my two hitchhiking policemen. Having organized the country, the Americans departed to be succeeded six years later by one of the finest examples of the abuse of power known to man. Rafael Trujillo came to power at the head of the military in 1930 and relinquished it with his death in 1961. Everything had to belong to Trujillo, symbolized by the renaming of Santo Domingo as Ciudad Trujillo.

Haitian immigrants – attracted by the relative wealth of the Dominican Republic and work on the sugar plantations – have been seen by leaders of a dictatorial inclination as a problem which needs to be solved. In 1937 Trujillo had about 10,000 rounded up and killed. By then Haiti was no longer the threat it had been: its population outnumbered the Dominicans by only three million to two and, thanks to a century devoted to anarchy and misrule, its once mighty economy lay in ruins.

Trujillo's death was, four years later, followed by a popular uprising quelled by the Marines whose Commander-in-Chief,

Lyndon B. Johnson, was obsessed with the recent memory of Castro's revolution, the Cuban missile crisis and the even more pressing fight against Communists in Vietnam. The Marines stayed just a year. Since then regular elections have alternated power between the Revolutionary Dominican Party and the Social Christian Reform Party in the person of Joaquin Ballaguer, a one-time Trujillo lackey. While for many years Balaguer played the political game on its own terms, his last three victories (1986, 1990 and 1994) have been narrowing to the point where ballot stuffing became the deciding factor. In 1991 Balaguer had a go at the Haitian immigrant 'problem' by the simple expedient of expelling all those under 16 or over 60, though with 28% unemployment and a population growing by 2.2% a year (the Republic's population now outnumbers Haiti's by 1.3 million), the country is not in a good position to take in outsiders.

Abandoned by Spain, against whom it has fought two revolutions, and invaded twice by Haiti and twice by the United States, the Dominicans have looked to their Taino roots – even if culturally and sanguinarily they have been diluted away to virtually nothing. Their Taino figurehead is Enriquillo, whose bronze statue stands bold and strong in a loin cloth outside the Museum of Dominican Man. He has been elevated to the status of a Boadicea by the Dominicans. So who was Enriquillo?

Enriquillo came from a *nitaino* (minor noble) family and was orphaned when Ovando's forces massacred the Xaragua Tainos in 1503. Franciscan friars brought up the boy as a Christian, taught him to read and write in Spanish and were favourably impressed by his intelligence and piety. Now in his teens, Enriquillo married a Taino girl, Mencía, and both he and his wife were allocated to an *encomendero* by the name of Valenzuela. Valenzuela took a fancy to Mencía, exercising his seignorial rights to keep her as his concubine. After confronting Valenzuela, and receiving a beating for his pains, Enriquillo fled to the mountains at the head of some other Indians and African slaves. The year is 1519. From then on the official history, first propagated by Bartolomé de Las Casas needing and, so he believed, discovering in Enriquillo a symbol of the Indian's proud and sporting resistance to the conquistador, is a mixture of fact and fiction.

According to Las Casas and official Dominican history, Enriquillo led a rebellion, holding the Spaniards at bay for fourteen years, using the classic techniques of guerrilla (the word is used by Las Casas) warfare. He cut out the tongues of his domestic animals so their bleating couldn't give him away, lit fires in caves so as not to reveal his refuge and stayed in remote mountain hideouts, protected by a system of lookouts, from where he would plan the ambush of Spanish forces sent out to capture him. Villages on the edge of the lake, which now bears his name, provided him and his men with food. He was constantly on the move. Enriquillo would send out small hunting and fishing parties, kept in ignorance of his whereabouts in case they were captured. After destroying a force of eighty Spaniards under the captaincy of Valenzuela, his old *encomendero*, who fled the island in shame, Indians flocked to his banner, so that Enriquillo had three hundred men at his command.

Finally, after spending a fortune on expeditionary forces which failed to trap him, the Spanish Crown offered Enriquillo a truce in 1533. This is when Las Casas met him, describing him as: *A tall and graceful man, with a well-proportioned body; his face was neither handsome nor ugly, but he seemed to be grave and stern.* Enriquillo won freedom for himself and his followers and was raised to the position of a District Commissioner, though four centuries would pass before he was elevated to the rank of a national hero.

Martínez Almánzar, a Dominican historian, has sifted through documents of the period and punctured the myth of Enriquillo. From 1519 to 1526 no one even mentions Enriquillo or his rebellion. In 1526 Enriquillo, who had been living peacefully in the mountains, was besieged by one of the forces sent out to put down armed uprisings mainly directed by fugitive African slaves. He asked for a truce, which Captain San Miguel conceded. Enriquillo broke the truce soon afterwards, attacking San Miguel's farm where he killed the Christianized Indians and stole women and horses. For the next couple of years his was one of many small bands which threatened the Spanish settlers, but he is not mentioned between 1529 and 1533 when, presumably, he was inactive. Captain Barrionuevo met him in 1533, when Enriquillo had about 400 followers, and negotiated his surrender. Enriquillo agreed to end the war, hand over fugitive black slaves, for which he would receive a reward, and return Indians to their feudal masters. In exchange, the Spaniards gave him cattle for his family and a village which a Spaniard could enter only on pain of death. Shortly before meeting Las Casas, Enriquillo had handed over a shipload of fugitive slaves to their Spanish masters.

For the remainder of 1533 and 1534, Enriquillo became a bounty hunter, leading what was effectively a rural police force under Spanish supervision. Not only did he turn in fugitive slaves, but he also asked to hunt down the Ciguayo rebel chief Tamayo. He died of tuberculosis in 1535, aged perhaps 36, after confessing and taking the holy sacrament. *Cimarrones* destroyed the village Enriquillo secured for his people, taking vengeance for his bounty-hunting activities.

Martínez Almánzar adds: 'The actions of the Negroes, Diego de Ocampo, Sebastian Lamba and so many others, appear in a partial manner in some writings. But this aspect of our history is still taboo in Dominican schools.' Nations have an insatiable appetite for national heroes and the Dominican Republic, with so few *bona fide* candidates, have settled on a perfectly innocuous figure in the Christian Taino Enriquillo.

On the road to Santo Domingo, it is impossible to appreciate the wonderful views of the greenest, most fertile land I have seen. Potholes, which would break an axle, keep your eye fixed to the road, minibuses, trucks, mules drive in from the right with little respect for something as small as my Toyota Starlet, and trucks and buses have a nasty habit of coming to a sudden, unannounced halt. My breaks made a new scraping noise and required a lot of effort on the pedal. Leaving Puerto Plata, tall, rich green sugar-cane shoots throng the hillsides, bending with the wind and disappearing darkly up through the clouds.

Approaching Santiago, banana plantations take over, stubby trunks on which huge leaves sprout like flags raised by an over-enthusiastic patriot. Rows of shacks appear, before which are planted twisting yuccas, their hard leaves ending in a crimson point as sharp as a bloodied dagger. Suddenly there's a clearing and a copse of coconut palms, tall and elegant with their bulbous green fruit hanging heavily beneath palm fronds, curving out high above the surrounding bushes. The soil is so fertile, the rain so frequent, that fence posts sprout shoots and grow into fully fledged trees. Between Santiago and La Vega a roadside market distracts the motorist. Each vendor places his produce as close to the tarmac as he dares: pyramids of green oranges, coconut stalls surrounded by green husks slashed open by the blow of a machete, rickety wooden kiosks serving refried chicken, sausages and *yaniqueques*, plastic frontages announcing Pepsi Cola and stands of green bananas pointing upward, as they grow.

To celebrate my safe arrival in Santo Domingo, I took the little Starlet for a spin around the colonial area. I turned left to reach the new Avenida del Puerto when I was stopped by a policeman. He was short and plump, reminding me of the indolent, see-nothing policemen in Lisbon. I thought of my guidebook's warning to negotiate the fine for a 'so-called infraction' and pay it on the spot. The policeman shook my hand through the open window. His was heavily calloused, a farmer's hand.

'You're driving the wrong way up a one-way street,' he announced. He was right, I hadn't noticed the sign and I said so. He contemplated me, and I thought he was working out how much he could sock me for.

'How long have you been in the country?' I told him a week.

'Well, I think we can excuse you this time,' and he shook my hand again.

I stopped at the hotel, meeting a tall, handsome woman, in a Caribbean coloured trouser suit, talking into a mobile phone. She wore a thick white band falling from her right shoulder to her left hip, on which was printed *Miss República Dominicana*. I picked up the latest *Listin Diario* and there she was on the front page – Patricia Bayonet, the 1995 beauty queen. The night before half the jury had walked out, the father of a favoured contender (pictured crying into her handkerchief) warned he would sue the organizers... How do you run a country where they can't even agree on a beauty queen?

Finally I dropped off the Starlet and when the black man, as tall and athletic as a basketball player, asked how it had gone, I told him it needed a complete overhaul. He noted transmission, clutch, breaks, tyres, rear lights, engine-cover on a piece of paper and handed it to a mechanic dressed in a spotless boiler suit.

Cheerfully, he knocked 20% off my bill and suggested I try a *sancocho* at *El Conuco*. Then he called a radio taxi for me from Apolo, who have a thousand taxis driving around the city and a branch in the Bronx.

My unshaven taxi driver was about thirty, with the colour and features of a chubby Sancho Panza, a talkative fellow: 'This government has left the country in ruins. They've sucked it dry.' And who is responsible? 'Balaguer.' The solution? 'Not Peña, we've had him as Mayor, he allowed it to happen.' Peynado? 'He's new, but do you think he's going to change the party's habits? Anyway he was born a millionaire, he knows nothing of the poor.' This leaves Leonel Fernández, a well-known lawyer and leader of the Liberal Democratic Party. 'We must give him a chance, but this country has never had a clean election. Top men in the military want Peynado's party to win.' Their fingers are sticky? 'Exactly. We'll know on May 16th.'

My paper's headline reported the Controller-General revealing that 2,400 million pesos was missing from the Reserve Bank (vigorously denied by the Bank's President next day). That's nearly $200 million, a huge sum for a country of seven million people. The woman in the gift shop watched me keenly. 'In December they indicted the woman who was head of the Customs Service for embezzling 1,000 million pesos. She was in prison for a couple of months, then released. Oh, there were lots of protests, but they say they didn't have enough evidence. Now she lives in Miami.'

I took up the suggestion of my rental-car owner to dine on *sancocho* at El Conuco. Sancocho is a stew made from six different meats, plantains, rice and potatoes. The meat is mainly bone and, even with Creole sauce, I found the dish far too stodgy for my taste. But merengue dancing, sometimes twisting one-legged on the spout of a bottle of Drambuie (chosen for its square base), and music, all performed by the enthusiastic staff of El Conuco, made the visit worthwhile. I lit up a Prince – the Republic is a major exporter of cigars – fantastic value at 6 pesos, apprehensive at the possible reaction of a table of Americans nearby. But I needn't have worried. The sweet scent of my Caribbean cigar proved contagious and soon two of the men had even larger Princes between their lips. All the little band's instruments looked homemade: they consisted of a kettledrum, a ridged stainless steel water jug which, when rubbed vigorously with a metal spatula, gave off a sound like a rattle, a pewter plate banged in time with a large spoon, a tambourine and a steel tube curling away, like a French horn, from its mouthpiece and ending in a small trumpet giving out a high, wheezing note. To add volume and depth, they performed karaoke-style against a background of taped merengue. After only three *amor del Conuco*, made with rum, *chinola* (passion-fruit juice), sugar and lime, I was ready for my Apolo taxi and bed.

Though it had rained heavily overnight and I had woken to subdued light filtered through heavy cloud, it had all cleared by breakfast. The sun had soaked up the puddles around the pool and the tiled terrace was as polished as ever. Sadly, this was my last morning in the Republic. I had grown fond of Dominicans, of their polite Spanish, their openness and ease with which they would strike up a conversation. Though their country was poor and their earnings a fraction of an American or European's, they never let it develop into a grudge or quell their enthusiasm for life.

My Apolo taxi driver, Señor Mora, had the features of Lawrence Olivier and the colour of Othello. 'My father was Spanish and my mother African, that's why I'm so black.' We discussed the election and he was for Peña. 'He was Mayor of Santo Domingo, has lots of experience and good contacts abroad. A President needs that.' What does he think of Columbus's memorial? 'It's an important memorial for our country and brings in tourists. Tourists are good, they leave money here.' And Columbus? 'They say he was Spanish. He's the father of our country like Duarte. Duarte's father was Spanish and his mother Dominican but after leading us to victory over the Haitian oppressors on the 27th February 1844, the others seized him and forced him out of the country. They said they didn't want a Spaniard as President.'

He was reading Balaguer's biography of Duarte. 'He went to Venezuela, but I don't know if he came back. I haven't got that far.' He passed me the book and I flicked through the pages past his bookmark. Duarte never returned and died in Caracas. His remains were brought back to Santo Domingo in 1888.

'My father never learnt to read and write, because his family wouldn't send him to school. Those were the Trujillo days, they were crazy. My family kept him hidden and if the soldiers came, they hid him under a bed. In those days many people couldn't read and write,' (today 90% of adults are literate), 'and the authorities would give a letter to a man to take to the police. The letter said he was to be executed. Sometimes they just pitched them into a crevice.'

I mentioned the Tainos. 'We are descended from Tainos, Africans and Spanish. You see some people with this dead, flat hair. And their skins, it's a beautiful colour. They say the Spaniards loved Indian women.'

I had taken a sceptical view of the Dominican's conviction that they were partly descended from Taino Indians. Dominicans run the colour spectrum from Mediterranean olive to African ebony and their features covered the continuum from European to African, without any noticeable oriental influence. Martínez Almánzar's comment that aristocratic Dominicans falsely claimed to be descended from Taino and European stock, seemed to confirm my opinion. But, on my last full day in the Republic, I came across two Dominicans who could have walked out of an Indian reservation in Arizona or New Mexico. The first, an imposing woman in her sixties, joined a table of hotel residents at breakfast. The second was my taxi driver, a permanent smile creased to his face, with the mild, slightly lilting tones so typical of Dominicans' speech. He was a Peynado supporter, 'His party has robbed us,' he admitted, 'but at least they've spent part of it on the country, and spent it well. You never know what the others might do.'[34]

He left me at the Faro de Colón, a hundred-metre long stone cross lying on its front, rising to a height of nearly thirty metres. Huge slabs are engraved with an evangelizing message from Pope John Paul, quotes from the Old Testament, Plato, Aristotle and Seneca which inspired Columbus, from Isabella and Columbus himself. One slab offers a homage to:

'The memory of the man who, with his vision, courage and faith, transformed the world and humanity'.

The monument is set in a park green with lawns and *flamboyan* trees running down to the sea, Columbus's true home.

Though the monument's exterior is too massive and austere to please the eye, it has captured the force of faith and seamanship – the cross rises along its length, imitating the upward curving deck of a seagoing vessel – that drove Columbus forward.

Inside, under the cross-piece, four naval ratings guard Columbus's tomb. A lead coffer sits behind a marble-fronted mausoleum, dating from 1892, protected by four bronze gates, before which stand the naval guard of honour. His coat of arms and his name – simply COLÓN – decorate the upper part of the mausoleum. The long arm of the cross is split in two, each side enclosing a series of rooms, on two floors, devoted to the Discovery of America. Nations from China to Israel have left exhibits from the Quincentenary. Only the British is empty, though its place is occupied by Spanish armour of the period, set against the backdrop of an unfurled Union Jack.

I could not think of anyone, other than a head of state or founder of a religion who, after 500 years, has such a large and well-guarded memorial to his life, and it is exactly where Columbus would have wished it, on his beloved island of Hispaniola. It is known as *El Faro de Colón*, 'Columbus's Lighthouse'.

What had my research revealed about Columbus? Columbus was a far more purposeful and constant man than he is generally given credit for. His concept of the world depended on intuition, experience gained at sea and the Atlantic ports, and, of course, Marco Polo's *Travels*. As early as 1477, at the age of twenty-six, he planned to make a great voyage westward across the supposedly uncrossable Ocean Sea, and undertook long sea voyages – to Guinea, Iceland and the Azores – which can best be explained by a desire to probe the extremities of the known world. By 1495, if not earlier, he extended his plan to circumnavigate the World, something he never abandoned until his death twenty-one years later. From very early on, with his sailor's nose for the sea, he realized that, to pick up a following wind, any discovery fleet had to set out from one of the Atlantic islands of the Iberian powers. For Columbus it was not a matter of opening up trade routes or converting the Chinese to Christianity, but an explorer's desire to discover *the secrets of this world,* as he so aptly wrote. Claims that his real motive was to enrich himself quickly break up on the rock of his eight or nine years importuning, no better off than a beggar, the Courts of Portugal and Castile. It was the explorer, with the romantic ideal of discovery almost for discovery's sake, that egged him on and led him to describe the people and the habitat he encountered at such length to Isabella and Ferdinand. Riches – whether they be in the form of gold, mastic, slaves, logwood or medicinal rhubarb – had to be promised and later delivered to Princes, without whom his venture was doomed.

Though his knowledge of the sea led him to scorn philosophers and mere seamen and his self-confidence in maritime affairs must have been infuriating to courtiers and scholars whose knowledge of ships ended at the nearest wharf, Columbus could be remarkably persuasive. He spoke well, knew the risks of ocean sailing and was evidently sincere; if the Courts of John and Ferdinand and his Genoese and Florentine investors wanted to know what he'd bring back, well everyone knew about Indian spices, pearls and gems and Cipangu's gold. He could offer Isabella the chance of converting the Chinese and both monarchs the chance of extending their prestige by discovering new lands and trade routes. If the commissions in Lisbon and Salamanca wanted scholarly support, he gathered it from whatever source came to hand, to the dismay of the scholars of his – and our – day. No wonder the bookworm historian is appalled by his 'inconsistencies' and 'half-baked scholarship'. Curiously, the one scholar who profoundly influenced his ideas was the one authority he never mentions – Paolo Toscanelli. He wanted to keep Toscanelli's ideas, ignored for nearly twenty years, to himself and hide his indiscretion of copying Toscanelli's map and letter from John II's archives.

His mastery of the sea liberated all that was best in his character – prevision, perseverance, stamina and adaptability – enabling him to become a great mariner, but in the difficult conditions of the Indies, his perseverance weakened and his adaptability came to be seen as weak irresolution. At sea, his knowledge of ships and navigation was unequalled and went, usually, unchallenged, but on land, where his military expertise couldn't match the Spaniards and where he had never had to govern anything larger than his own house, his resolution and self-confidence deserted him. On Hispaniola he relied on the men he knew he could trust – his brothers – opening himself to charges that he had won the Indies for his family and that *he loved foreigners*. His intelligence, sobriety and enormous drive to accomplish the unaccomplishable kept him aloof from his men and this aloofness, together with his foreignness, distanced him dangerously from the proud conquistador.

In his personal habits Columbus was, for the contrary historian, disappointingly modest. His house at Isabela was too small to satisfy the needs of the most insignificant Castilian merchant. He cared so little for clothes that he often wore a monk's habit or a seaman's cloak, scandalizing a Court which expected its Grandees to be richly dressed. He ate sparingly, drank little, failed to womanize, disliked swearing and didn't gamble. He preferred the comfort of a mule to the prestige of a horse, showed no interest in hunting and enjoyed the company of friars, seaman and his Genoese friends. He was a misfit, and he didn't seem to care. Yet he gained the respect and friendship, perhaps even affection of Isabella, the respect of the scholars Las Casas and Peter Martyr, the envy of Vespucci, the loyalty of brave men like Méndez and Fieschi, the friendship of religious men from Bishop Deza to the chronicler Bernaldéz and the friars at La Rábida and the love and admiration of his brothers and sons. He was as loyal as the circumstances would permit to Beatriz Enriquez, the mother of his younger son.

Columbus was, as Las Casas recognized, the Indian's friend, interested in their *beliefs and traditions* to the extent that he would instruct Fr. Pané to spend years investigating them, the first of a great line of friars to compile invaluable reports on the cultures the Spaniards encountered in the Americas. Columbus went to great extremes to avoid confrontation and bloodshed, and his survival from a year marooned on Jamaica was not the product of luck, but of self-discipline and imagination – to whom but Columbus would it have occurred the ruse of an eclipse of the Moon to gain provisions and respect from unfriendly natives? Everywhere Columbus landed, his instinct was to negotiate with the native inhabitants, but the demands from Castile to justify the expense of his venture sometimes pushed him to be aggressive – noticeably on the occasions he enslaved Tainos and imposed the Gold Tax – only to regret it later. His generous reports of the Tainos, extolling their virtues and sympathetically explaining their failings, encouraged Isabella's evangelization and desire to bring them into her kingdom on an equal footing with her Spanish subjects. Hers was the first voice to call for the respect of the Indians' properties and persons, *as the free men they are*, and she and Columbus can hardly be blamed for their extinction (which occurred long after both were dead), due as much to the novel circumstances of the first encounter between the Old and New worlds as to the greed and ambition that form part of human nature.

Through thick and thin Columbus was loyal to his adopted Queen and country, though this didn't stop him from criticizing – and a lot less obliquely than is generally noticed – the expulsion of the Jews. Was he swayed by his own Judeo-Spanish origins? I think not; as he said himself, he had *shipped with Latins, Greeks, Moors and Jews*, the four religions dominating the Mediterranean and wrote to Isabella (one wonders what she made of it) *that the Holy Spirit works in Christians, Jews, Moors and in all others of all other sects.* Columbus is distinguished from earlier mariner-explorers pushed on by Princes keen to enrich their coffers: Columbus was fired by the desire to know and explain the world; Columbus believed that God was working through him, granting him powers beyond the reach of other mortals, and so he let Isabella know. This discovery-fire and God-willed empowerment was a heady mixture igniting the great and single-minded energy with which Columbus overcame so many obstacles to discover America. Coupled with an enormous sense of righteousness, this led him to insist that only his understanding of the location of the Indies in the world was the correct one and to the ridiculous spectacle of dragging the chains Bobadilla had placed on him in Hispaniola through the orange tree-shaded streets of Seville.

Columbus, collector of books on cosmography and painter of maps, retained a close interest in discovery to the end of his life: he had John Day, an English merchant in Seville, look for a copy of John Cabot's chart to Newfoundland (Day couldn't find one); he corresponded with Santostefano, a Genoese merchant who sailed as far as Burma (this in 1498, only a year after Vasco da

Gama's arrival in India), was in Lisbon to see *with my own eyes* the chart Batolomeu Dias drew of his 1488 rounding of the Cape of Good Hope, shared his house with Vespucci, who had sailed on three voyages of discovery, and closely followed the exploits of his contemporaries in Portugal and Castile. The first world map to include parts of Brazil and the West Indies, long thought to be the work of Juan de la Cosa, was painted under Columbus's direction, yet further proof of his navigational virtuosity.

Genoa, with her tradition of maritime discovery and trade and her Bank, and the open-mindedness which often accompanies such seagoing and commercial activities, left its mark on Columbus. But in the infrequent moments when he writes about his past, it is to justify his nautical experience to his King and Queen or to confirm – or not – something he read in one of his books. At the back of his mind there lurked the memory of the anarchy, violence and poverty of his childhood in Genoa. No wonder he never returned to Genoa after the age of twenty-seven, no wonder he never wrote of his Genoese origins or maintained any contact with anyone he'd known, in the old days, in that city. It was this almost-amnesia, including the complete disuse of the language of his home country, that encouraged Columbus always to look ahead – to the next voyage, the next discovery, the next challenge, even the distant and impossible plan to recover Jerusalem for Christianity. A great sailor-discoverer, more than a dreamer, must be a man of practical common sense and authority, with the strength of personality and conviction to lead men where men have never gone. Such a man was Columbus.

NOTES

[1] There are also Corsican, French, German, English, Greek and Armenian candidates, though it is the Iberians who are the most insistent. Macaranhas Barreto has recently published a 572-page tract 'proving' that Columbus, son of a Portuguese prince by the name of Salvador Fernandes Zarco, was a secret agent of John of Portugal (incidently convincing the editors of the *Blue Guide* to rebaptize Columbus as Cristóbal Colón-Zarco). To doubly ensure that the credit for the discovery of America goes to the Portuguese, Barreto has two sea-captains discovering Newfoundland in 1473. Unlikely though it may seem, Portuguese fishermen may have known of Newfoundland – known in Portuguese as Bacalaos, or Codland – twenty years before Columbus's discovery of the Caribbean islands. If so, they kept their discovery to themselves.

[2] I rely on Juan Gil's study of Columbus's language in his introduction to *Textos*, pp. 30-63.

[3] Madariaga, writing in 1940, and Juan Gil, in 1992, are notable exceptions. They offer further evidence pointing towards Columbus's Jewish origins, which I find interesting but not conclusive. Morison's only reference to the issue, citing Menéndez Pidal is, 'The Discoverer did not write Jewish-Spanish, or Italian-Spanish, but Portuguese-Spanish'. Taviani dismisses Madariaga's Jewish Columbus as 'A theory based on the linguistic argument, which is quite unfounded, and on others quite unsupported by specific evidence.' Fernández-Armesto ignores the whole question of Columbus's language and Jewish origin. However, the evidence cannot be wished away, nor can its significance to a 15th-Century figure living in Catholic Genoa, Portugal and Spain be ignored. See also the next footnote.

[4] I should mention one other objection which borders on the ridiculous. Columbus is said not to have used Judeo-Spanish (which Menéndez Pidal never argues); can one seriously suggest that all Spanish Jews spoke and wrote in a different manner from all Spanish Christians?

[5] Everyone has a favourite interpretation, but, other than Xpo Ferens (Christbearer or Christopher) there is no way of knowing whether the monogram is Cabbalistic, in Latin, Spanish, or Greek, or what Columbus wished to convey.

[6] As this is the only source for Columbus's arrival in Portugal, it has been challenged by historians. Fernández-Armesto distrusts Fernando's biography and has Columbus arriving on a trading vessel, for which there is no evidence at all. For the early part of *The History*, Fernando had to rely on his father's or uncles' memory to complete his story. Hence the various places he might have been born, the uncertainty with which he tackled his family and, I suspect, his decision to have Columbus attend Pavia University – whose records prove he didn't. But when Fernando is unsure of events, he qualifies them – the birthplace, his name and family. His father's attendance at the University of Pavia is too specific claim to have come unprompted to Fernando's hand, though as a scholar he would have needed little persuading. The accidental landing at Lagos is quite a different matter: what possible advantage could Columbus gain by telling a lie?

7 A Genoese notarial document, dated 25th August 1479, states that Columbus, then 27 years old, brought sugar from Madeira in 1478 for the trading house of Di Negro. The following day he would depart for Lisbon. Also, on his Third Voyage he put into Funchal where he was received with great fanfare by his old friends.

8 The Iceland voyage is hotly debated because, other than fish, the island offered nothing in the way of trade and had become a complete backwater after the extinction of its Greenland colonies and the ravage of the Plague (1403). Also, February was an unlikely month for a voyage since ships avoided sailing in the winter months, and, as a hundred leagues west of Iceland would have taken him to Greenland, he either sailed in a different direction or less than a hundred leagues. These inconsistencies could be explained by the 22 years separating his voyage from his description of it to Ferdinand and Isabella which reads: *In February 1477 I sailed a hundred leagues beyond Iceland, whose southern coast is 73 degrees north of the equator and not 63 degrees as some say [63 degrees is correct]. It is not in the Western hemisphere, as Ptolemy says, but much further west. The English, especially from Bristol, come to this island which is as big as England and when I was there the sea was not frozen though the tides were huge.* Taviani suggests Columbus might have signed up as a seaman on an English fishing boat.

9 Paolo del Pozzo Toscanelli (1397-1482) was an eminent physician, astronomer and philosopher as well as mathematician, who was forced by the Medici to read their horoscopes, for which he was condemned by the Church. He met John of Portugal in Rome and encouraged him to seek the east by sailing to the west, grossly underestimating the distance from Lisbon to China. Toscanelli's dedication to scholarship, 'purity of mind' and repulsive features encouraged contemporaries to claim that he remained a virgin all his eighty-four years.

10 The curious issue of Columbus's correspondence with Toscanelli has vexed many an historian. Inconsistencies in both of Toscanelli's letters imply forgery, which could be explained by Columbus's reticence to mention him, a reticense caused by his unauthorized copy of Toscanelli's letter and map to King John II. On this reasoning, Columbus invented the correspondence to avoid awkward questions about Toscanelli's map which at some point he used to back up his venture.

11 Morison suggests his encounter with the westerlies on the return voyage was fortuitous, but a man who had worked out one set of trade winds would have worked out the other.

12 Something like 300,000 Moriscos – baptized Moors – were expelled by Philip III between 1609 and 1614, though a few remained, the last recorded case of Moslem apostasy being recorded in 1728. Intolerance was not one-sided; in 1126 the Almoravids deported many Christians to Morocco.

13 Though an odious institution, the Inquisition was lenient by 20th-century standards. 73 Conversos suffered an auto-da-fé between 1490 and 1500 and, in

over three centuries, about 10,000 people suffered an auto-da-fé, an average of thirty a year.

14 In terms of climate, Gran Canaria, Tenerife, Hierro, La Gomera and La Palma with their steady rainfall and luxuriant vegetation are markedly different from the arid, almost barren deserts of Lanzarote and Fuerteventura to the east, close to the African coast.

Notes to Chapter 5:

15 The November 1986 issue of the *National Geographic* magazine revived the debate by supporting Samana Cay as the Landfall. However, the bases for this election are unconvincing. The magazine's study relied on a computerized reconstruction of Columbus's course which, due to probable errors in the Journal's course markings and uncertainty of the ships' leeway, could equally have him landing hundreds of miles north or south of Samana Cay. A second 'proof' – archaeological excavations of probable landing sites recorded by Columbus coincide with Lucayan villages on Samana – could equally well confirm any other candidate, since all the islands were occupied by Indian villages. Finally linguistic errors by one of the magazine's consultants, Fuson, do not help the case for Samana; Fuson (1992) asserts that Columbus called Guanahani 'isleta', or islet, favouring the smaller Samana candidate. Actually Columbus refers to Guanahani as both 'isleta' and 'isla', island. Then Fuson argues that the *laguna* Columbus reports finding on the island was a sea-water lagoon, fitting Samana but not San Salvador (which has a freshwater lake). In fact, when Columbus wished to describe a sea-water lagoon he called it *laguna del mar* and laguna meant and still means in Castile an inland freshwater lake. Also Las Casas reports seaman drinking water from this laguna of Ganahani. As Landfall theorists will quickly point out, none of this proves San Salvador or definitively disproves Samana Cay.

Notes to Chapter 7:

16 Americans are reluctant to accept that such a venal disease was transmitted to Europeans by native Americans and not the other way around. However, the first major recorded outbreak of syphilis in Europe (Northern Italy in 1494-5 among Charles VIII's army) coincides all too closely with Dr. Ruiz de Isla's observations in Barcelona the preceeding year.

17 Diego was the only brother to become a naturalized Spanish citizen, in 1504, taking holy orders. Bartolomé Colón, still in France, would join his brothers in Hispaniola.

Notes to Chapter 9:

18 The city was repopulated by immigrants from Asturias.

19 Columbus, after his return from his last voyage, never mentions the Indians, not even in his will. The most charitable explanation is that after the battle at Belén, where he lost fifteen of his men to the Indians of Veragua, and a year marooned on Jamaica, where his very survival depended on the Tainos, he was happy to see the back of them.

264

[20] Regular attacks by Algonquin Indians drove the Vikings out of Newfoundland. In the last battle, Karlsefani and his men were saved by the bravery of a pregnant woman, Freydis, who snatched up a sword from a dead Norseman and faced her attackers, pulling out her big breast and slapping it with the flat of the blade. This so terrified the Indians that they fled to their canoes and paddled away. Freydis, illegitimate daughter of Eric the Red, was by all accounts a fearsome woman, cutting down all the other women in the settlement with her axe.

Notes to Chapter 10:
[21] At first, Guacanagari, shamed by the murder of Columbus's men near his village and frightened of possible reprisals, claimed he couldn't see Columbus because of leg wounds he'd sustained fighting Cahonaboa. Columbus sent the ship's surgeon to look at the cacique's wounds, and when he stripped off Guacanagari's bandages, he found no wound at all.

Notes to Chapter 11:
[22] Here the Duke of Medina Sidonia, one of Columbus's backers, had a palace which can still be seen, a pleasant white-washed mansion in a small square with views to the Atlantic. Columbus undoubtedly stayed here, watching ships entering and leaving the Guadalquivir, wondering when he could finally assemble a discovery fleet.
[23] On the reasonable grounds that malaria was endemic in Andalusia, American archaeologists have speculated that malaria was brought to America by the early colonizers. If this is the case, then one wonders why no widespread outbreak was recorded among the Indians.
[24] Las Casas recalls talking to this Indian in Castile.
[25] He applied oil from the ash of goat's horn, saltpetre, tamarind seed, butter and oil to his hair and a paste of stag's horn ash to his gums; cuttlefish eggs purge the kidneys, water snake liver alleviates gall stones. The remedy for a woman's lust sounds very effective – smear the blood of ticks, which have fed on a savage black bullock, on her hips; men should drink ram's urine.

Notes to Chapter 12:
[26] Also from Italy and now Columbus's confessor and aid.
[27] Both maps were discovered in unusual circumstances in the 19th century. Found by the Italian scholar, Boni, hanging in a butcher's stall, the Cantino map was painted by an unknown Portuguese cartographer at the request of Alberto Cantino in Lisbon on the instructions of the Duke of Ferrara. Juan de la Cosa's map was found in a Paris bookstall by Baron Walckener, Dutch chargé d'affaires to Paris in 1832, and subsequently purchased by the Spanish State. I have a facsimile hanging at the end of my bed.
[28] Ferdinand did not deign to reply.

Notes to Chapter 14:
[29] In subsequent editions of his map, Waldseemüller stopped calling the new con-

tinent America, replacing it with *Mundus Novus*, but the name had stuck.

[30] Duarte Leite in 1959. For a concise discussion of Vespucci's voyages see Morison, *The European Discovery of America, Southern Voyages*.

Notes to Chapter 15:

[31] 5th December 1492, Cuba: *As it was getting dark, I ordered the caravel* Niña *to go ahead and find a harbour by daylight, because she was a faster sailor than the* Santa María. *As it was already night by the time they reached a harbour, which was like Cadiz Bay, the* Niña *sent her small boat carrying a light to take soundings. Before I reached the place where the* Niña *was beating about, waiting for a signal from the small boat, the light went out. The* Niña *then showed a light and came to me to explain what was happening. While this was going on, the men in the small boat rekindled the light. The* Niña *was able to go to it, but I was afraid to attempt this at night with the larger ship. So I jogged to and fro all night.*

[32] Appropriately, Spain represents him on the 5,000 peseta banknote, the second largest denomination after the 10,000 peseta banknote which bears a portrait of King Juan Carlos. The 1,000 peseta bill is shared by Cortés and Pizarro. The only other banknote, the 2,000 peseta, represents a certain José Celestino Mutis observing an open flower with a magnifying glass.

Notes to Chapter 17:

[33] But not the first. In 1505 Cristóbal Rodriguéz, known as 'The Tongue' for his knowledge of Arawak, protested to Ferdinand about the ill treatment being meted out to the Tainos on Hispaniola. Ferdinand remitted his protest to Ovando who had Rodriguéz banished from the island.

[34] The election results of 16th May 1996 were: Peña Gomez 46%, Leonel Fernández 39%, Jacinto Peynado 15%. Under the new election rules, Peña and Leonel were forced to a runoff. Balaguer, who had kept aloof from the campaign before the first round, came out in favour of Leonel Fernández, with veiled allusions to Peña's supposed Haitian origins. Leonel's earlier criticism of Balaguer changed to admiration (he was 'an historical figure'), and he won the election on 30th June with 51% of the vote. Many Dominicans believed that the true winner was Balaguer.

SELECTED BIBLIOGRAPHY

A young generation of Spanish scholars have, thanks to the support of Madrid - based publishers Alianza Editorial and Cambio 16, opened up the Columbian Archives to the general reader. Their commentaries and footnotes have been fundamental for the preparation of this book. My thanks to C. Varelo, J. Gil, L. Arranz, A. Ramírez de Verger, F. Socas, J. Fernández Valverde, M.A. Medina, J.A. Barreda, and I. Pérez Fernández.

I have translated from the following sources:

Joâm de Barros: *Da Asia. Dos fectos que os Portuguses fizeram no descubrimento e conquista dos mares e terras do Oriente.* (Lisbon, 1552).

Andrés Bernáldez: *Historia de los Reyes Católicos Don Fernando y Doña Isabel...* Ed. Sociedad de Bibliófilos Andaluces (Seville, 1870).

Biblioteca de Colón: Vol. I: *El Libro de Marco Polo, Las Apostillas a la Historia Natural de Plinio el Viejo,* ed. Juan Gil. Vol. II: Pierre d'Ailly, *Ymago Mundi,* ed. A. Ramírez de Verger. Vol. III: E.S. Piccolómini (Pope Pius II), *Descripción de Asia,* ed. F. Socas. Vol. IV: Cristóbal Colón, *Libros de las Profecias,* ed. J. Fernández Valverde.), (Madrid, 1992).

Cartas de particulares a Colón y relaciones coetáneas: Ed. Juan Gil y C. Varela (Madrid, 1984).

Cristóbal Colón: Textos y documentos completos: Nuevas Cartas: Ed. C. Varelo y Juan Gil (Madrid, 1992).

Cristóbal Colón, *Diario de a bordo,* ed. L. Arranz (Madrid, 1985).

Hernando Colón, *Historia del Almirante,* ed. L. Arranz (Madrid, 1984).

G. Fernández de Oviedo, *Sumario de la natural historia de las Indias,* ed. M. Ballesteros (Madrid, 1986).

The Four Voyages of Columbus, ed. C. Jane (New York, 1988).

B. de Las Casas, *Historia de las Indias (Obras Completas,* Vols. III & IV). Ed. Medina, Barreda & Fernández (Madrid, 1994), and, *Brevísima relación de la destrucción de las Indias,* ed. I. Pérez Fernández (Madrid, 1992).

Historia de España en sus documentos: Siglo XV, F. Diaz-Plaja (Madrid, 1984)

P. Mártir de Anglería, *Décadas del Nuevo Mundo* (Madrid, 1989) and *Epistolario* (Madrid, 1892).

Ruy de Pina: *Crónica d'El Rey D. Joâo II. Colleçâo de Livros Ineditos de Historia Portuguesa,* (Lisbon, 1792).

Hernando del Pulgar: *Cronica de los Señores Reyes Católicos Don Fernando y Doña Isabel de Castilla y de Aragón...* (Valencia, 1870).

OTHER SOURCES:

J. F. Amler, *Christopher Columbus's Jewish Roots* (New Jersey, 1991).

L. Arranz Márquez – *Repartimientos y encomiendas en la isla Española* (Madrid, 1991)

M. Barreto, *The Portuguese Columbus: Secret Agent of King John II* (New York, 1992).

J. Brondsted, *The Vikings* (London, 1965).

R. Cassa, *Los Tainos de La Española* (Santo Domingo, 1974), and *Los Indios de las Antillas* (Madrid, 1992).

Christopher Columbus: The Four Voyages. Edited and translated by J.M. Cohen (London, 1969).

S. de Madariaga, *Vida del muy magnifico señor don Cristóbal Colón*, quinta edición (Madrid, 1992). Also published in English.

C. Dobal, *Como pudo ser La Isabela* (Santiago, Dominican Republic, 1988).

El Dorado, text by Clemencia Plazas (Bogota, 1975).

J. H. Elliott, *Imperial Spain 1469-1716* (London, 1970).

F. Fernández-Armesto, *Columbus* (Oxford, 1991).

R. Fletcher, *Moorish Spain* (London, 1992).

R. H. Fuson, *The Log of Christopher Columbus* (Camden, Maine, 1992).

Juan Gil, *Mitos y utopías del Descubrimiento: 1 Colón y su tiempo* (Madrid, 1992).

G. Granzotto, *Christopher Columbus* (New York, 1985).

National Geographic, November 1986 and January 1992.

J. Manzano Manzano, *Cristóbal Colón: siete años decisivos de su vida 1485-92* (Madrid, 1964), and *Colón descubrio America del Sur en 1494* (Caracas, 1972).

J.F. Martinez Almánzar, *Enriquillo: Idolo de Barro* (Santo Domingo, 1986).

R. Menéndez Pidal, *La lengua de Cristóbal Colón*, (Madrid, 1942).

S.E. Morison, *Admiral of the Ocean Sea* (Boston, 1942), *The European Discovery of America, The Northern Voyages* (New York, 1971) and The *European Discovery of America, the Southern Voyages* (New York, 1974).

F. Moya Pons, *Indios y Españoles en el repartimiento de 1514 en La Española* (Santo Domingo, 1996)

H. O'Donnell Y Duque de Estrada, *El Mapamundi denominado Carta de Juan de la Cosa* (Madrid, 1992).

Michael Paiewonsky, *Conquest of Eden 1493-1515* (Rome, 1991).

J. Pérez, *Isabel y Fernando* (Madrid, 1988).

El Primer Viaje de Cristóbal Colón, ed. J.F. Guillén (Madrid, 1943).

Rex and Thea Rienits, *The Voyages of Columbus* (New York, 1989).

J. S. Romm, *The Edges of the Earth in Ancient Thought* (Princeton, 1992).

K. Sale, *Christopher Columbus and the Columbian Legacy*, (New York, 1990).

D. E. Stannard, *American Holocaust* (Oxford, 1992).

The Vinland Sagas: The Norse Discovery of America, Translated by M. Magnusson and H. Palsson (London, 1965).

P.E. Taviani, *Christopher Columbus: The Grand Design* (London, 1985).

J. Urrea, *Guia Artistica de Valladolid* (Valladolid, 1990).

Amerigo Vespucci: Cartas de viaje, ed. L. Formisano (Madrid, 1986).

J. Wasserman, *Columbus, Don Quixote of the Sea* (Boston, 1930).

INDEX

Aguado, Juan 145-146
Alexander IV, Pope 56, 113, 115
Alfraganus 37-38, 42
Anacoana 227
Antilla 7, 37, 39, 41, 45-46, 147
Arana, Diego de 76, 142
Arranz, Luis 210
Azores 32, 37, 41, 46, 61, 108-111, 115, 149, 195, 197, 257

Bahamas 41, 87, 88, 123-124, 127, 194, 199, 211; & Landfall 83-84
Balaguer, Joachin 215, 218, 230, 234, 250, 254, 255
Balboa, Vasco Nuñez de 174, 191
Banco di San Giorgio 10, 12, 17-18, 23, 167
Barros, Joâo de 45, 111
Bastidas, Rodrigo de 178, 223-224
Bavarello, Giacomo 9
Bay Islands & Guanaje 172
Behaim, Martin 39
Behechío 96
Bellini, Father Francisco de 224, 230
Berardi, Juanoto 63, 134, 138, 144
Bernaldéz, Andrés 8, 12, 71, 201, 259
Bermejo, Juan Rodríguez 80
Bobadilla, Beatriz de 77, 117-118
Bobadilla, Francisco de 136, 157-159, 161, 163, 171, 186, 210, 223
Buil, Fr. 132-134, 145-146

Cabot, John 25, 191, 195, 260
Cabot, Sebastian 106
Cabral, Pedro Alvares 165, 191
Cabrero, Juan 58, 63
Cahonaboa 126, 142-144
Cartier, Jacques 191
Caicihu's prophecies 92, 227
Canary Islands & islanders (Guanches) 16, 37, 41, 49, 53, 60, 76-77, 86, 99, 117, 131, 195; slavery at 135-137
cannibalism 5, 92, 107, 133, 137, 150, 206; in Americas 105-106; Caribs 102-105
Cantino map 165
Cape St. Vincent 27, 30-31, 38, 199
Carib Indians 5, 92, 95-96, 132, 137, 141, 191, 205-206; & cannibalism 101-107
Cassa, Roberto 212
Centurione 34
Chanca, Dr. D. Alvarez 102-104, 105, 141, 197
Charles VIII of France 65, 262

Cheng Ho 34
China 37, 39, 41, 77-78, 80, 98, 106, 149, 151, 165, 173, 189, 257
Chios 15, 36
Cibao 125-126, 143, 154, 173, 204, 209, 210, 238
Ciboneye Indians 84, 235
Ciguayo Indians 85, 209, 235, 247, 252
Cipangu/o (Japan) 37, 39, 41, 45-46, 56, 62, 68, 77, 80, 124-125, 173, 189, 258
Colombo, Domenico 9-10
Colombo, Giovanni 186
Colón, Bartolomé (brother) 9; description 33; 39, 60, 96, 100, 133, 146, 151-152, 154, 170, 188, 190, 201, 218, 221, 227 ; at Veragua 173-176; on Jamaica 180-183
Colón, Diego (brother) 9, 117, 133, 158, 170, 188, 201
Colón, Diego (son) 33, 46, 50, 61, 63, 112-114, 116, 167, 185-188, 190-191; as Governor 211; 216, 221, 228, 231-232
'Colón, Diego' (interpreter) 88, 202-203
Colón, Diego of Larreategui, 176
Colón, Fernando (Son) 5, 10, 12-13, 17, 20, 26-27, 32-33, 37, 41, 45-46, 51, 57-61, 63, 81, 89, 105, 113-114, 116, 139, 156-157, 159, 164-165, 168, 170-172, 175, 177, 179-183, 188, 190, 197
Colón, Felipa 232
Colón, María 232
Colón de Portugal, J.F. Fitzjames Stuardo 189
Colón of Córdoba, Domingo 176
Colón of Portugal, Pedro 176
Columbian Archives (Genoa) 22-25

COLUMBUS, CHRISTOPHER
appearance & character 45, 257-261; Barcelona 114; Capitulations of Santa Fé 63-66, 163, 185; Caribs 102-103; Cardinal's hat for Diego 112-113; Converso 20-21; death 188; descendants 189-190; financial affairs 58-59, 185-187; geographical ideas 37-41, 62, 148, 165-168, 173-174; gold 122-124, 128-129; health 151, 161; inspirations 34-41; Jews 73-74; King John's conspiracy 109-112, 162; language 18-20; map making 200; marooned 177-183; mental health 97, 178-180; modern myths

6-8; navigation & seamanship 195-201; origins 9-13; in Portugal 27-32, 44-48; prophecies 164; religious beliefs 21, 34, 36, 45; remains & ashes 25, 191-192, 257; shackles 157-159; in Spain (1486-92) 49-51, 56-68; slavery 130-139, 157; Tainos 85-89, 91-92, 101, 142-144, 209-210; Vespucci 192-194; wind system 41; women 33, 35, 39, 57-58, 62-63, 77, 117-118, 195;

VOYAGES: prediscovery 36-37; First 78-81, cost of 64, fleet & crew 74-76, Landfall 83, monuments to 76-77; Second 116-117; Third 146-152, discovers mainland 149-151; Fourth 170-177; Cuban 201-203

WRITINGS: Book of Privileges 24, 163-164; Book of Prohecies 163-164; Journal 65-66, 73, 79-80, 86-88, 102-103, 108-112, 123-125, 130-131, 140-141, 196-197, 199, 240, 245, 266; Libro Copiador (Copybook) 91-92, 101, 129, 138, 141-142, 154, 200-203;

LETTERS to: Bank of St. George 23, 167; Bartolomé (brother) 146; Diego (son) 61, 185-186, 193-194; Father Gorricio 167-168; Bishop Deza 187; Juana de Torres 152, 158, 161-162; Isabella & Ferdinand 36, 50, 74, 89, 103, 122-123, 125, 128, 133, 135, 143-144, 147-153, 156, 163, 165, 173, 178-179, 195, 198; Postils 35, 47, 62, 161; Will 188, 238

Coma, Dr. G. 104, 147
Contarini & Rosselli map 189
Conversos 6, 8, 20-21, 63, 69-74, 88, 156
Cortés, Hernan 172, 217, 232
Cosa, Juan de la & map 76, 84, 151, 165, 191, 200, 223, 261
Cuba 8, 84-85, 88, 93, 102, 112, 146, 138, 145, 147, 165, 172-173, 177, 189, 192, 199, 213, 231; & discovery 123-124; & CC's voyage 172-173
Cuneo, Michele de 95, 104, 117, 134, 198

D'Ailly, P. & Ymago Mundi 35, 37, 42, 47, 62, 146, 199
Day, John 260
Deza, Diego 63, 70, 187, 208, 259
Dias, Bartolomeu 47, 59, 109, 166, 261

Di Noli 34, 262
Drake, Sir Francis 216, 222, 224, 231, 248
Duarte, Juan Pablo 233, 248, 255

encomienda 130, 152, 208-213, 220, 247
England 16, 36, 49-50, 60, 62-62, 73, 75, 135, 195
Enriquez, Beatriz 57-58, 60-61, 76, 81, 114, 118, 188, 190, 259
Enriquillo 235, 250-252
Eric the Red 34
Eriksson, Leif 34, 140
Ezra (Esdras) 37, 42, 150

Ferdinand, King (for joint acts see Isabella) 53, 65, 68, 77, 99, 104, 114, 116, 131, 168, 184-188, 190, 210, 217, 221, 223, 229; CC's imprisonment 157-159; description 54-58
Fermor, Patrick Leigh 101, 242
Fernández-Armesto, F. 36, 49, 63, 97, 102, 111, 130, 150, 151, 154
Fieschi, Bartolomé 170, 178, 180-182, 188, 259
Flanders 16, 50, 135, 184
Fonseca, Juan de 115-116, 134, 146, 245
Fontanarossa, Susanna 9
France 8, 16, 49, 50, 60, 62-63, 73, 135, 191, 248
Franciscan Order 11, 50, 60, 146, 231, 250
Fregoso, Doge Pietro 15

Gallo, Antonio 12
Gama, Vasco da 34, 43, 112, 165-166, 169, 195, 261
Garay, Francisco 231-232, 245
Genoa 5, 33, 36, 40, 49, 62, 73, 129, 131, 135, 167, 191-192, 261; description 62-68
Gil, Juan 18, 262
gold 120-129
Gold Tax 126, 128, 171, 260
Gorricio, Father Gaspar 164, 167-168, 178
Granada 55, 58-59, 70-73, 137, 171; description 62-68
Greenland 7, 34, 43, 99
Grimaldo, J.F. 10
Guacanagari 88, 140-142, 209
Guadeloupe 102-106, 175, 191
Guanahaní 83, 85, 86, 124
Guanches – see Canary Islands
Guarionex 89, 100, 126, 171
Gunnbjörn 34

Haiti – see Hispaniola
Hamilton, Charles 19
Havana 8, 192
Helluland 34
Henry IV of Spain 52-53, 56
Henry VII of England 60, 65, 191
Henry 'The Navigator' 27, 30-31, 44
Herjofson, Bjarni 34
Hispaniola 5, 8, 39, 83-85, 88-89, 91-
  95, 101-103, 112, 121, 161, 163,
  170, 172-173, 185-188, 190-191,
  197-198, 201, 208; discovery of
  124-139; CC as Governor 140-
  145; CC relieved of Governorship
  146-159; & 4th Voyage 175-183; &
  Tainos 204-214; at end of 20th
  Century 204-214
Hojeda, Alonso de 143, 152-153, 167,
  176, 178, 191

Iceland 34, 36, 41, 257
India 7, 39, 43, 47, 73, 110, 112, 147,
  165, 166, 169, 173; distance from
  Spain 62; objective 66
Ireland 36
Inquisition 20-21, 56, 70, 72, 74, 246
Isabela (town) 126, 133, 134, 143,
  144, 153, 200, 218, 220, 239, 241-
  245, 259; site 154-156
Isabella, Queen 8, 24, 54, 68, 77, 99,
  101, 109, 111, 117, 119, 127, 138,
  145; as Queen of Spain 54-57;
  CC's venture 49, 57-65, 74; death
  & will 184-187; description 51-53;
  & Jews, Moors 70-72; Letters from
  CC 36, 50, 65-66, 73, 91, 106,
  113, 125, 128, 129, 135, 140, 143,
  146-147, 151-153, 158, 161-163,
  171, 178, 200; Letters to CC 100,
  115, 132, 168; receives CC in
  Barcelona 113-116; receives CC in
  Alcalá de Henares 51, 56; slavery
  & 131-136, 157
Isaiah 42, 162, 164

Jamaica 84, 122, 145, 170, 171, 173,
  184, 189, 190, 194, 199, 201, 202,
  214, 221, 223, 231, 232, 259; CC
  marooned on 177-183
Jerusalem 113, 123, 131, 136, 144,
  164, 261
Jews 6, 20-21, 33, 36, 40, 49, 53, 55,
  56, 76, 101, 135, 188, 189, 246,
  260; expulsion of 69-74
John II, King of Portugal 18, 27, 31-
  32, 35, 38, 40, 42, 53, 65, 73, 115,
  149; & CC 46-47, 59-60;
  description 44-45; Lisbon
  conspiracy 109-112

Juan, Infante of Spain 99, 114, 116,
  118, 184
Juana 'la loca' (Queen of Spain) 136,
  184, 187-188
Juana (wife of Henry IV) 52-53
Juana (daughter of Henry IV) 53-55

Karlsefani 99, 140

Las Casas, Bartolomé 5, 8, 41, 63, 83,
  89, 93, 96, 106, 109, 115, 117,
  127, 144, 157, 178, 193, 201, 208-
  209, 212-213, 226-228, 230-231,
  250-252, 259; & CC's character
  138-139; & CC's religion 21;
  describes Bartolomé Colón 33
Libro Copiador (Copybook) 6, 91, 101,
  113, 117, 129, 138, 141, 154, 195,
  200-203
Lisbon 13, 18, 39, 41, 46-47, 62, 131,
  132, 136, 162, 197; CC's home
  32-33; CC takes refuge 109-112;
  description 32, 43-44

Machiavelli, Nicòlo 44-45, 53-54
Macorix Indians 84, 85, 89, 100, 235,
  247
Madariaga, Salvador 20, 35, 42, 49,
  64, 83, 102, 111, 130, 150
Madeira 16, 18, 32-33, 62, 197
Majd, Ibn 34
Maldonado, Rodrigo 57
Mandeville, Sir John & Travels 107
Manzano, J. Manzano 51, 57-59, 64
Marchena, Fr. Antonio de 50, 56, 61,
  63, 147
Margarit, Mosén Pedro 104, 133, 143,
  146
Markland 34
Martyr, Peter 8, 104, 106, 147, 171,
  184, 259
'Mateo, Juan' (Guaticaba) 100, 238
Maya Indians 93, 105, 106, 138, 171-
  172, 219-220
Méndez, Diego 178, 180-183, 186,
  259
Mendoza, Alonso Vélez de 165
Mendoza, Cardinal 58, 59, 114
Menéndez Pidal 18-19
Mina, El 16, 37, 41, 43, 126
Molina, Tirso de 231
Moniz (Muniz), Felipa 33, 35, 49
Moniz, Violeta 50
Montesino, Fr. Antón de 227-229
Morgan, Robert 37
Morison, S. E. 5-6, 30, 35, 37, 41, 43,
  46, 64, 69, 83-84, 102, 106, 111,
  130, 150, 155, 195, 198
Mugica, Adrian de 152, 158

Nadd-Odd 34
Navidad 101, 140-141, 143-144, 155, 176, 180, 208, 209
Neco, King of Egypt 31
Norsemen – see Vikings

Oderigo, Nicòlo de 23, 167
Ojeda – see Hojeda
Ovando, Nicolás de 136, 161, 170, 178, 182-183, 186, 210-211, 218, 221-223, 227, 232, 250
Oviedo, G. Fernández de 8, 93, 216, 219

Palos de la Frontera 49-50, 62, 64, 65, 69, 75-76, 81, 112; description 50
Panama 122, 128, 137, 165, 170, 173-175
Paria 105, 137, 149, 152, 165, 167, 176, 178, 193, 198
Phoenicians 31, 34
Piccolomini, E. S. (Pius II) 35, 40, 42, 147
Pina, Ruy de 44
Pineda, Alvarez 231-232
Pinello, Francesco 63
Pinzón, Francisco Martín 76
Pinzón, Martín Alonso 39, 75-76, 79, 80, 108-109, 112, 124, 129
Pinzón, Vicente Yañez 76, 152-153, 165, 176, 191
Pliny 42, 161
Polo, Marco & *Travels* 24, 37, 42, 66, 106, 146, 257,
Pons, Frank M. 212
Porras, Francisco & rebellion 180-183, 186
Porto Santo 18, 33, 37, 199
Portugal 5, 10, 18-20, 49, 53, 55, 72, 74, 76, 115, 135, 140, 156, 168, 195; CC and 30-48; CC arrives 26-28
Puerto Rico 84, 85, 95, 145, 147
Pulgar, Hernando de 51-52

René of Anjou 27
Roldán, Francisco & rebellion 148, 151-152, 156, 158, 171, 186, 210, 238

St. Thomas Fort 101, 126, 133, 143-144; site 237-238
Salamanca Commission 57, 136, 258
Santa Fé, Capitulations of 64-66, 118
Santángel, Luis de 63, 64
Santo Domingo 8, 25, 88, 157-158, 170, 176, 181-183, 186, 191-192, 198, 204-205, 245; description 215-236; history 247-255

Santostefano, Geronimo 129, 260
Sargasso Sea 41, 79
Satespes 31-32
Savona 10-11, 13, 117
Seville 8, 10, 23, 47, 58, 61, 63, 116, 139, 146, 159, 185, 187, 191-192; slavery 130-139
Spain & CC 5, 7, 9, 18, 22, 46, 79, 88, 135, 162, 165; CC's home 49-68; CC between 2nd & 3rd Voyages 146-149; last months in 184-188
syphilis 90, 114, 133, 153, 232

Taino Indians 5, 74, 99-105, 113, 121, 126, 130, 134-137, 143, 145, 155, 171, 173, 177, 189, 218-221, 225-227, 232, 234-236, 238, 241-248, 250-252, 256, 259-260; mythology & customs 83-98; extinction 204-214
Talavera, Hernando de 70
Taprobana 148, 166, 173
Taviani, P. E. 12, 20, 23, 36, 49, 195
Tordesillas Treaty 115
Torfaeus, Thormodus 7
Torres, Juana de 152, 158, 161, 179
Toscanelli, Paolo 42, 45, 56, 62, 66, 189, 258; letter copied by CC 38-39; map 40-41
Trinidad 85, 149-151, 194, 211
Trujillo, Rafael 215, 219, 243-244, 248-250, 256

Urrea, Jesús 190

Valladolid 138, 187, 191; description 188-190
Vega Real 126, 210, 237, 238, 247
Venice 13, 22, 49, 62, 76, 135, 173, 191
Veragua & Duchy of 128, 137, 165, 173-176, 183, 190, 198, 213
Verrazzano, Giovanni da 106, 191
Vespucci, Amerigo 105, 153; CC and 185, 192-194, 259, 261
Vinland & Vinland map 7, 34, 42-43
Vikings 7, 34, 99, 101, 122

Waldseemüller, Martin 192-194
Watson, Lyall 107

Xaragua 96, 127, 158, 211, 250